WHO'S WHO IN TRACK AND FIELD

WHO'S WHO IN TRACK AND FIELD

Reid M. Hanley

ARLINGTON HOUSE New Rochelle, New York

Library of Congress Catalog Card Number 73-11872

MANUFACTURED IN THE UNITED STATES OF AMERICA

Library of Congress Cataloging in Publication Data

Hanley, Reid M 1945-
Who's who in track and field.

1. Track-athletics--Biography. I. Title.
GV697.A1H34 796.4'2'0922 [B] 73-11872
ISBN 0-87000-219-8

FOREWORD

It was interesting that Reid Hanley, author of *Who's Who in Track and Field*, should invite me to write the foreword for his book—for I have been long hoping that someone would produce such a book, for which there is need.

There are many record books, even those which cover the sport of track and field, but there are so few volumes which bind together the biographical sketches of illustrious athletes and coaches, particularly so in track and field.

I am pleased that Reid Hanley, in producing *Who's Who in Track and Field*, has eliminated the need.

As director of what is probably the most complete sports library in existence, that now funded by Citizens Savings Athletic Foundation, Los Angeles, I shall be looking forward to placing copies of *Who's Who in Track and Field* upon our shelves for constant reference and research.

I am impressed with the fact that more than 400 biographical sketches on renowned track and field athletes and coaches appear in Hanley's *Who's Who*, many of whom have claimed awards from Citizens Savings Athletic Foundation, for election to its track and field Hall of Fame, or as World Trophy winners.

The *Who's Who* sketches highlight the backgrounds and subsequent achievements not only by famed American athletes, both men and women, and coaches, but by those of all areas of the world as well.

When did Paavo Nurmi establish the world record for the two-mile run? Did Jesse Owens really create three new world records and tie another all in one afternoon in 1935? How old was Bob Mathias when he won his first Olympic Games Decathlon crown in 1948? Was Emil Zatopek the only Olympian who ever scored a grand-slam in long-distance running events? In how many Olympic Games did Lord Burghley compete? Who was the only woman ever to win four gold medals in Olympic Games track and field competition? ...

All of these questions and countless more are readily answered in *Who's Who in Track and Field.*

I can well imagine that Mr. Hanley has devoted years of time and effort in conducting research for his book. Now that it is published, it will be welcomed by members of the press media, libraries, sports historians, and track and field followers in the five continents and Australasia, not to forget the points in between.

For those of us who are members of the sports fraternity, who follow extremely busy schedules daily, most frequently pointing toward deadlines, *Who's Who in Track and Field* will serve as an appreciated time-saver—an authoritative ready reference. I shall make use of my copy often.

Finally, I should note, Mr. Hanley hasn't packed his *Who's Who* with merely factual text. To the contrary, he has brightened it with incidents of note and descriptive passages. It provides enjoyable reading.

W. R. "BILL" SCHROEDER
Managing Director

Citizens Savings Athletic Foundation
Los Angeles, Calif.
March 1973

PREFACE

Much of the success of any reference book must be attributed to the author's sources. *Who's Who in Track and Field* is no exception. As a full-time project in addition to my regular duties as a sports writer, it would have been difficult to compile any information without the help of my sources throughout the world.

The task seemed monumental when I agreed to compile information and write biographies on many of the world's greatest track and field performers of all time. Who would be included in such a book? World record holders, Olympic gold medalists, those honored by the United Savings (Helms) Hall of Fame, successful coaches were obvious candidates. World leaders who did not fall into any of the other categories would also be considered. With these things in mind I set a goal of 750 biographies, realistically knowing various factors might cut this number in half.

Letters were sent to the various athletic bodies throughout the world, requesting information on Olympic medalists and world record holders. The response was not always immediate, nor the information always what was requested. A big reason for the confusion was simple—the language barrier. The French had trouble with my English and I had trouble with their French. German wasn't much better. But with the help of my wife and friends, the language barrier on this side of the Atlantic was solved.

The greatest responses I received came from Bill Schroeder of the Citizens Savings (Helms) Hall of Fame and C. Robert Paul of the United States Olympic Committee. Mr. Schroeder supplied valuable information on the members of the United Savings (Helms) Track and Field Hall of Fame. Birth dates were the most difficult bits of information to find and he obliged with a long list of athletes from the U.S. and the rest of the world. As mentioned before, the Hall of Fame list was beneficial in determining who was included in the book.

Despite mountains of work with the 1972 Olympics, Mr. Paul contributed pertinent information on U.S. Olympians. The USOC Information Director provided much intersting data, adding life to many biographies. For instance, who knew that A. C. Gilbert, who tied for the gold medal in the pole vault (12′2 1/16″) in the 1908 Olympics, invented the erector set?

Messrs. Paul and Schroeder have my sincerest thanks and I will always be grateful for their tremendous help. Without their unselfish hours of devotion to the sport of track and field, this book would have never left the typewriter.

Other help came from national athletic bodies of 16 countries: Poland, Greece, West Germany, East Germany, Czechoslovakia, New Zealand, Finland, Belgium, Australia, Rumania, Italy, Japan, France, Norway, England, and Canada. The Olympic organizations from Sweden, West and East Germany also came through with priceless information. The efforts of these people are much appreciated.

Sports information directors from U.S. colleges and universities also did their part. Some took time from the busy football and basketball seasons to unearth information. Some, including a few from athletically prominent schools, were unresponsive.

The replies were as interesting as the athletes themselves. Many were contacted personally when information sources could only furnish addresses. Extremely interesting letters were received from Ernie Shelton, Larry Snyder, Mrs. Brutus Hamilton, and many others, including several from West German women Olympians. I even received an autographed picture of Christiane Krause, a member of the gold-medal-winning 400-m relay team.

Some athletes were eliminated from consideration when all possible sources were used up with no results. A letter was sent to the U.S. ambassador to Russia, requesting help in obtaining more information on Soviet athletes. The good ambassador, like the Russians, kept mum.

Still, some 420 of the world's greatest athletes of all time are covered in this book. Of the 460 gold medals awarded in the history of the Olympic Games (including the 1906 Athens Games, which are not officially recognized), 352 are accounted for. This included events such as the standing high jump, 10,000-m cross-country race, Greek-style discus, and other events long discontinued. A comparable percentage of world record holders are included in this volume.

Extended effort was made to include all Olympic winners and world record holders but, unfortunately, many track and field performers just run off into the sunset and disappear from sight following their careers in the sport. To those men and women, I apologize.

Also deserving of thanks are my wife, for typing and proofreading assistance, and Ron Mendell, for bringing this project to my attention.

My hope is that this book will help fill the void in the area of track and field sports reference, by making easily available biographical and statistical information to journalists, fans and athletes.

REID M. HANLEY

April 1973

EDITOR'S NOTE

As every sports buff knows, the records of athletes and coaches are sometimes in dispute. Add to this the possibility of human error and you can see why the author is asking every reader of this work to pass on any corrections he might discover.

Beyond that, can you think of any significant omissions? These will normally fall into the gray "matter of opinion" area. But if sentiment does build for including a particular athlete or official in a revised edition, the author will want to.

If you have any suggestions or corrections, please write to the author in care of Arlington House, New Rochelle, N. Y. 10801. Since this volume is likely to become one of the established sources, you will be making a significant contribution to sports research. Everyone who helps will be given a credit line in the revised, enlarged, updated edition we hope to bring out in the later 1970s.

ABRAHAMS, HAROLD B. 12/15/99, Bedford, England. Member 1920, 24 British Olympic teams. In 1920 was chosen by Amateur Athletic Association of Britain for Olympics because of success at Cambridge University. Unsuccessful in 1920 Olympics, but began training with more intensity for '24 Games. Had improved his 10.0 time in 100-yd and ran 9.6 which would have tied world record had it not been wind-aided. Was British champion and consistent 10.6 in 100-m as 1924 Paris Olympics opened. Was decided underdog to Charlie Paddock and other better known sprinters. Ran 10.6 in prelims and semis. In finals ran 10.6 again and took gold medal with ease. Received silver medal as member of British 400-m relay team. Same team set world mark of 42.0 day before finals, only to have it broken by U.S. team with 41.0. Long jump actually his specialty. Jumped 24′2½″ in 1924 for British record. Mark stood 34 years. Track career ended in 1925 when he broke leg. Lawyer with part-time career as sports writer and broadcaster.

ADAMS, PLATT B. unknown. D. 2/27/61. Member U.S. 1908, 12 Olympic teams. One of great all-round jumpers in early track history. Primarily triple jumper, first achieved fame by winning 1907 AAU TJ with 44′9″. In 1908 won event in AAU championship at 44.19′ and also long jump with 21′6½″. Won AAU LJ in 1911 with 23′⅖″. In 1912 won both LJ and TJ in AAU. Went 22.4′ in LJ and 45.07′ in TJ. Made 1908 Olympic team and was 5th in TJ. In 1912 Olympics at Stockholm won standing high jump at 5′4⅛″. Missed gold medal in standing long jump by 1 centimeter with 11′⅖″. Was 5th in TJ. Member Citizens Savings (Helms) Hall of Fame.

AGOSTINI, MIKE B. 1/23/35, Port of Spain, Trinidad. Member 1956 Trinidad Olympic team. One of top non-American sprinters in world during 1950s. In 1953 ran 9.4 in 100-yd and 21.1 in 200-yd on straightaway at Bakersfield, Calif. In 1956 Melbourne Olympics competed in 100-m and 200-m. In 100-m finished 6th behind Germar of Germany, Murchison of U.S., Hogan of Ausralia, Thane Baker of U.S. and winner Bobby Morrow of U.S. In 200-m did better against another classy field. Finished 4th behind U.S. sweep of Baker, Stanfield and Morrow. Competed among best in world and made many meets in U.S. In 1955 Pan-Am Games was 2nd in 100-m in 10.4 and 3rd in 200-m in 21.4. In 1959 was again 2nd in Pan Am 100-m in 10.4 and was 3rd in 200-m in 21.1.

AHEARN, DANIEL B. 4/2/88, County Limerick, Ireland. Member 1920 U.S. Olympic team. Only American to ever hold world triple jump record. Hopped-stepped-jumped 50′11″ in New York on May 5, 1911 for world mark. Beat former record of 48′11 ¼″ held by brother Timothy Ahearne competing for native Ireland in 1908. Dan emigrated from Ireland to U.S. and dropped "e" from last name. Completely dominated TJ in U.S. from 1910–18. Won AAU 8 times: 1910–11, 1913–18. Jumped 50' in 1913 AAU which stood as record 22 years. Went wind-aided 50′11 ½″ in 1915 AAU at San Francisco, which was not bettered until 1941. Did not compete in 1912 Stockholm Olympics. No Olympics in 1916 because of WWI. Made 1920 team but finished 6th at Antwerp. One of many great Irish-American track stars in early 1900s.

AKII-BUA, JOHN B. 12/3/50, Uganda. Member 1972 Uganda Olympic team. Holds world 400-m hurdle record. Ran 47.82 at 1972 Munich Olympics for world record, gold medal. Akii-Bua came into prominence in 1971 at Pan African-USA meet. Ran 49.0 defeating Americans and Kenyans. In U.S.-USSR World All-Star Meet same summer ran 50.1 over Americans and Russians. In 1970 Commonwealth Games was 4th in 51.1. Was originally high hurdler but tried intermediates when saw high standard in 1970 Commonwealth Games was tough. Qualified for both, but did not make 110-m finals. In Munich Olympics ran 50.35 in winning first heat. Won semifinal in 49.25. Set world record in becoming Uganda's 1st track medalist. Policeman by vocation. Winner 1972 Citizens Savings (Helms) World Trophy Award, Africa.

ALBRITTON, DAVID B. 4/13/13, Danville, Ala. Member 1936 Olympic team. Co-held world high jump record with Cornelius Johnson. Both cleared 6′9 ¾″ at 1936 Olympic trials in Los Angeles, July 12, 1936.

Finished second to Johnson in 1936 Berlin Olympics. Hitler watched as two black American high jumpers took top honors in high jump. Had extremely long career. Won or tied for 7 AAU outdoor titles from 1936–50. Best AAU effort 6′8 ⅝″ in 1937. Born in same town as Olympic and Ohio State teammate Jesse Owens. At OSU tied for NCAA high jump title 1936–38. Was one of first world class high jumpers to straddle bar. Member Citizens Savings (Helms) Hall of Fame.

ANDERSON, JOHN B. 7/4/07, Cincinnati, Ohio. Member 1928, 32 Olympic teams. Won gold medal in 1932 Olympic discus throw. Broke Olympic record by over 7′ with toss of 162′4 ⅞″. In 1928 was 5th at Amsterdam with toss of 147′2 ½″. Was 1932 AAU champion with 165′6″. Won title again in 1933 with 165′1″. A 6′3″, 215-pounder when competed for Cornell U. and New York Athletic Club.

ANTAO, SERAPHINO B. 10/30/37, Goa, India. Member 1960, 64 Kenya Olympic teams. One of first sprinters from African nations to compete on international scale. After competing in 1960 Rome Olympics where won first qualifying heat in 10.5, won two gold medals in 1962 British Empire Games. Won 100-yd in 9.5 and 220-yd in 21.1. Before Empire Games double, ran 9.3 and 20.1 (wind-aided) at Nairobi on Sept. 9, 1962. That 9.3 still stands, although tied, as Kenya record. Made 1964 Olympic team but ran 10.7 in qualifying heat and was 4th.

ASHENFELTER, HORACE (Nip) B. 1/23/23, Collegeville, Pa. Member 1952, 56 Olympic teams. Only American to win gold medal in 3000-m steeplechase. In 1952 Helsinki Olympic prelim won heat with 8:51.0, .15 seconds better than previous best. In finals passed Kazontsev of Russia and won gold medal with world best of 8:45.4. World record was not recognized at that time in steeplechase. Competed in 1956 Games but failed to make finals. Holder of many national titles from 2-mile to 6-mile. Was AAU steeplechase winner in 1951, 53, 56; took 3-mile in 1954, 55 and 6-mile in 1950. Won AAU 3-mile indoor 1952–56. At Penn State was 1949 NCAA 2-mile champ. Took IC4A outdoor 2-mile in 1948, 49 and indoor in 1948. FBI agent at time of historic Olympic victory. Member Citizens Savings (Helms) Hall of Fame.

ATTLESEY, RICHARD B. 5/10/29, Compton, Calif. Held world 110-m and 120-yd hurdle records. Ran 13.5 at West Coast Relays May 13, 1950 to break 120-yd record. Set 110-m record of 13.6 at AAU championships at College Park, Md., June 24, 1950. Ran 13.5 in Helsinki to break 110-m mark and tie 120-yd mark July 10, 1950. Won 1950, 51 AAU outdoor championships. While at Southern Cal won 1950 NCAA with 14.0 time. Injuries forced career to end before possible Olympic glory and further world records. Had average speed but used 6′3½″ stature and form to break records.

AVILOV, NIKOLOY B. 8/6/48, Russia. Member 1968, 72 USSR Olympic teams. Won gold medal in decathlon at 1972 Munich Olympics, setting world record of 8454 points. Set personal bests in seven events and tied in another. Ran 11.0 in 100-m to open competition, then long jumped 25′2½″ (career best); put shot 47′1″ for another best; high jumped career top 6′11½″ and ran 48.5 for best in 400-m on first day. Total was 4345 for first day. Second day ran 14.3 hurdles, best of the day; tossed discus 154′1½″, personal high; pole vaulted 14′11″, his best; threw javelin 203′½″, another best; and finished with personal record 4:22.8 in 1500-m. Was 4th in 1968 Olympics with 7905. Placed 4th in 1969 European Championships with 7779. In 1971 had best of 8096 going into Olympics.

BABCOCK, HARRY B. 12/15/90, Pelham Manor, N.Y. D. 6/5/65, Norwalk, Conn. Member 1912 Olympic team. Won gold medal in pole vault at 1912 Stockholm Olympics. Vaulted 12′11½″ for Olympic record. Competed at Columbia U. where graduated as civil engineer. Pursued engineering as career. Was 1910 AAU champion at 12′1″. Took AAU 2 years later at 12′.

BABKA, RINK B. 9/23/36, Cheyenne, Wyo. Member 1960 Olympic team. Co-held world discus record. Had toss of 196′6″ at Walnut, Calif., on Aug. 12, 1960 to tie Edmund Piatkowski's record. Was 1958 AAU champion with throw of 187′10″, which broke record by more than 3 feet. Same year, while competing for Southern Cal, won NCAA with rival Al Oerter. Both threw disc 186′2″. Was great rival of Oerter and was second to the Kansas star often. Finished 2nd in 1960 Rome Olympics to Oerter. Had throw of 190′4″ for silver medal. A 6′5″, 267-lb giant.

BACON, CHARLES B. 1/9/85, Brooklyn, N.Y. D. 1/15/68. Member 1908 Olympic team. Won gold medal in 400-m hurdles in London Olympics. In final on July 22 set world record of 55.0. Was neck-and-neck with Harry Hillman but nosed him out at tape. Competed in 1906 unofficial Olympics at Athens. Competed for New York Athletic Club. Was sales executive.

BAKER, THANE B. 10/4/31, Elkhart, Kans. Member 1952, 56 Olympic teams. Co-held world 200-m record. Ran 20.6 at Bakersfield, Calif. on June 6, 1956 at AAU Championships. Made 1952 Olympic team in 200-m, took silver medal behind Andy Stanfield at Helsinki in 20.8. In 1953 NCAA, running for Kansas State, won 220 in 21.5. Stayed in competition and made 1956 Olympic team in 100-m (10.4) and 200-m (20.7). In 1956 Melbourne Games won gold, silver and bronze medals. In 100-m got silver behind Bobby Morrow in 10.5. Bronze came in 200-m behind Morrow and Stanfield. Got gold as member of U.S. 400-m relay. U.S. team, with Baker running third, ran 39.5 for world mark. Also ran on U.S. team that set 800-m and 880-yd relay world records of 1:23.8 on Dec. 12, 1956 at Sydney, Australia. Member Citizens Savings (Helms) Hall of Fame. Now supervisor for Mobil Research and Development Corp., field laboratory in Dallas. Still active in track as official.

BALAS, IOLANDA B. 12/12/36, Rumania. Member 1956, 60, 64 Rumanian Olympic teams. Won gold medals in women's high jump at 1960 Rome, 1964 Tokyo Olympics. In 1960 set Olympic record with leap of 6′ ½″. Bettered it in 1964 with jump of 6′2 ¾″. In 1956 was 5th. Won European Championships in 1958 and 1962. Broke world high jump record 14 times. First claimed mark in 1956 at Bucharest on July 14 with leap of 5′8 ¾″. Lost record, regained it, lost it again in next 1 ½ years. On June 22, 1958, reclaimed record with jump of 5′10″ at Bucharest. Then broke mark 11 times in 3 years. Moved record to 6′3 ¼″ on July 16, 1961 at Sofia.

BALZER, KARIN B. 6/5/38, Magdeburg, West Germany. Member 1964, 68 German Olympic teams; 1972 West German Olympic team. Won gold medal in 80-m hurdles at 1964 Tokyo Olympics. Ran 10.5 and won in dead heat with Teresa Ciepla of Poland, Pamela Kilbourn of Australia. In 1968 Mexico City Olympics was 5th in 10.6. In 1972 Munich Olympics won bronze medal in 100-m hurdles with 12.90. Co-held world records in 80-m and set world 100-m hurdles record. Ran 10.5 at Leipzig on May 23, 1964 to tie 80-m record. At Warsaw ran 13.3, as did Teresa Sukniewicz, on June 20, 1969 to set 100-m hurdle mark. Was 1966 and 1971 European champion. Physical education instructor.

BANNISTER, ROGER B. 3/23/29, Harlow, England. First man to break 4-minute mile. Broke barrier May 6, 1954 at Oxford. Paced by Oxford teammates in first 3 laps, ran 3:59.4. Lap splits of 57.5, 60.7, 62.3, 58.9. Greatest flood of publicity in track history followed. Was also timed 3:43 in 1,500 meters in same race. Record lasted short time before John Landy ran 3:58 on June 21, 1954. In Fifth British Empire Games in Vancouver, B. C., Aug. 7, 1954, Bannister met Landy in "Mile of Century". Using patented speed at finish, overtook Landy for victory.

Timed at 3:58.8 with Landy at 3:59.6. Also won European Championships in 1500 meters Aug. 29 that year. Ran 54.7 on last lap for 3:43.8 over tough competition. Retired after fantastic season. Said to have lost only one race, his first. Physician in his native country.

BARBUTI, RAYMOND (Ray) B. 6/12/05, Brooklyn, N.Y. Member 1928 Olympic team. Only American to win a running event at Amsterdam Olympics. Ran 47.8 to win 400-m. Dove across finish line to win gold medal over James Ball of Canada. Ran anchor on U.S. 1600-m relay team that won gold medal. U.S. team set world record of 3:14.2. A football-track star at Syracuse U., won 1928 IC4A 440-yd in 48.8. Was 1928 AAU titlist in 51.4. Represented New York Athletic Club. Worked for N.Y. State Civil Defense Commission, now retired. Member Citizens Savings (Helms) Hall of Fame.

BARNES, LEE B. 7/16/06, Salt Lake City, Utah. Member 1924, 28 Olympic teams. Held world pole vault record. Vaulted 14′1 ½″ at Fresno on Apr. 28, 1928. As a 17-year-old student at Hollywood H.S. won gold medal in 1924 Olympics. Tied with Glenn Graham at 12′11 ½″ and won jump-off for gold. Competed for Southern Cal and Los Angeles Athletic Club after high school. Won 1927 AAU at 13′ and 1928 AAU at 13′9″. Fifth in 1928 Amsterdam Games at 12′11 ½″, same height that won gold medal 4 years earlier. Headed own manufacturing company in Oxnard, Calif., until retirement. Member Citizens Savings (Helms) Hall of Fame.

BARTHEL, JOSEPH B. 4/27/27, Mamer, Luxemburg. Member 1948, 52, 56 Luxemburg Olympic teams. Finished 9th in 1948 London Olympic 1500-m. Going into London Games had 800-m best of 1:51.0 and 1500-m of 3:51.0. Seemingly made little progress in preparation for 1952 Helsinki Olympics. Was not leading contender in 1500-m, despite a 3:48.5 in June. Won both prelim heat and semifinals. In finals met Roger Bannister of Britain, who was to become world's first 4-minute miler; Aberg of Sweden and Lamers of Germany. Took lead in last 50-meters and held off McMillan of U.S. for gold medal. Both timed at 3:45.2. In post-Olympic meetings proved worthiness of gold medal. In 1956 Melbourne Olympics lost out in prelims. Had been clocked around 3:41 before Games. His gold medal is only one in his country's history.

BAUSCH, JAMES B. 3/29/06, Marion, S. Dak. Member 1932 Olympic team. Held world decathlon record with 8462.235 (on 1920 point scale) in 1932 Los Angeles Olympics. Was tremendous all-round athlete at Kansas. Was great fullback for KU and is member of Big Eight Football Hall of Fame. "Jarring Jim" set Jayhawk school scoring mark in 1930. Was primarily weight man with tremendous ability in pole vault.

Prior to 1932 L.A. Olympics, could not decide whether to enter discus, shot, javelin or decathlon. Chose all-round event and made history with gold medal performance. Great performances in field events enabled him to break record. Jumped 22′10 13/16″ in long jump, 5′6 15/16″ in high jump and vaulted amazing 13′1 7/16″. Tremendous weight performances (50′3 1/8″ in shot, 146′3 1/8″ in discus and 203′1 3/8″ in javelin). One reason scoring tables were revised to give running performances more point value. Was better than average hurdler in his time, fair in sprints but weak in 1500-m with 5:17.0 in record performance. Won 1932 Sullivan award as top amateur athlete of year. Worked for U.S. Department of Agriculture 30 years. Retired, living in Hot Springs, Ark.

BAXTER, IRVING B. 1876. D. 6/13/57. Member 1900 Olympic team. Great Penn trackman who had much success in Olympic competition. IC4A high jump champion in 1899, won 2 gold medals and 3 silver in 1900 Paris Olympics. Was Olympic high jump winner with leap of 6′2 4/5″. Bettered previous Olympic best by over 3″. Took other gold medal in pole vault with Olympic record leap of 10′9 9/10″. Ruled high jump for several years. Was AAU champion in 1907-10, '12. Jumped 6′2 1/4″ in '07. Was also one of world's best pole vaulters and won 1899 AAU with 10′9″.

BEAMON, BOB B. 8/29/46, Jamacia, N.Y. Member 1968 Olympic team. Holds world long jump record. Set mark at 1968 Mexico City Olympic Games on Oct. 18. In preliminary rounds, scratched twice. On last try, landing far behind board, went 26′10 1/2″ to qualify easily for finals. On first jump of finals, hit take-off board just right. Soared to American, Olympic and world record of 29′2 1/2″. Leap has been called the perfect long jump and greatest track mark of all-time. Bettered Ralph Boston's world of 27′5″ mark by nearly 2′. Boston had set Olympic record of 27′1″ in qualifying, but his mark sank into oblivion with Beamon's "perfect" jump. Conditions for the jump (maximum wind, low wind resistance) and tremendous ability and technique of Beamon added up to great feat. Was named Track & Field Athlete of 1968 by *Track & Field News.* Was 1st in every outdoor meet competed in during 1968 season. Won AAU with 27′4″ and Olympic trials at 27′6 1/2″ with wind, along with Olympic and U.S. relay titles. Competed sporadically after 1968 gold medal. Made attempt for comeback in 1972, but retired before Olympic trials. Had best of 25′1″ before hanging up spikes as amateur. Winner 1968 Citizen Savings (Helms) World Trophy Award, North America. Turned pro 1973.

BEARD, PERCY B. 1/26/08, Hardinsburg, Ky. Member 1932 Olympic team. Held world 120-yd and 110-m hurdle records. Broke 120-yd mark with 14.2 in 1931 AAU championships at Lincoln, Nebr. Tied record in 1934. Broke 110-m record in 1932 with 14.4 clocking. Broke own mark in 1934 with 14.3 then 14.2. Won 1931, '34, '35 AAU championships, running 14.2 in 1931 and '35. In 1932 Los Angeles Olympics hit hurdle and finished second to teammate George Saling. Saling timed in 14.6, Beard 14.7. Did not have outstanding college career, but became world's best when in prime.

BEATTY, JIM B. 10/28/34, New York, N.Y. Member 1960 Olympic team. Held world 2-mile record with 8:29.8 on June 6, 1962, at Los Angeles. Was first miler in history to run 4-minute mile indoors. Ran 3:58.9 at L.A. Times indoor meet Feb. 10, 1962. In spring of 1960 lowered U.S. mile mark to 3:58.0 and 5000-m to 13:51.7. Won 1960 Olympic trials in 5000-m with 14:13.6. In Rome Olympics was eliminated in qualifying heat with 14:43.8. In 1962 set U.S. records in 1500-m with 3:39.4 and mile in 3:56.3. Concentrated on 5000-m for 1964 Olympics but had bad luck. Dropped out of trials with 2½ laps to go. Hampered by heat and injury to right foot. Had cut foot in winter and had 12 stitches taken. Finished 3rd in 1964 AAU 5000-m. Won 1961–63 AAU indoor mile titles. Won 1962 outdoor with 3:57.9. Fair miler in college with 4:13.1 best, came to world prominence under guidance of Milhaly Igloi.

BECCALI, LUIGI B. 11/19/07, Milan, Italy. Member 1928, 32, 36 Italian Olympic teams. Held world 1500-m record. Ran 3:49.2 at Turin on Sept. 9, 1933, to tie record set by Ladoumegue. Eight days later broke record at Turin with 3:49.0. In first Olympics at Amsterdam was eliminated in prelims. Improved between Olympics. Had world best of 3:52.2 prior to 1932 Los Angeles Olympics. In L.A. ran away from Glenn Cunningham and other leaders to win gold medal and break Olympic record. Time of 3:51.2 was 4th best time in history. In 1936 Olympics was 3rd behind Jack Lovelock and Glenn Cunningham. Lovelock set world record with 3:47.8 as Cunningham, San Romani, Edwards and Beccali all beat previous Olympic record set by the Italian in 1932. Came to U.S. in 1937 and ran 4:09.6. Became member of New York Athletic Club, lives in U.S. Has distinction of winning 1500-m in both Olympics and European Championships.

BELL, GREG B. 11/7/30, Terre Haute, Ind. Member 1956 Olympic team. Won gold medal in 1956 Melbourne Olympic long jump with leap of 25′8¼″. Was 1955 AAU champion with 26′½″ and 1959 champion with 26′1¼″ jump. Won 1957 NCAA LJ with 26′7″, only 1′¼″ off Jesse Owens' world record. Took 1958 NCAA title for Indiana U. with 25′9″. Won silver medal in 1959 Pan-Am Games jumping 24′11¼″. Made attempt for 1960 Rome Olympics but was 4th in tryouts with 25′4″. At peak was only inches away from Owen's world record 26′8 ¼″.

BERRUTI, LIVIO B. 5/19/39, Turin, Italy. Member 1960, 64 Olympic teams. Co-held world 200-m record, with 20.5 in 1960 Rome Olympics semifinals and finals. In finals was underdog to Ray Norton, Stone Johnson and Les Carney of U.S. Wearing sunglasses, Italian thrilled home crowd by tying world record of 20.5 and winning gold medal. Only European to win gold medal in 200-m. In 1964 Olympics finished 5th in defense of 200-m crown. Also fine 100-m man. Best of 10.2 done in Verona on May 26, 1960, still Italian record. Winner 1960 Citizens Savings (Helms) World Trophy Award, Europe.

BESSON, COLETTE B. 4/7/46, Saint-Georges de Didonne, France. Member 1968 French Olympic team. Won gold medal in Mexico City Olympics in 400-m. Ran 52.0 to collect unexpected medal. In 1969 tied world 400-m record. Ran 51.7 at Athens on Sept. 18 to share mark with countrywoman Nicole Duclos. French 400-m champ 1968–71. Was 800-m champ in 1970 and won cross country title in 1971. Third in 1970 European indoor 400-m with 53.6, ran 3rd leg of winning French 1600-m relay team.

BIFFLE, JEROME B. 3/20/28, Denver, Colo. Member 1952 Olympic team. Won 1950 NCAA long jump for Denver U. with leap of 25′4¾″. After career at Denver was drafted into Army. During most of time in Army was retired from competition. Tried out for 1952 Olympic team and made squad. At Helsinki not one of favorites. George Brown, also of U.S., was favored but fouled on all jumps. Biffle rose to occasion and won gold medal with jump of 24′10″.

BIKILA, ABEBE B. 8/7/32, Addis Ababa, Ethiopia. Member 1960, 64, 68 Ethiopian Olympic teams. In 1960 Rome Olympics scored surprising win in marathon. Running barefoot, set Olympic mark of 2:15:15.2 over 26-mile course. Running his 3rd marathon, was with leaders all the way and took lead with about mile to go. Only 25 years earlier, Games host Italy conquered Ethiopia. In 1964 Tokyo Olympics won gold medal in great performance. Beat nearest competitor by 4:07 for world best and Olympic record of 2:12:11.2. First man to win marathon twice. Had appendix out 40 days before Games. In Tokyo wore shoes and socks. Tried for 3rd gold medal in 1968 Olympics at Mexico City but failed. Dropped out after 10 miles because of broken fibia. Countryman Mamo Walde won gold medal. One of Emperor Haile Selassie's palace guards when won first gold medal. Now captain holding desk job. Confined to wheelchair and visited by emperor weekly. Winner 1960 Citizens Savings (Helms) World Trophy Award, Africa.

BLACK, LARRY B. 7/20/51, Miami, Fla. Member 1972 Olympic team. Versatile sprinter, ran 200-m and leg of 400-m relay in 1972 Munich Olympics. Primarily 200-m and 220-yd man. In 1971 won NAIA for North Carolina Central with wind-aided 20.4. Also took NCAA College Division title in 20.9. NCAA University champ with 20.5. Placed 2nd in AAU with wind-aided 20.5. Took 3rd in U.S.-USSR-World All-Star meet. In 1972 on N.C. Central relay team, ran 43.8 440-yd. Won 1972 NAIA 200-m in 20.2 and ran on 2 winning relays. At U.S. Olympic trials made team finishing 2nd in 20.7. In Munich Olympics won silver medal in 200-m with 20.19 time. Ran leadoff leg of U.S. 400-m relay team that tied world record of 38.19 and won gold medal.

BLANKERS-KOEN, FANNY B. 4/26/18, Amsterdam, Netherlands. Member 1948, 52 Dutch Olympic teams. Held world 100-yd, 100-m, 220-yd, 80-m hurdle, high jump and pentathlon records. Also ran on world record 440-yd and 800-m relay teams. Had following bests: 10.8 in 100-yd, 11.5 in 100-m, 24.2 in 220-yd, 11.0 in 80-m hurdles, 20′6″ in long jump, 5′7 ¼″ in high jump. Set pentathlon record of 4692 points. In 1948 Olympics won 4 gold medals, tops of any track and field performer. First won 100-m in 11.9, then set world mark in 80-m hurdles of 11.2; 200-m was next in 24.4, gained 4th gold medal by anchoring 400-m relay team. Won 5 gold medals in European Championship competition. In 1950 won 100-m, 200-m and hurdles; in 1946 won hurdles and relay. Married Jan Blankers, a former triple jumper now sports writer.

BLOZIS, AL B. 1/5/19, Garfield, N.J. D. 1/31/45, in combat. Top shot putter of 1940s. Won 3 NCAA championships for Georgetown U. In 1940 won with meet record 56′ ½″. Record stood 9 years. Also took 1941, 42 NCAA crowns. Won everything in sight 1940–42 and was good bet to beat Jack Torrance's world record. Had best of 56′6 ⅛″ outdoors to Torrance's 57′1″. Won 3 AAU outdoor and indoor crowns, 55′ ⅜″ in 1940 AAU best championship performance outdoors. Had indoors best of 57′ ¾″ in 1942. The huge Blozis (6′6″, 240) played pro football for the N.Y. Giants. Died on Western Front in WW II. Member Citizens Savings (Helms) Hall of Fame.

BOLOTNIKOV, PYOTR B. 3/8/30, Zanovkino, Russia. Member 1956, 60 USSR Olympic teams. Held world 10,000-m record. Broke countryman Kuts' record by 12.4 seconds with 28:18.8 on Oct. 15, 1960, in Kiev. In 1962 broke own record with 28:18.2 in Moscow on Aug. 11. In 1956 Olympics was unimpressive in 5000-m and 10,000-m. Was 9th in 5000-m and 16th in 10,000-m. Was USSR 10,000-m champ in 1957 over

Kuts. In 1960 Rome Olympics passed up 5000-m and concentrated on 10,000-m. In finals ran away from Hans Grodatzki of Germany for gold medal. Time of 28:32.2 broke Kuts' Olympic record. Won 1962 European Championship in 10,000-m but failed double in 5000-m; was 3rd.

BONDARCHUK, ANATOTIY B. 5/31/40, Russia. Member 1972 USSR Olympic team. Won gold medal in hammer throw at Munich with Olympic record of 247′8½″. In 1969 at Athens on Sept. 20, set world mark of 245′0″. Later that year increased mark to 247′7½″. Was 3rd in 1971 European Championships with 234′3″. Was 1972 Soviet Union champ at 247′10″. Had best of 248′6½″ going to Munich Games, tops in world.

BONHAG, GEORGE B. 1881, New York, N.Y. D. 10/30/60. Member 1904, 08, 12 Olympic teams. Primarily long distance runner, won gold medal in 1906 unofficial Olympics 1500-m walk in 7:12.6. Had never competed in walking race before. Disappointed in showing in 1500-m (6th) and specialty 5-mile run where was 4th. Won gold medal as most competitors were disqualified because of technique. In 1904 Olympics was 5th in 2500-m steeplechase. In 1908 was member of 3-mile team and collected only medal when team was 2nd. Carried U.S. flag in 1912. Was 4th in 5000-m and 5th in 3000-m team race. Won 1911 AAU 5-mile with time of 25:50.04.

BONTHRON, WILLIAM (Bill) B. 11/1/12, Detroit, Mich. Held world 1500-m record, running 3:34.8 on June 30, 1934 at Milwaukee. Was a top collegiate miler at Princeton. IC4A outdoor 880-yd and mile champ 1933, 34. Took IC4A indoor mile title in 1934. In 1933 met Jack Loveland of New Zealand at Princeton in historic mile. Bonthron led most of way but Lovelock won in 4:07.6. Bonthron ran 4:08.7 as both men beat Jules Ladomege's world record of 4:09.2. In NCAA mile in 1934, his best year, defeated great Glenn Cunningham with 4:08.9. At AAU won 1500-m from Cunningham with great kick and set world record of 3:48.8. Was winner of Sullivan Memorial trophy as athlete of year in 1934. In 1936 Olympic trials finished 4th and did not make team. Accountant living in Princeton, N.J. Member Citizens Savings (Helms) Hall of Fame.

BORZOV, VALERI B. 10/20/49. Russia. Member 1972 USSR Olympic team. Won impressive sprint double at Munich Olympics. Took 100-m in 10.14. Won all prelim heats, finals with no trouble. Much the same in 200-m. Ran 20.00 to win by almost .2. Again won all his heats. Ran anchor leg on Russian 400-m team that won silver medal behind U.S.

team which tied world mark of 38.19. Was 1971 European champion in both sprints (10.0 and 20.3). Took 1969 100-m title in 10.0 which set European record. Was awarded Order of Lenin, one of highest awards bestowed on Soviet citizen, following Olympic triumphs.

BOSTON, RALPH B. 5/9/39, Laurel, Miss. Member 1960, 64, 68 Olympic teams. Held world long jump record. First set mark at Walnut, Calif., Aug. 8, 1960 with leap of 26′11¼″. Improved to 27′½″ at Modesto, Calif., May 27, 1961. In Moscow on July 16, 1961, defeated rival Ter-Ovanesyan and advanced record to 27′2″. Ter-Ovanesyan took record away with 27′3¼″ in 1962. Boston tied mark in Jamaica on Aug. 15, 1964. At 1964 final Olympic trials at Los Angeles on Aug. 12, regained sole possession of record with 27′4¼″ jump. Last record jump of 27′5″ at Modesto, on May 29, 1965. Took gold medal in 1960 Rome Olympics, breaking Jesse Owens' record with 26′7¾″. In 1964 Tokyo Olympics took silver medal behind Davies of Great Britain. In 1968 Mexico City Games jumped 26′9½″ but settled for bronze medal. Bob Beamon's unbelievable 29′2½″ and German Klaus Beer's 26′10½″ topped effort. While student at Tenn. A & I was 1960 NCAA titlist. Holds American collegiate record with 27′½″ in 1961. Won 1961–66 AAU outdoor championships. Was bio-chemist, now administrator at Tenn. U. and television track commentator. Top long jumper of decade. Member Citizens Savings (Helms) Hall of Fame. Winner 1961 Citizens Savings World Trophy Award, North America.

BOURLAND, CLIFFORD B. 1/1/21, Los Angeles, Calif. Member 1948 Olympic team. Standout quarter-miler in early 1940s. Won 1942 NCAA championship while at Southern Cal in 440-yd with 48.2. Took NCAA again in 1943 with 48.5. Had outstanding college career. In 1941 AAU ran 46.1 but only finished 3rd. Ran 45.8 split on USC mile relay team in 1941. Trojans ran 3:09.4 which bettered world mark, but lost to UCLA in race. Was 1942 AAU champion with 46.7 and repeated in 1943 with 47.7. War interrupted career for several years, but came back to qualify for 1948 Olympics. Made team in 200-m with 21.0 in tryouts. Made finals in London but was 5th. Got gold medal as member of U.S. 1600-m relay team.

BOWDEN, DON B. 8/8/36, San Jose, Calif. Member 1956 Olympic team. First American to run 4-minute mile. Ran 3:58.7 at Stockton, Calif., June 1, 1957. Member California U. world record 2-mile relay team which ran 7:21.0 at Los Angeles, May 16, 1958. Was 1957 NCAA 880-yd champ with 1:47.2. Had 800-m best of 1:46.5 and 880-yd best of 1:47.2, both in 1957 NCAA at Austin, Tex., June 15, 1957. Did not surpass 1957 performances in short career. Was 1500-m representative for U.S. in 1956 Melbourne Olympics but ran 4:00 and did not qualify.

BOWERMAN, BILL B. 2/19/11, Fossil, Oreg. Coach 1972 Olympic team. Head coach at Oregon, 1948–72. Oregon teams won NCAA titles in 1962, 64, 65. Teams were in NCAA top 10 in 14 of last 19 years. Has produced 23 NCAA individual winners and 37 conference champions. Coached 56 all-Americans at Oregon. Has had outstanding distance runners, including Dyrol Burleson, Bill Dellinger, Jim Grelle, and Steve Prefontaine. Has coached 10 sub-4-minute milers. His 1962 440-yd relay team of Mel Renfro, Mike Gaetcher, Jerry Tarr and Harry Jerome set world record of 40.0. In same year his 4-mile relay team ran 16:09.0 for world mark. Sent 11 runners to Olympic Games. With Bowerman as head coach, U.S. won 6 gold medals. Political rulings, schedule mixups, alleged protests and upsets, all beyond Bowerman's control, kept team from winning at least 4 more gold medals. Was star football player at Oregon in 1930s. Assistant director of athletics and professor of physical education at Oregon, along with track duties.

BRAGG, DON (Tarzan) B. 5/15/35, Penns Grove, N.J. Member 1960 Olympic team. Held world pole vault record of 15′9 ¼″ in 1960. Last of metal pole record-holders. Called Tarzan because of 6′3″, 197–lb stature, large for vaulter. In 1959 set indoor world record with 15′9 ⅝″. Won 1960 Olympic tryouts with world mark of 15′9 ¼″. Won gold medal at Rome Olympics with record 15′5 ⅛″. Won 1959 Pan-Am Games with 15′2 ½″, also meet record. Won 3 straight IC4A outdoor titles at Villanova from 1955–57 and 2 indoor IC4A titles and tied for a third in same period. Set NCAA record of 15′1″ in 1955. Won 3 indoor AAU championships and tied for 2 more. Won 1959 AAU outdoor title with 15′3″. Outspoken critic of fiberglass poles. Member Citizens Savings (Helms) Hall of Fame.

BRASHER, CHRIS B. 8/20/28, Georgetown, British Guiana. Member 1952 British Olympic team. Fine all-round distance runner who had greatest moment in steeplechase. Close friend and teammate of Roger Bannister, helped Bannister in historic mile. Set pace for first 2 ½ laps in first sub 4-minute mile. In 1956 Melbourne Olympics climbed out of Bannister's shadow. Won gold medal in 3000-m steeplechase in Olympic best of 8:41.2 in mass of confusion. Was disqualified, charged with interfering with Ernst Larsen of Norway. After hearing both Larsen and Brasher, Jury of Appeal gave Brasher back gold medal.

BRIX, HERMAN (Bruce Bennett) B. 1909. Member 1928 Olympic team. Won silver medal in shot with toss of 51′8 $\frac{1}{16}$″. Was 4-time AAU champion. Took 1928–31 titles with toss of 52′5 ¾″ in 1930 his best. Was

1930 AAU indoor champ with 51′2½″. Won 1932 AAU indoor, setting meet record of 51′4½″. Was 1927 NCAA champion while at Washington U. Winning put was 46′7⅜″. Was 3rd in 1928 and 5th in 1926. Was 1928 Pac Coast Conference champion. After track career, went into movies as actor. Played Tarzan in 12-episode series of *New Adventures of Tarzan* in 1935. Played Kioga in highly successful series *Hawk of the Wilderness*. Well known as supporting character in movies of 1940s and 50s. Member Citizens Savings (Helms) Hall of Fame.

BROWN, EARLENE B. 7/11/35, Latexo, Tex. Member 1956, 60, 64 Olympic teams. Holds American citizen outdoor records in shot and discus. Threw disc 176′10″ at Abilene, Tex. on July 16, 1960, shot 54′9″ on Sept. 21, 1960, at Frankfurt, Germany. Also held indoor mark in shot (49′6″) and basketball throw (135′2″), both set in Akron, Ohio, on March 22, 1958, at AAU indoor. Was AAU champion in shot 8 times. Took 1st crown in 1956 with toss of 45′, then won 6 more in a row with 49′8½″ in 1960 best. Last took championship in 1964. Won AAU discus in '58, '59 '61 with 153′8″ in '59 her best. Was 1957 AAU baseball throw champ with record 271′10″. In 1958 U.S.-USSR duel in Moscow took 1st in shot with 54′3″ and 2nd in discus with 162′1¼″. Was 2nd in 1959 duel in shot. Was 1959 Pan-Am shot and discus champion. In 1st Olympic competition in 1956 at Melbourne was 6th in shot with 49′7¼″ and 4th in discus with 168′5½″. In 1960 Rome Olympics took bronze medal in shot with 53′10⅜″. Was again 4th in discus with 168′3¼″. In 1964 was disappointing 12th with toss of 48′6½″. Member Citizens Savings (Helms) Hall of Fame. Beautician and housewife in Los Angeles.

BRUCH, RICHARD (Ricky) B. 7/2/46, Göteborg, Sweden. Member 1968, 72 Swedish Olympic teams. Won bronze medal in '72 Munich Games in discus with 208′0″. In '68 Mexico City Olympics, was 8th with 194′6″. In 1971 matched Jay Silvester's world mark of 224′5″. Set European record of 223′3½″ in 1969. Second in 1971 European championships. Swedish national discus champion in '67, '69, '70, '72. Was shot put champ in 1970, '72. Holds national shot record of 65′9″. A giant 6′6¼″, 298-pounder, has been member of 19 Swedish national teams. Physical education instructor.

BRUMEL, VALERY B. 4/14/42, Tolbuzhino, Siberia. Member 1960, 64 Russian Olympic teams. Broke world record high jump mark with 7′4″ jump June 18, 1961 in Moscow. Came to world attention in 1960 Rome Olympics with silver medal finish over John Thomas of U.S. who held world record. Brumel and Russian gold winner Shavlakadze scored one of track's greatest upsets in Rome. Raised his world record to 7′4½″ at Sofia in August of 1961. In Palo Alto, Calif., in U.S.-USSR duel raised mark to 7′5″ on July 22, 1962. Jump of 7′5½″ at Moscow on Sept 29, 1962, raised mark again. Won 1964 Tokyo gold medal over arch-rival Thomas at 7′1⅞″ on fewest misses. Broke leg in 3 places in motorcycle accident, ending career for all intents and purposes. Recovered to jump again but not at world class level. Had leg operated on 29 times. Winner 1961 Citizens Savings (Helms) World Trophy Award, Europe.

BRUNDAGE, AVERY B. 9/28/87. Member 1912 U.S. Olympic team. Former president (1952–72) International Olympic Committee. Before IOC post was president of U.S. Olympic Committee 1929–53. Served 7 terms as president of AAU. While Olympic head, tried with religious fervor to keep Games pure and free from commercialism. Criticized many times for idealistic views. Standout decathlon man. Won national titles in "all-round", decathlon and pentathlon. Finished 22nd in discus, 5th in pentathlon, 14th in decathlon in 1912 Stockholm Olympics. Graduated from Illinois with degree in civil engineering. Multimillionaire contractor, devoted much time and money to Olympic Games.

BUDD, FRANK B. 7/20/39, Long Branch, N. J. Member 1960 Olympic team. Held world 100-yd and 220-yd records. Ran 9.3 in 1961 to tie record. At AAU championships June 24, 1961, in New York ran first official 9.2. On May 12, 1962, at Villanova, Pa., equalled Dave Sime's 220-yd record with 20.0. At Villanova U. won 1961, 62 NCAA double in 100-yd and 220-yd with 9.4s each year. Won IC4A 100-yd and 220-yd in same years. Competed only in 1960 Rome Olympics. Finished 5th but time of 10.3 equalled Olympic 100-m record. Also ran on 400-m relay team which was disqualified. Tried luck in pro football before reaching possible peak. Failed to make pros as have most trackmen.

BURGHLEY, LORD DAVID B. 2/9/05, Stamford, England. Member 1928, 32 British Olympic teams. Held world 440-yd hurdle record. Ran 54.2 at London on July 2, 1927. Record lasted only few hours. Was chopped to 52.6 by John Gibson of U.S. same day. Had great impact on British athletics with his skill. In 1928 Olympics defeated world record-holder F. Morgan Taylor and Bab Cuhel, both of U.S., for gold medal in 53.4. In 1932 Olympics finished 4th with personal best time of 52.2. Best all-round hurdler in England for many years and won many titles. Had best of 14.5 in high hurdles, 24.3 in lows and 52.2 in 400-m. Still active as one of two vice-presidents of International Olympic Committee. Chairman of 1948 British Olympic Committee. Did excellent job in preparing still-scarred Britain for Games.

BURKE, EDWARD B. 3/4/40, Ukiah, Calif. Member 1964, 68 Olympic teams. Holds American hammer throw mark with toss of 235′11″ at

Bakersfield, Calif., on June 22, 1967, at AAU championships. Won 1966, 68 AAU titles. Great competitor, had shoulder injury in 1968 that would have put many into retirement. But won AAU and Olympic trials. However, in Mexico City Games was 12th with best of 215′7 ½″. College history professor. Member Citizens Savings (Helms) Hall of Fame.

BURLESON, DYROL B. 4/27/40, Saginaw, Oreg. Member 1960, 64 Olympic teams. One of U.S. 's 1st sub 4-minute milers. Ran for Oregon 1960–62. While at Oregon won 1960 NCAA 1500-m with 3:44.2, 1961 mile at 4:00.5 and 1962 mile. Was 1959 AAU 1500-m champ with 3:47.5. Won 1961 AAU mile with 4:04.9. Set AAU meet record with 3:56.7 mile in 1963. Set American Collegiate 2-mile record with 8:42.6 at Eugene, Oreg, on April 7, 1962. In 1960, trying for first gold medal for U.S. in 1500-m since 1908, was 6th, even though bettering Olympic record. Herb Elliott set world record of 3:35.6 for gold medal. In 1964 ran 3:40.0 but was 5th, only 1.9 off winning time. Was 1959 Pan-Am 1500-m champion. Insurance salesman in Cottage Grove, Oreg.

BUSCH, JIM B. 9/15/26, Cleveland, Ohio. Track coach at UCLA since 1964; has taken Bruins to top of U.S. collegiate ranks. UCLA has won 4 NCAA outdoor titles (1966, 71–73) and 6 Pac-8 titles under Busch. First year at UCLA, team set world distance medley record (9:33.9) and U.S. mile and 2-mile records. Team won 1966 NCAA by 48 points, largest margin ever. Became only school to win 440-yd and mile relay in same meet. In 1967, 440-yd team tied world mark of 39.6. Mile relay team set American record in 1967, 3:03.4. Bruins were unbeaten in dual competition in '66, '67, '70. Coached 7 NCAA individual champs. 1972 NCAA title team won 3 individual events and mile relay 4th time in row. Named 1971 "Coach of Year" by National Collegiate Track Field Coaches Association (NCTFCA). Called honor "highest point" of career. Highly successful coach at Fullerton High School and Junior College before moving on to Occidental in 1962 where teams recorded 3 straight dual wins over UCLA. Coached John Smith, world record-holder in 440-yd, and 1972 Munich Olympic 400-m silver medalist Wayne Collett. President NCTFCA.

CAIRD (JONES), MAUREEN B. 9/29/51, Sydney, Australia. Member 1968 Australian Olympic team. Won gold medal in 1968 Olympics, running 10.3 in 80-m hurdles to win handily over Pat Kilborn and Chi Cheng. Held world 200-m hurdle record with 27.1 at Sydney on May 24, 1969. In 1970 Australian championships won 100-m hurdles and 200-m hurdles with 13.3 and 26.3. Was 1970 Australian 200-m hurdle champ in 27.0. Her 10.3 in 1968 Olympics is Australian record.

CALHOUN, LEE B. 2/23/33, Laurel, Miss. Member 1956, 60 Olympic teams. Co-holder world 120-yd and 110-meter high hurdles with 13.2 on Aug. 21, 1960. Only man to win 2 gold medals in Olympic 110-meter hurdles. Won with Olympic record 13.5 in 1956, 13.8 in 1960 at Rome Olympics. Won both by slim margins over U.S. teammates in 1–2–3 sweeps. Won AAU outdoor hurdles in '56, '57, '59; 13.6 in 1956 best. Won AAU indoor 60-yd hurdles in 1956, 57. While at North Carolina College won 1956, 57 NCAA 120-yd hurdles, 13.6 in '57. World record still stands. Citizens Savings (Helms) Hall of Fame. Now assistant track coach at Yale.

CAMPBELL, MILTON B. 12/9/33, Plainfield, N.J. Member 1952, 56 Olympic teams. Co-held world 120-yd hurdle record. Ran 13.4 at Compton, Calif, on May 31, 1957, to tie Jack Davis' record. Although great hurdler, decathlon was his forte. Did, however, take 1955 NCAA and AAU 120-yd hurdle titles with 13.9 in both races. In 1952 Helsinki Olympics was 18-year-old schoolboy, but took decathlon silver medal with 6975 points behind Bob Mathias. In 1956 Melbourne Olympics big (6′3″, 215-lb) ex-Indiana football player took decathlon gold medal with great performance. Won first event, 100-m, with 10.8; 2nd in long jump with 24′ 5/8″; 1st in shot with 48′5″; 2nd in high jump at 6′2 1/4″; and 2nd in 400-m with 48.8. Gave him 4564 points at halfway point of 10-event test. Was on world record pace. Took 1st in 110-m hurdles with 14.0 to start second day of competition. Was then 2nd in discus with 147′6 3/4″. But in pole vault made only 11′1 3/4″ for 476 which cost him world record. Did well enough in javelin and 1500-m to set Olympic record of 7937. Director of program for underprivileged in New Jersey.

CANTELLO, ALBERT B. 6/9/33, Norristown, Pa. Member 1960 Olympic team. Held world javelin record. Threw spear 282′3″ on June 5, 1959, at Compton, Calif. Was 1959 AAU champion with 246′9″ and 1960 with 271′9″. In 1960 Olympics was 10th with throw of 245′1″, more than 30′ behind winner. Won 1956 U.S.-USSR dual meet with throw of 262′5″. Only second U.S. javelin thrower to hold the world record.

CARLOS, JOHN B. 6/5/45, New York, N.Y. Member 1968 Olympic team. Co-holds world 100-yd record. Ran 9.1 at Fresno, Calif., on May 10, 1969. Ran 200-m with illegal shoes in 19.7 at South Lake Tahoe Olympic trials Sept. 12, 1968. Won gold medal in 1967 Pan Am Games in Winnipeg with 20.5 in 200-m. In 1968 Mexico City Olympics was 3rd behind Tommie Smith of U.S. and Peter Norman of Australia. On award stand Smith and Carlos staged protest of treatment of blacks in U.S. Lowered heads during National Anthem and raised gloved, clenched fists. Both expelled from team with protest approved by some, blasted by others. In 1969 Carlos was world's leading sprinter in both 100-yd and 220-yd. Ran 9.2 for San Jose St. in 1969 NCAA 100-yd and 20.2 in 220-yd. Ran 9.1 with wind in NCAA prelim. Lost AAU 100-yd but won 220-yd with 20.2. Was double winner in U.S.-USSR, U.S.-Europe, U.S.-W. Germany meets. Ran 10.1 in 100-m and 20.3 against Germany. In Indian Summer Meet ran 9.9 with wind and 20.0. Tried pro football in 1970 but failed.

CARPENTER, KENNETH (Ken) B. 4/19/13, Compton, Calif. Member 1936 Olympic team. Two-time collegiate discus champ at Southern Cal. Won 1935 NCAA title with throw of 157′11″ and was 1936 NCAA titlist with meet record toss of 173′, beating record by nearly 10′. Was 1935 AAU champion with 158′11″. Took 1936 AAU title with throw of 166′2″. In 1936 Berlin Olympics took gold medal with throw of 165′7 3/8″, new Olympic record by over 3′. Gordon Dunn of U.S. won silver medal 3 1/2′ back. Resides in Compton, Calif. Member Citizens Savings (Helms) Hall of Fame.

CARR, HENRY B. 11/27/42 Montgomery, Ala. Member 1964 Olympic team. Held world 200-m, 220-yd records. Ran 20.3 at Tempe, Ariz., on June 23, 1963, to get name in record books at both distances. Ran 20.2 April 4, 1964, at Tempe. AAU co-titlist at 220-yd in 1963 with Paul Drayton at 20.4. Took 1964 AAU with 20.6. In 1964 Tokyo Olympics was gold medalist at 200-m. Set Olympic record with 20.3 in finals. Anchored U.S. 1600-m team to gold medal with world and Olympic record 3:00.7. Won 1963 NCAA 220-yd for Arizona State with 20.5 clocking. Fine all-round sprinter with 9.4 in 100-yd and 440 relay laps just over 45.0. Ran on ASU mile relay team that set world record of 3:04.5 on April 27, 1963, at Walnut, Calif. Turned to pro football after Olympics. Defensive back for New York Giants several seasons.

CARR, SABIN B. 9/4/04, Dubuque, Iowa. Member 1928 Olympic team. Held world pole vault record. Was world's first 14′ vaulter. Went 14′0″ at Philadelphia in IC4A meet on May 25, 1927, for world mark. Collegiate vaulter for Yale. Won '26, '27, '28 IC4A outdoor championships. Tied for 1927 indoor IC4A and won 1928 crown with 13′3¾″. Went 13′0″ in 1925, 13′3″ in '26 prior to world best. Set American indoor record and world best with vault of 14′1″ in 1928. Later that year lost world record to Lee Barnes who went 14′1¾″. Made Olympic team along with Barnes, William Droegemuller and Charles McGinnis. In Amsterdam competition Carr came out with gold medal. Went 13′9½″ for Olympic record. Droegemuller won silver, McGinnis bronze. Barnes was 5th. Member Citizens Savings (Helms) Hall of Fame.

CARR, WILLIAM B. 10/24/09. D. 1/14/66. Member 1932 U.S. Olympic team. Held world 400-m record. Set mark in 1932 Olympic finals at Los Angeles, Aug. 5, with 46.2. Had broken Olympic record with 47.2 in semifinals. Came into limelight as runner for Penn in 1932 IC4A championships at Berkeley, Calif. Took on Ben Eastman, then holder of world 400-m and 440-yd records. Defeated Eastman, 47.0 to 47.2. Won 1932 AAU (Olympic trials), again beating Eastman with meet record 46.9. In Olympic finals came from behind to defeat Eastman again, breaking world and Olympic records. Also ran on gold medal U.S. 1600-m team. Seriously injured in car accident that ended career shortly after great Olympic performance.

CAWLEY, WARREN (Rex) B. 6/7/40, Detroit, Mich. Member 1964 Olympic team. Held 400-m hurdle world record, running 49.1 at Los Angeles on Sept. 13, 1964, in the final Olympic trials. In 1963 won NCAA 440-yd hurdles in 49.6. Was 2nd in USSR-USA dual. In 1964 had mixed success in early season with wins at Coliseum Relays (51.0) and

Cal Relays (51.5). Then went 5 meets without win. Was 4th in AAU. Finished 2nd in early Olympic trials and was picked for USSR-USA dual meet. In meet, held in L.A. took 1st with 49.5. Then won at Carreras Invitational and final Olympic trials. In 1964 Tokyo Olympics won prelim heat in 50.8 and semi with 49.8. In finals was slow first 5 hurdles, but moved up to 2nd by the 7th hurdle. Passed Frinolli of Italy at 9th hurdle for lead and won going away with 49.6. Selected top 400-m-440-yd hurdle man of 1964 by *Track & Field News.*

CHATAWAY, CHRIS B. 1/31/31, Chelsea, England. Member 1952, 56 British Olympic teams. Held world records in 3-mile, 5000-m. Member British 4-mile relay team that set world mark of 16:41.0 at London in 1953 with Roger Bannister running anchor. Set 3-mile record at London with 13:32.2 on July 10, 1954. Lost record to Kuts of USSR but regained it about year later with 13:26.4. Ran 13:51.6 to set 5000-m mark at London on Oct. 13, 1954. Helped college teammate Bannister break 4-minute mile. Was 2nd in historic race with 4:07.2. Also 2nd in second 4-minute mile to John Landy. Landy ran 3:58.0, Chataway 4:04.4. Ran 3:59.8 in 1955 but was 3rd in race. In 1952 Helsinki Olympics Chataway fell on final turn in 5000-m in jam for lead. Won 1954 British Empire Games at Vancouver in 5000-m with 13:35.2. Defeated Kuts in world record performance at London in 1954. Said to be greatest victory for British athlete at home. In 1956 Melbourne Olympics was disappointing 11th in 5000-m. Was one athlete who considered track "just" sport. Did not push himself in training, but had great career.

CHENG (REEL), CHI B. 3/15/44, Formosa. Member 1968 Formosa Olympic team. Won bronze medal in 80-m hurdles with 10.4. Holds numerous women's sprint records. In 1970 set or tied four world records in unbelievable season. Tied Wyomia Tyus' 100-m record of 11.0 on July 18, at Vienna. Set 200-m record of 22.4 on July 7 at Munich. On June 13 set 100-yd mark of 10.0 at Portland. At Westwood, Calif. on July 3, set 220-yd record with 22.6. Started off great 1970 with U.S. AAU 60-yd title with 6.7. Also won 60-yd hurdles in 7.6. In 1970 AAU outdoor won 100-yd and 220-yd. Ran 10.2 in 100-yd and 22.4 in 220-yd in meet held at Los Angeles. Represented L.A. Track Club. Voted Woman Athlete of the Year by Associated Press in 1970. In 1971 came up with mysterious leg ailment. Had surgery, tried acupunture, but pain remained. Unable to compete in 1972 Olympics. Has been residing in U.S. for last 10 years. Married to Vince Reel, women's track coach of fine repute and editor of *Women's Track & Field World.* Winner 1969 Citizens Savings (Helms) World Trophy Award, Asia.

CLARK, ELLERY B. 3/13/74, West Roxbury, Mass. D. 7/27/49.

Member 1896 Olympic team. One of fine Boston Athletic Association athletes sent to first Olympic Games held in Athens. Gold medalist in high jump with 5′11 ¼″. Took second gold medal in long jump at 20′9 ¾″. Despite international success, was never national title-holder at home.

CLARKE, RON B. 2/2/37. Member 1964, 68 Australian Olympic teams. Set 17 world distance records from 2-mile to 20,000-m. First record came on Dec. 18, 1963, at Melbourne with 27:17.8 in 6-mile. Beat record by 26 seconds. Set 10,000-m mark of 28:15.6 in same race. Set 3-mile mark of 13:07.6 at Melbourne on Dec. 3, 1964. Had records in 2-mile, 3-mile, 5000-m, 6-mile, 10,000-m, 10-mile, 20,000-m and 1-hr run. Records in all but 20,000-m and 1-hr run still stand. Best of 8:19.6 in 2-mile, 12:50.4 in 3-mile, 13:16.6 in 5000-m, 26:47.0 in 6-mile, and 27:39.4 in 10,000-m still stand as world records. In 1965 set 11 world records in 7 distance events. In 1964 qualified in 3 events in Tokyo Olympics. Ninth in 5000-m. Possibly best race was 10,000-m but was 3rd behind American Billy Mills and Mohamed Gammoudi of Tunisia in one of greatest upsets in Olympic history. Also ninth in marathon. In 1968 Mexico City Olympics was entered in 5000-m and 10,000-m. In 10,000-m could not take altitude and finished 6th. Collapsed after finish and was unconscious for 10 minutes. Recovered and ran 5000-m prelims and qualified for finals. In finals had lead at 9 laps but could not answer on final lap and was 6th. Although never won a major championship, has to be considered one of greatest distance men in history. Held decisive edges in meetings with Olympic champions Gammoudi, Mills, Roelants, Temu. Named *Track & Field News* Athlete of 1966. Lit torch at 1956 Melbourne Olympics. Winner 1965 Citizens Savings (Helms) World Trophy Award, Australasia.

COACHMAN, ALICE B. 11/9/23, Albany, Ga. Member 1948 Olympic team. Won gold medal in London Olympics in high jump. Set Olympic record with leap of 5′6 ⅛″. Won AAU HJ crown 3 times. Won in 1941 at 5′1″, 1945 at 4′8″, and 1946 at 4′6 ⅞″. No competition was held in 1938–40 and 1942–44, robbing her of valuable competition and possible honors. Now schoolteacher in Atlanta, Ga. Member Citizens Savings (Helms) Hall of Fame.

COCHRAN, ROY B. 1/6/19, Richton, Miss. Member 1948 Olympic team. First big win 1939 AAU 400-m hurdles in 51.9, only .1 off world record. Set 440-yd hurdle record at 1942 Drake Relays with 52.2. Career interupted by WW II stint in navy. Returned to track after war. At age 29 won 2 gold medals in 1948 London Olympics. Won 400-m hurdles in Olympic record 51.1. Also ran on winning 1600-m relay team. Exceptionally long, successful career. Named outstanding 440-yd hurdle man in first 50 years of Drake Relays. Won AAU as Indiana U. hurdler in 1940 and in 1942 while in navy. Member Citizens Savings (Helms) Hall of Fame.

COLLETT, WAYNE B. 10/20/49, Los Angeles, Calif. Member 1972 Olympic team. Versatile sprinter with top times in 200-m, 440-yd hurdles, and 400-m. As UCLA freshman at 1968 U.S. Olympic trials training camp ran 20.2. In 1970 NCAA championship ran 49.2 440-yd hurdles in rain and was 2nd to Ralph Mann. In 1971 was rated No. 2 man in 400-m, 440-yd by *Track & Field News*. In 1971 won Pacific-8 440-yd title over favored teammate John Smith in 45.4. In NCAA finished 4th in 46.2. Took 2nd in AAU in 44.7, his best time of year. In 1972, as UCLA graduate student, trained for Olympic team. In Olympic trials ran 44.1, best sea level 400-m in history, to win. In Olympic Games ran 44.80 for silver medal. On victory stand, along with Vince Matthews, did not stand at attention and was banned from further competition. Both Collett and Matthews denied any protest motive.

CONNOLLY, HAROLD B. 8/1/31, Somerville, Mass. Member 1956, 60, 64, 68 Olympic teams. Held world hammer throw record. First set mark in 1956 with throw of 224′10″ at Los Angeles on Nov. 2. Improved mark to 225′4″ in 1958, 230′2″ at Ceres, Calif., on May 29. On June 20 at Walnut, Calif., improved record to 233′9″. In 1956 Olympics was matched against Russian rival Mikhail Krivonosov, former world record-holder. Russian was early leader in finals, but Connolly won with Olympic record 207′3½″. Krivonosov fouled on last three tosses. Connolly won hand of Olga Fikotova, women's discus gold medalist from Czechoslovakia, in story book romance. In 1960 Olympics was favored since he had increased world record shortly before Games. But finished 8th with a poor toss of 208′6″. His Olympic record was broken by Russian Vasily Rudenkov at 220′2¼″. In 1964 Tokyo Olympics was 6th with best of 218′8″. In 1968 Mexico City Olympics did not qualify for finals. Tried out for 1972 Olympic team, but did not make top 3. AAU champion 1955–61, 64, 65. Threw 232′1″ in '65 championship. Was 1959 Pan-Am hammer champ. Took 1st in 1958 and 1963 U.S.-USSR dual meets. Took up hammer throw to strengthen left arm which was slightly withered at birth. Also broke arm several times competing in other sports. Teacher by profession. Member Citizens Savings (Helms) Hall of Fame.

CONNOLLY, JAMES B. 1868, S. Boston, Mass. D. 1/20/57. Member 1896, 1900 Olympic teams. First man to win gold medal in modern Olympic Games. Won triple jump, opening event of Athens Olympics, with leap of 45′0″. Was 2nd in high jump with 5′9 ¼″ performance. Won 3rd medal of Games with bronze in long jump with 19′1 ⅞″. Member of Boston Athletic Association team sent to first modern Olympics. Went to 1900 Paris Olympics on his own since there were no official teams. Competed in only triple jump and was 2nd behind Myer Prinstein, despite improved jump of 45′9 ⅞″. Made trip to 1906 Olympics in hopes of competing but injured knee and had to watch competition. Became writer of note, specializing in sea stories.

CONNOLLY (FIKOTOVA), OLGA B. 11/13/32, Praha, Czechoslovakia. Member 1956 Czechoslovakian Olympic team; member 1960, 64, 68 72 U.S. Olympic teams. In 1956 Olympics was in news on and off field of competition. In specialty, discus, upset Nina Ponomareva of USSR for gold medal. Toss of 176′1 ½″ bettered Nina's Olympic mark by over 8′. Off track, Olga fell in love with Harold Connolly, U.S. gold medal winner in hammer throw. Were married after Games and Olga became an American citizen. Was AAU discus champ in '57, '60, '62, '64, '68. In 1962 set meet record of 172′2″. In 1960 Olympics was 7th with throw of 167′1 ⅞″. In 1964 Games did not take a medal, also shut out in 68, 72 Games. Mother of four and author of *Rings of Destiny*, which details her life.

CONSOLINI, ADOLPHO B. 1/5/17, Verona, Italy. Member 1948, 52, 56, 60 Italian Olympic teams. Held world discus record. First set mark in Milan on Oct. 26, 1941, with toss of 175′0″. Improved to 177′11″ on April 14, 1946, also at Milan. Lost record two months later but regained it in 1948 with throw of 181′6″ on Oct. 10 at Milan. Started throwing at late age of 20, but was in top ten of Italian disc men his first year, 1937. Second year was 5th in 1938 European championships with 157′6 ½″. Did win AAA Championship at London with 162′5″ in 1938. From then on was world class competitor. On track scene for amazing 25 years. Won European Championships 3 times: '46, '50, '54. Best of 176′4″ in European Championships. Was 5th in 1938 and 6th in 1958. In 1948 took Olympic gold medal with record-breaking toss of 173′2″. Was silver medalist in 1952 behind Sim Inness. Sixth in 1956 and 17th in 1960. European record-holder for nearly 18 years (1941–1959). Had best throw at age of 38 years, 11 months. Tossed disc 186′11″ for his last European record.

COOKE, EDWARD B. 11/27/88, Chillicothe, Ohio. D. 10/18/72. Member 1906 Olympic team. Won gold medal in pole vault when tied with A. C. Gilbert. Pair cleared 12′2 $\frac{1}{16}$″ without aid of box. Won 1907 AAU title at 12′3″, breaking record by 9″. In 1911 tied with H. Coyle for AAU title at 12′6″. Competed for Cornell when student there. Graduated in 1910. High school athletic director in Ohio until retirement.

COPELAND, LILLIAN B. 11/25/04, New York, N.Y. D. 2/7/64. Member 1928, 32 Olympic teams. Standout in weight events. One of first women to win medal in Olympics. Took silver medal in discus in 1928 Amsterdam Olympics, first year women were allowed to compete. Throw of 121′7⅞″ took medal. In 1932 L.A. Olympics bettered world best in discus and took gold medal with 133′1⅝″. Took many AAU titles in career. AAU shot put champion 1925–28, 31. Had best of 40′4¼″ in 1928. Was AAU discus winner in 1926, 27 in early stage of career. Won AAU javelin in 1926, 31. At Southern Cal won every event she participated in. Member Citizens Savings (Helms) Hall of Fame.

COURTNEY, TOM B. 8/17/33, Newark, N.J. Member 1956 Olympic team. Held world 880-yd record with 1:46.8 in Los Angeles, May 24, 1957. Had great rivalry with Arnie Sowell of Pitt. Was seeing lot of Sowell's heels until 1956. First win came in U.S. Olympic trials in 1956 at L.A. Ran 1:46.4 in 800-m and beat Sowell. Had concentrated on speed and won AAU 400-m title with 45.8. Won gold medal in 1956 Melbourne Olympics in record 1:47.7. Made stretch run early and had to fight off Sowell and Johnson of Great Britain. Made another stretch drive 10 yds from tape to win. Was 1957, 58 AAU 880-yd champion. Took 1955 NCAA crown for Fordham with 1:49.6. Was 1954 IC4A indoor 1000-yd champ. Won 2nd gold medal with anchor leg of 45.8 on U.S. 1600-m relay. Member Citizens Savings (Helms) Hall of Fame.

CRAIG, RALPH B. 6/21/89, Detroit, Mich. D. 1972. Member 1912 Olympic team. Co-held world 200-m and 220-yd (straight) records. Ran 21.2 at Philadelphia on May 28, 1910. Became second man in Olympics to win both 100-m and 200-m. Seven men have scored sprint double in Olympics. Howard Drew, top U.S. sprinter, pulled up lame in semi heat of 100-m, putting pressure on Craig and D. F. Lippincott. Pair ran entire course after false start and had to run again. In "real" race Craig won gold medal in 10.8. Lippincott was 3rd as Alvin Meyer was 2nd in U.S. sweep. In 200-m, Craig won in 21.7 with Lippincott 2nd. Competed for Michigan and graduated in 1911. Won IC4A in 1910, 11 at 21.2 both years. Worked for state of New York as administrator. Member Citizens Savings (Helms) Hall of Fame.

CROMWELL, DEAN (The Dean) B. 9/20/79, Turner, Oreg. D. 8/3/62, Los Angeles. Coach 1948 Olympic team. At Occidental College, had outstanding athletic career from 1898 to 1902 in football and track. Appointed Southern Cal head track, football coach in 1909. Southern Cal grid coach for 5 seasons and had 21–8–6 record. As track coach, The

Dean had no peer. In his 39 years as USC track coach, team won 12 NCAA titles, 9 in row. Trojans also won 9 IC4A team titles. From 1930–48 teams lost only 3 dual meets. His performers won 33 NCAA individual events, 39 IC4A crowns, and 38 AAU titles. List of pupils long and impressive. Charlie Paddock, Bud Houser, Mel Patton, Frank Wycoff, Earle Meadows and Bill Sefton are just few pupils of the "Maker of Champions." His Trojans set 14 individual world records, plus world records in 440-yd, 880-yd and mile relays. Coached 10 Olympic gold medal winners and 36 U.S. Olympic team members from 1912–48. Olympic team won 10 gold medals in 1948 under his direction. Retired from Southern Cal in 1948, same year was elected to Citizens Savings (Helms) Hall of Fame.

CSERMAK, JOZEF B. 2/14/32, Szentes, Hungary. Member 1952 Hungarian Olympic team. Held world hammer throw record. Set record of 197′11″ in 1952 Helsinki Olympics on July 24. Student of 1948 Hungarian Olympic winner Imre Nemeth. Student got gold medal and world record, teacher got bronze medal. Started throwing hammer in 1950 and had throw of 183′2½″ in 1951. In 1954 European Championships was 3rd with 195′11″.

CULBREATH, JOSH B. 9/14/32, Norristown, Pa. Member 1956 Olympic team. Held world 440-yd hurdle record. Ran 50.5 on Aug. 9, 1957, at Oslo. One of top 3 intermediate hurdlers in 1950s. Won 1953 AAU championship with 52.5 clocking, repeating in 1954, 55 with 52.0 times. In 1956 lost AAU crown to Glenn Davis. Made 1956 Olympic team as Marine in what was then greatest 400-m hurdle race in history. Davis won in 49.5, followed by Eddie Southern in 49.7 and Culbreath in 50.6. In Olympic finals came in 3rd with 51.6 behind Southern and gold medal winner Davis. Was one of first specialists in this grueling event and was the world's best from 1953–55.

CUNNINGHAM, GLENN (Kansas Ironman) B. 8/4/09, Atlanta, Kans. Member 1932, 36 Olympic teams. Held world mile record with 4:06.7 in 1934 which stood 3 years. Overcame severe burns on legs to become one of all-time greats. Won first major race in 1932 AAU 1500-m championship. Also won NCAA 1500-m for Kansas in 1932. Made 1932 Olympic team and finished 4th in 1500-m. In 1933 won AAU 1500-m in 3:52.3 and 800-m in 1:51.8. Won 2nd NCAA for KU in 1933 with 4:09.8 mile. In 1934 Princeton Invitational set world and American mile records with 4:06.7. Lap splits were 61.8, 64.0, 61.8, and 59.1 in record effort. Lost to rival Bill Bonthron in 1934 NCAA and AAU. Came back strong to take 1935, 36 AAU 1500-m. Won 1936 Olympic tryouts with 3:49.9 time in 1500-m. In 1936 Berlin Olympics tried to outrun field on 3rd lap but Lovelock of New Zealand out-sprinted Kansas Ironman in world record 3:47.8. Added 1937, 38 AAU titles to collection. March 5, 1938, ran indoor mile of 4:04.4 on oversized track. Ran fastest 1500-m in last major competition with 3:48.0 but finished 2nd. Now operates youth ranch in Kansas. Member Citizens Savings (Helms) Hall of Fame.

CUTHBERT, BETTY B. 4/20/38, Sydney, Australia. Member 1956, 60, 64 Australian Olympic teams. Won 3 gold medals in Melbourne Olympics. Won 100-m in 11.5 to tie Olympic record. In 200-m tied Olympic and world record of 23.4. Anchored Australian 400-m relay team to gold medal in 44.5, world and Olympic record. In 1960 was injured and could not compete in Rome Olympics. In 1964 Tokyo Olympics won gold medal in 400-m with 52.0 clocking. Best marks were 10.4 in 100-yd, 23.3 in 200-m and 220-yd, and 53.3 in 440-yd. In 1958 set 100-yd and 220-yd records. Improved 220-yd mark twice. In 1963 set 440-yd mark of 54.3 and improved it to 53.3. Had set two 440-yd world records in 1959 with 55.6 and 54.3. Set total of 16 world marks. Won Australian national titles in 220-yd in 1956, 60, and 440-yd title in 1963. Set national records in 220-yd, 400-m, 440-yd. Best was 23.5 for 220-yd in 1958, and 53.1 for 400-m in 1963. Saleswoman. Winner 1964 Citizens Savings (Helms) World Trophy Award, Australasia.

DANEK, LUDVIK B. 1/6/37. Member 1964, 68, 72 Czechoslovakian Olympic teams. Won gold medal in discus in 1972 Munich Olympics after taking silver medal in 1964 and bronze in 1968. Tossed disc 211′3½″ on final throw to defeat Jay Silvester for gold medal. Led qualifiers with toss of 211′. In 1968 Olympics was 3rd with throw of 201′3″. One of favorites in 1964 Tokyo Olympics but was beaten by Al Oerter, 200′1½″. Both passed Olympic record. Twice set world records. In 1964 at Turnov broke Oerter's record by over 5′ with toss of 211′9″ on Aug. 2. Improved mark to 213′11″ on Oct. 12, 1965, at Sakalov. Was 1971 European champion at 211′9½″ after subpar showings in three previous (meets).

DANIELSEN, EGIL B. 11/9/33, Hamar, Norway. Member 1956 Norwegian Olympic team. Held world javelin record. Threw spear 281′2″ in 1956 Olympics in Melbourne on Nov. 26. Made world record on 4th throw. Defeated Janusv Sidlo of Poland, world record-holder and 3-time Olympian, for gold medal. His second-best throw in the competition was 238′2″. Had fantastic year. Unbeaten in 37 competitions and was over 262′5½″ on 11 throws. Second to Sidlo in 1958 European Championships. After that, distance and interest declined. Had potential to be even greater than he was.

DA SILVA, FERREIRA ADHEMAR B. 9/29/27, Brazil. Member 1948, 52, 56, 60 Brazil Olympic teams. Held world triple jump record. Equalled world mark of 52′6″ on Dec. 3, 1950, at Sao Paulo. Became sole owner of record on Sept. 30, 1951, at Rio de Janeiro with 52′6¼″. Due to lack of competition in South America, concentrated on international events. Won gold medal at 1952 Helsinki Olympics with world record 53′2½″. Beat world mark 4 times during competition in Helsinki. Lost record in 1953. Regained it in 1955 Pan-Am Games with 54′4″ (20′7¼″ hop, 16′3″ step, 17′5¾″ jump). Also won 1951, 59 Pan-Am gold medals. Won 1956 Melbourne Olympics gold medal with 53′7¾″. Also competed in 1948 London (11th place) and 1960 Rome (14th place) Olympics. Greatest athlete in South American history. Furthered triple jump world record over 2′ in long career.

DAVENPORT, WILLIE B. 6/8/43, Troy, Ala. Member 1964, 68, 72 Olympic teams. Won gold medal in 1968 Olympics in 110-m hurdles. Was AAU outdoor champion 1965–67 with 13.3 times in last 2 wins. Won AAU indoor 60-yd hurdles in 1966–67, 69–71. Ran 6.9 in 1966 and 7.0 in '67, '71. In 1964 Olympics ran 14.4 in first heat to make semis. But ran 7th and did not make finals. Was injured at time. In 1968 Mexico City Olympics made up for Rome failure. Ran 13.6 in first heat, 13.5 in semis to make finals. In finals streaked to Olympic record 13.3 and gold medal. In 1972 was 2nd in AAU with 13.6. In 1972 Olympic trials was 2nd in 13.5. In Munich Olympics was 4th in 13.50. Was in contention until hit hurdle late in race. Member Citizens Savings (Helms) Hall of Fame.

DAVIES, LYNN B. 5/20/42. Member 1964, 68, 72 British Olympic teams. Won gold medal in 1964 Olympic long jump over Ralph Boston and Igor Ter-Ovanesyan at Tokyo Games. Jumped 26′5 ¾″ to take gold medal on a cold rainy day. First gained prominence by winning 1962 British Commonwealth with record 25′4″. Was 1966 European champion with 26′2¼″ and won British Commonwealth with 26′2¾″. In 1968 set British record with personal best of 27′. In 1968 Mexico City Olympics was so dejected after seeing Bob Beamon's world record-shattering 29′2½″ that he took only three jumps: 21′1¼″, 26′½″ and foul. Best jump produced 9th place. In 1971 took 4th in European Championships with jump of 25′9″. Did not qualify for finals in 1972 Olympics at Munich. Best jump was 25′9″.

DAVIS, GLENN B. 9/12/34, Wellsburg, W. Va. Member 1956, 60 Olympic teams. Held world 400-m hurdle record with 49.5 in 1956 and 49.2 in 1958. Also world 440-yd hurdle mark with 49.9. Broke world 440-yd dash mark in 1958 with 45.7 in NCAA Championships. Won gold medal in 1956 Melbourne Olympics in 400-m hurdles in Olympic record 50.1. In 1960 Rome Olympics won 400-m hurdles in Games record 49.3. Ran on 1600-m relay that took gold medal. While at Ohio State won

1958 NCAA 440-yd dash in world record time 45.7. Won AAU 440 hurdles 1956–58 with world mark of 49.9 in 1958. At Ohio State ran high hurdles, low hurdles, sprints and long jumped. Tried pro football but failed to make Detroit Lions. Member Citizens Savings (Helms) Hall of Fame.

DAVIS, HAROLD B. 1/5/21, Salinas, Calif. Co-held world 100-m record. Ran 10.2 June 6, 1941, at Compton, Calif. to tie record set by Jesse Owens in 1936. King of American sprinters for 4 years. Won AAU 100-m in '40, '42, '43. Ran 10.3 in 1940 at age of 19. In 200-m was invincible. Took AAU crowns 1940–43. In 1940 ran 20.4 to complete first sprint double. Ran 20.2 with wind in 1943 national championships. Actually lost only one important race in whole career. Barney Ewell defeated him in 1941 AAU 100-m to ruin what would have been 4-year sweep of sprints. Bad start caused him to lag 3 meters behind Ewell at 50-m mark. Was never good starter, average at best, came on unbelievably strong in second half of races. Had a 9.4 legal 100-yd mark never accepted for world record. WW II prevented from obtaining Olympic and world recognition due him. Was 1942, 43 NCAA 100-yd and 220-yd champion for Cal. Member Citizens Savings (Helms) Hall of Fame.

DAVIS, IRIS B. 4/30/50, Pompano Beach, Fla. Member 1968, 72 Olympic teams. Holds American female 100-yd record with 10.2 at Champaign, Ill., on June 20, 1971. Alternate on 1968 Olympic team and did not compete in Games. Was 2nd in 1964, 70 AAU 100-m. Won 1970 U.S.-USSR 100-m in 11.7 at Leningrad. Took 1971 AAU 100-m in 11.2. Won 1971 Pan-Am Games 100-m and ran on 400-m relay team that took gold medal. Named North America Female Athlete of Year by Helms Foundation. Was 3rd in 1972 AAU and took 2nd in Olympic trials. In 1972 Olympic 100-m finals was 4th in 11.3.

DAVIS, JACK B. 9/11/30, Amarillo, Tex. Member 1952, 56 Olympic teams. Held world 120-yd and 110-m hurdles records with 13.4 in 1956 AAU prelim heat. Finished 2nd to Harrison Dillard in 1952 Helsinki Olympics with both timed in Olympic record 13.7. Won 3 straight NCAA high hurdle championships 1951–53 at Southern Cal. Won 1953 NCAA lows. In 1956 Olympic trials Davis and Lee Calhoun tied with 13.8. Before Melbourne Games Davis ran 13.4 with slight wind. Two watches caught him at 13.3. In Melbourne Olympics history repeated as Davis and Calhoun both timed in 13.5 against wind. Calhoun received gold medal and for second time Davis received silver medal. Photo finish necessary to determine winner. Besides 1956 world mark in 120-yd and 110-m, set 220-yd low hurdle record of 22.2. Won 1953, 54 AAU high and low hurdle championships. Member Citizens Savings (Helms) Hall of Fame. President of California resort.

DAVIS, OTIS B. 7/12/32, Tuscaloosa, Ala. Member 1960 Olympic team. Won 400-m dash gold medal and set world record in doing so. Edged German Kaufman with 44.91 to Kaufman's 44.93. Equaled Olympic record in quarterfinal heat with 45.9. Broke record in semi heat in 45.5 before record 44.91 performance. Won with great spurt on turn and held off German's challenge at finish. All six finalists beat Olympic record of 45.9. Ran 45.6 in Berne prior to Games in August to give indication he was gold medal threat. Anchored U.S. 1600-m relay team that set world and Olympic record of 3:02.2. Held off rival Kaufman with 45.0 anchor lap. Germans also broke old mark. Davis 1960, 61 AAU champion in specialty, 45.8 in 1960 was AAU record.

DAVIS, WALTER B. 1/5/31, Beaumont, Tex. Member 1952 Olympic team. Held world high jump record with 6′11½″ on June 27, 1953, at Dayton, Ohio, in AAU outdoor championships. Jumped 6′10½″ in 1952 AAU championships. Set Olympic record of 6′8¼″ in 1952 Helsinki Olympics. Tied for 1952 NCAA title while at Texas A&M with jump of 6′8″. Stricken with polio as boy, used athletics as rehabilitation. At 6′8″ was one of tallest world class high jumpers. Also played basketball for Texas Aggies.

DELANY, RON B. 3/6/35, Arklow, County Wicklow, Ireland. Member 1956 Irish Olympic team. Won gold medal in 1500-m in Olympic record, 3:41.2. Ran last lap in .54. All 8 runners broke record in final. Ran 3:59.0 mile in 1956, but ran to win, not for time. Won most of big races in career, biggest being 1956 Olympics. Went to college in U.S. at Villanova. Won NCAA mile titles in 1957, 58, and 1500-m in 1956. Won 880 in 1958. Won 4 AAU indoor mile titles from 1956–59, 4:02.5 best in 1959. Member Citizens Savings (Helms) Hall of Fame.

DILLARD, HARRISON B. 7/8/23, Cleveland, Ohio. Member 1948, 52 Olympic teams. Only man ever to win gold medals in sprints (100-m in 1948) and hurdles (110-m in 1952). Held world record in 120-yd highs with 13.6 in 1948 Kansas Relays. Had won 82 straight races before loss one week before 1948 Olympic trials. Hit hurdle and dropped out of trials in hurdles, but qualified in 100-m. In London came in first, tying Jesse Owens' Olympic record of 10.3, upsetting Barney Ewell and Mel Patton. In 1952 Dillard took aim on hurdles medal. Edged Jack Davis in trials and repeated performance in Helsinki Olympics with 13.7 clocking. Also ran on 400-m relay teams, bringing gold medal total to 4. Used tremendous speed (10.3 in 100-m) to offset lack of height (5′10″). While at Baldwin Wallace won both 120-yd highs and 220-yd lows in 1946, 47 NCAA and AAU meets. Held world record in 120 highs with 13.6 and 220 lows at 22.3. Employed by Cleveland schools, also writes sports column for *Cleveland Press*. Member Citizens Savings (Helms) Hall of Fame.

DOUBELL, RALPH B. 2/11/45, Melbourne, Australia. Member 1968 Australian Olympic team. Won gold medal in 1968 Mexico City Olympics in 800-m. Not one of favorites but equaled world record 1:44.3 in winning gold medal. Trained at sea level and defeated Wilson Kiprugut of Kenya who trained at high altitude much like Mexico City. Australian national 800-m champ from 1966–70. Best mark in meet was 1:47.3 in 1966, good for national record. Lowered mark, which he had originally claimed with 1:47.7 in 1966, to 1:47.2 in 1968. Also set 880-yd mark of 1:48 in 1967 and 1000-m with 2:20.8 in 1970. Systems analyst.

DREW, HOWARD B. 6/28/90, Lexington, Ky. Member 1912 Olympic team. Co-held world 100-yd, 220-yd, and 200-m records. Ran 21.2 at Claremont, Calif., on Feb. 2, 1914, to equal record in 200-m and 220-yd. At Berkeley, Calif., March 29, 1914, tied 100-yd mark with 9.6. In 1912 Stockholm Olympics ran well in 100-m prelims, but pulled a tendon in semifinals. Tried to run in finals but had to be carried to dressing room. First of long line of great black sprinters. Was AAU champ in 100-yd in 1911, 12. Took 220-yd AAU championship in 1913.

DUMAS, CHARLES B. 12/2/37, Tulsa, Okla. Member 1956, 60 Olympic teams. World's first 7′ high jumper. Went from 6′5½″ best jump to 6′10¼″ in 1954. Went 7′0¼″ in 1956 Game trials. At Melbourne Olympics made Olympic record 6′11¼″ on last try for gold medal. Finished 6th in 1960 Games with 6′7⅞″. Won 1956–59 AAU titles. Consistant in big ones at 6′10″ or better. Used slow approach, great spring. Breaking great psychological barrier, Dumas' 7′ jump opened door for others. Member Citizens Savings (Helms) Hall of Fame.

EASTMAN, BEN B. 7/9/11, Burlingame, Calif. Member 1932 Olympic team. Held world records in 440-yd, 400-m, 880-yd, 800-m. Gained world acclaim first as quarter man. Set first world record with 47.4 time in 440-yd at Palo Alto, Calif., May 16, 1931. On March 26, 1932, at Stanford U. track in Palo Alto, chopped full second off 440-yd record with 46.4. Time also good for 400-m record. Favored in 1932 Olympics until defeats in IC4A and Olympic tryouts by Bill Carr of Penn. In Olympic 400-m finals Carr grabbed gold medal with Eastman 2nd. After 1932 Olympics, Eastman turned to 880-yd and 800-m. Set 800-m and 880-yd record at Princeton, N.J., with 1:49.8 on June 16, 1934. Won 1934 AAU in 1:50.8. In 1936 ran 1:50.1 in 800-m in preparation for Berlin Olympics. Failed to make team. Held 8 world marks, including anchoring Stanford mile and 1600-m relay teams that ran 3:12.6 at Fresno, Calif., May 8, 1931. Member Citizens Savings (Helms) Hall of Fame.

EASTON, M. E. (Bill) B. 9/13/06, Stinesville, Ind. Coach 1968 Mexican Olympic team. One of top U.S. collegiate coaches for 3 decades. Track coach at Drake from 1941–47. Also director of Drake Relays during that time. While at Drake his cross-country teams won 3 NCAA titles. Moved to Kansas in 1947 and built medal-winning machine. From 1947–56 KU teams won 39 Big 8 team titles in cross country, indoor and outdoor track. In 1950s Jayhawks won Big 8 cross country, indoor and outdoor track 8 years in row. Teams won NCAA outdoor team titles in 1959, 60. Won NCAA cross-country title in 1953 with team led by Wes Santee. Voted top college coach in 1960. Coached 32 All-Americans and 8 Olympians. Some of his top performers were Bill Nieder, Al Oerter and Billy Mills, all world record-setters. Athletes broke 4 world records, 14 American records and 14 intercollegiate marks. Mills, Nieder and Oerter all won Olympic gold medals. Oerter won 4. Named honorary referee of 1970 Kansas Relays and 1970 NCAA Championships. Member Citizens Savings (Helms) Hall of Fame. Assistant professor of physical education at KU.

EHRHARDT, ANNELIE B. 6/18/50, Ohrsleben, E. Germany. Member 1972 E. German Olympic team. Won gold medal in Womens 100-m hurdles at Munich. Ran 12.59 to win over Valeria Bufanu of Rumania and Karin Balzer of E. Germany. In 1970 equaled world record in 200-m hurdles with 25.8 at GDR Championships where also won 100-m hurdles over Balzer. In 1972 set 100-m hurdle world record of 12.5. Was 1972 GDR 100-m hurdle champion. Is photographic lab assistant, married to racing canoeist.

ELLERBE, MOZEL B. 6/17/13, Palatka, Fla. One of greatest collegiate sprinters in late 1930s. Won 2 NCAA 100-yd dash crowns for Tuskegee Institute in Alabama. In 1938 won with 9.7 in finals, in 1939 with 9.8. In 1938 Drake Relays ran 9.6 to win. Only Jesse Owens and Ralph Metcalfe had run better times at Drake. Ran well, winning many important races over top foes in 1940. But WW II ruled out any Olympic honors.

ELLIOT, JAMES F. (Jumbo) B. 8/8/15, Philadelphia, Pa. Head track coach at Villanova. One of most successful track coaches in U.S. Has coached more Olympic team members (22) than any other U.S. coach. Five won gold medals and 3 silver medals. Ron Delany won gold in 1500-m for Ireland in 1956. Charlie Jenkins won 400-m same year. Don Bragg won 1960 pole vault. Paul Drayton won gold in 1964 as member of 400-m team. In 1968 Larry James won gold as member of 1600-m relay. Elliot's Wildcat teams have won 30 IC4A outdoor, indoor and cross country team titles. His teams have captured one NCAA outdoor crown, two indoor NCAA titles and 203 IC4A individual crowns. Fourteen world records have been set by Jumbo's athletes and 31 American indoor marks. A 1935 graduate of Villanova where he was a standout 220, 440, and 880 man, coaches "part-time" and runs a highly successful company which deals in contracting equipment. Member Citizens Savings (Helms) Hall of Fame.

ELLIOTT, HERB B. 2/25/38, Subiaco, Australia. Member 1960 Australian Olympic team. Held world mile and 1500-m records. Broke Derek

Ibbotson's mile world record by over 2.5 seconds with 3:54.5 in Dublin on Aug. 6, 1958. Ran 3:36.0 in Göteborg on Aug. 28, 1958, in 1500-m to break previous record by 2.1 seconds. In 1960 Rome Olympics ran race of his life and bettered own 1500-m world record with 3:35.6 for gold medal. Had run 1:49.3 in 880-yd and 3:59.0 mile to win gold medals in 1958 British Empire Games. Had possibly greatest career of any distance runner. Ran 17 four-minute miles from 1958–60. Never lost in international competition from 1957–60. Had great speed and stamina, cultivated by Coach Percy Cerutty into unbeatable combination. At peak was virtually unbeatable and unchallenged in any race.

EVANS, LEE B. 2/25/47, Mandena, Calif. Member 1968, 72 Olympic teams. Holds world 400-m record. Ran 43.8 in 1968 Mexico City Olympics on Oct. 18. Anchored U.S. Olympic 1600-m relay team that set world mark of 2:56.1. Broke old mark by 3.5 seconds. Won 1966 AAU 440-yd in 45.9 and 1967 in 45.3. In 1967 Pan-Am Games won 400-m gold medal in 44.9. In 1968 NCAA ran 45.0 and won title as San Jose State student. Won 1968 AAU in 45.0. In final Olympic trials at South Lake Tahoe, ran 44.0 to beat world mark. In Olympic finals set world mark, edging Larry James who ran 43.9. Anchored winning U.S. 1600-m relay team with 44.1 leg. Continued to run following Olympics. In 1969 won AAU after finishing 2nd in NCAA. Also won U.S.-USSR dual in 45.3. Ran 44.5 in Indian Summer meet. Ran in 1970, 71 with Olympics of 1972 in mind. Did not win titles, but competed when not injured. In 1972 ran 44.9 as his year's best. Won 1972 AAU in 45.0. In Olympic trials was 4th in 45.1. Was selected for U.S. 1600-m relay. Team did not run when Wayne Collett and Vince Matthews were banned because of "demonstration" on victory stand and John Smith was injured. Pro 1973.

EWELL, NORWOOD (Barney) B. 2/25/18, Harrisburg, Pa. Member 1948 Olympic team. Held 100-m world record. Long (11-year), successful sprint career. Deprived of competing in Olympics during peak because of WW II. Always among top in world during career. Won AAU 100-m in 1941, 45 in 10.3, and 1948 in 10.6. Won 200-m in 1939 with 21.0, 1946 with 21.2, and 1947 with 21.0. Had chance for 1948 London Olympic sprint gold medals but had to settle for silver in both 100-m with 10.4 and 200-m with 21.1. Did run on winning 400-m relay team. Had run world record 10.2 in trials for career best. Nipped at tape by Harrison Dillard in 100-m, but thought he had won. Won NCAA sprint double while at Penn State in 1940, 41. In IC4A won sprint double in 1940–42. Member Citizens Savings (Helms) Hall of Fame.

EWRY, RAY B. 10/14/73, Lafayette, Ind. Member 1900, 04, 06, 08 Olympic teams. Holds all-time high of 8 gold medals as standing jump specialist. Won standing long jump with 10′6 ⅜″, standing high jump at 5′5″, standing triple jump with 34′8 ½″ in 1900 Paris Games. At St. Louis in 1904 Games won same 3 events. Improved standing long jump to 11′4 ⅞″ but fell off in other two. In 1906 unofficial Games in Athens won standing long jump & high jump. In final Games appearance at London in 1908 won same 2 events. Event bests: 5′5″ standing high jump, standing long jump 11′4 ⅞″ and 34′8 ½″ standing triple jump. Legend in now extinct events. Won virtually every championship during career. Member Citizens Savings (Helms) Hall of Fame.

FAGGS, HERIWENTHA MAE B. 4/10/32, Mays Landing, N.J. Member 1948, 52, 56 Olympic teams. Member world record 400-m relay team that ran 45.9 on July 27, 1952, at Helsinki Olympics for gold medal. Also member world record U.S. 880-yd relay team that ran 1:40.0 on Aug. 4, 1952, at London. Was AAU indoor 100-yd champ in 1952 with 11.1. But 220-yd was more her race. Won indoor AAU in 1949–52, 54, 56, with meet record 25.9 in 1949 her best. Record stood until 1960 when Wilma Rudolph ran 25.7. Took AAU outdoor 100-yd in 1955 with 10.8 and in 1956 in 11.7 for 100-m. Was AAU 200-m champ in 1954, 56 and 220-yd champ in 1955. In 1948 London Olympics failed to qualify for 200-m finals. In 1952 Helsinki Games was 6th in 100-m finals and failed to make 200-m finals, but led off gold medal 400-m relay team. Failed in 1956 Melbourne Olympics in 100-m and 200-m, but was on bronze medal-winning 400-m team. Won silver medal in 1955 Pan-Am Games and was on winning U.S. 400-m relay team. Member Citizens Savings (Helms) Hall of Fame.

FALCK, HILDEGARD B. 6/8/49, Nettelrede, W. Germany. Member 1972 West German Olympic team. Won gold medal in 800-m at Munich Olympics. Ran 1:58.6 to set Olympic record. Holds world 800-m record with 1:58.3 at Stuttgart on July 11, 1971. Set world indoor record for 800-m same year with 2:03.3 on Dec. 27 at Kiel. Ran third leg of German 1600-m relay team that won bronze medal in 1972 Olympics. Won 1970 European Cup. Was 1970 German 800-m champion, and in 1972.

FERRELL, BARBARA B. 7/28/47, Hattiesburg, Miss. Member 1968, 72 Olympic teams. Held world 100-m record. Ran 11.1 in 1967 at Santa Barbara on July 2. Holds American 200-m record with 22.8 in 1968 Olympics. In 1968 took silver medal in 100-m in 11.1 and was 4th in 200-m. Ran on U.S. gold medal-winning 400-m relay team. Was 1967 AAU 100-m champ in 11.1. Won AAU 100-yd and 220-yd in 1969 in 10.7 and 23.8. Won gold medal in 1967 Pan-Am Games in 11.5. In 1972 was 5th in AAU, but ran 11.3 in Olympic trials to take 1st. Was 2nd in 200-m. In 1972 Munich Olympic 100-m finals was 7th. Did not qualify for 200-m finals. Ran 3rd leg on U.S. 400-m relay team that was 4th.

FEUERBACH, ALLAN B. 1/14/48, Preston, Iowa. Member 1972 Olympic team. One of 3 men to throw shot 70′. Threw 70′ ½″ in March of 1972 at Walnut, Calif. Toss was then 2nd best of all-time. Increased his best to 70′3 ½″ at UCLA Meet of Champions in April. Broke world record with toss of 71′7″ May 5, 1973, at San Jose, Calif. In Olympic trials finished 2nd to George Woods with throw of 68′10 ½″. Prior to Olympics had put of 70′7 ¼″ at Long Beach, Calif., on Aug. 6. In Munich Olympics finished 5th with put of 68′11 ¼″. In 1971 had great indoor season. Set world mark of 68′11″, but was less successful outdoors. Equally successful in 1972 indoor season. Had put of 69′ ¼″ at Los Angeles Times Meet and 69′4″ at Pocatello, Idaho. Was 1970 NAIA champion for Emporia (Kans.) State. Third in 1971 AAU with put of 66′1″. Was 1971 Pan-Am Games champion despite subpar toss of 64′10″. Improved from a 60′ thrower (12 lb) in senior year in high school to 56′ (16 lb) as college frosh. As college senior had best of 65′. Following college graduation, devoted time to shot. Put self among top men in history through weight training and dedication. Said to be one of quickest weight men in world.

FLANAGAN, JOHN B. 1873, County Limerick, Ireland. D. 1938. Member 1900, 04, 08 U.S. Olympic teams. Held world record in hammer throw. In 1897 set record with throw of 150′8″ at Bayonne, N.J., then went on to break 160′, 170′, 180′ barriers. Best toss was 184′4″ at New Haven, Conn., July 24, 1909. In 1900 Paris Olympics was only non-collegian on U.S. team. Irish-American was New York City policeman. Won hammer with toss of 167′4″. In 1904 St. Louis Olympics competed in 3 events. As ususal came in 1st in hammer with winning toss of 168′1″. Placed 2nd in 56-lb weight throw with 33′4″. Was 4th in discus. In 1908 won hammer for 3rd time. Throw of 170′4 ¼″ put him in rare circle of athletes who won 3 gold medals in same event. Was AAU hammer throw champ 1897–99, 1901–02, 06–07. Took 56-lb weight throw in AAU in '99, '01, '04, '06, '07, '08. Best of 38′8″ in 1907 lasted as meet record for 35 years. After retiring from police force, returned to Ireland and coached 2-time Olympic gold medal winner Dr. Patrick O'Callaghan. Member Citizens Savings (Helms) Hall of Fame.

FONVILLE, CHARLES B. 4/27/27, Birmingham, Ala. Held world shot put record. Threw 16-lb iron ball 58′0 ¼″ on April 17, 1948, at Kansas Relays. Small for shot putter (6′2″, 195 lbs). Only black shot putter to hold world record. Was 10.0 100-yd dashman. Improved from 52′ at age 19 to nearly 55′ at 20. Hurt spine prior to 1948 Olympic trials. Injury kept him from making team. Was 4th at trials with 54′1 ⅜″, great put considering injury. Tried to make comeback in 1950 but could not return to form.

FOSBURY, DICK B. 3/6/47, Portland, Oreg. Member 1968 Olympic team. Held American citizen high jump record. Went 7′4 ¼″ in 1968 Mexico City Olympics on Oct. 10. Started back-over flop style known now as "Fosbury Flop." Went over 7′ for first time in winter of 1968 and won NCAA indoor title for Oregon State at 7′0″. Won NCAA outdoor at 7′2 ¼″. Made 7′3″ at Olympic trials and made team, although was 3rd on misses. In Mexico City Games electrified world with gold medal-winning 7′4 ¼″ for Olympic and American record. One of only 6 competitors to clear 7′ ¼″ to qualify for finals. Fosbury did not miss until record jump. Kicked bar off with heel on first try and also missed second jump. On third try made record height for gold medal. Ranked No. 1 high jumper in 1968 by *Track & Field News*. In 1969 won NCAA outdoor at 7′2 ½″ and was 2nd in AAU at 7′0″. More or less dropped out of competition until 1972 when failed to make Olympic team.

FOSS, FRANK B. 5/9/95, Chicago, Ill. Member 1920 Olympic team. Held world pole vault record. Vaulted 13′5″ at Antwerp on June 20, for gold medal in 1920 Olympic Games. Was AAU champion in 1919 at 12′9″ and in 1920 tied for title at 13′1″. Retired, was vice president of Wilson Company packers.

FRENKEL, PETER B. 5/13/39, Eckartsberga, E. Germany. Member 1968 German, 1972 East German Olympic teams. Won 1972 Olympic gold medal in 20,000-m walk. Scored upset over Vladimir Golubnichiy with Olympic best of 1:26:42.4. Also in 1972 tied world mark with 1:25:19.4. In 1971 European Championships was 4th in 1:27:52.8. In 1970 set world record of 1:25:50.0. Is decorator-designer. In 1968 Mexico City Olympics was 10th in 10,000-m walk with 1:37:20.8.

FRIGERIO, UGO B. 9/16/01. Member 1920, 24, 32 Italian Olympic teams. Won 3 gold medals and bronze in Olympic walking competition.

At Antwerp in 1920 won both 3000-m and 10,000-m walk. Had time of 48:06.20 in 10,000 and 13:14.20 in 3000-m. In 1924 at Paris Olympics was timed in 47:49.00 for gold medal, bettering 1920 time. In 1932 at Los Angeles took bronze medal in 50,000-m walk. Timed in 4:59:06.0, 9 minutes behind winner in race which was staged on streets of L.A. Very popular performer, among top Olympians with his 4 medals.

FUCHS, JIM B. 12/6/27, Chicago, Ill. Member 1948, 52 Olympic teams. Held world shot put record with 58′4 ½″ in June of 1949 at Oslo, Norway. In 1950 advanced mark to 58′5 ½″ at Los Angeles, April 29; 58′8 ¾″ at Visby, Sweden, Aug. 20; and finally 58′10 ¾″ at Eskilstuna, Sweden, two days later. In 1948 London Olympics was 3rd with 53′10 ½″ that bettered Olympic record. In 1952 won bronze again with 55′11 ¾″. Both times placed 3rd in 1–2–3 U.S. sweeps. Was 1949, 50 IC4A champ with 57′9 ¼″ best in 1950. Also won 1949, 50 NCAA for Yale with best of 56′11′ in 1950. Won AAU indoor 1950–52 with record 57′11 ⅜″ in 1951. AAU outdoor champ in 1949, 50. Yale football star as well as track.

GARDNER, ROBERT B. 4/9/1890, Hinsdale, Ill. D. 6/21/56. Held world pole vault record. First man to pole vault over 13′. Jumped 13′1″ in 1912 IC4A championship at Philadelphia on June 1 for world record. Lasted only week as Marc Wright of Dartmouth went 13′2 ¼″ at 1912 Olympic trials at Cambridge, Mass. After graduation from Yale in 1912, turned athletic interests to tennis and golf. In 1926 was national doubles rackets champion with Howard Linn. Had been national amateur golf champ while at Yale in 1909 and won again in 1915. Runner-up in 1916, 22. Member Walker Cup team 1922–24, 26, captain last 3 years. Partner in Mitchell, Hutchens & Co. investment firm.

GARRETT, ROBERT B. 6/24/75, Baltimore County, Md. D. 4/25/61. Member 1896, 1900 Olympic teams. One of pioneers of Olympic competition. Paid own way to first modern Olympics. Captain of Princeton track team as weightman. Heard discus was going to be on Olympic program and had crude disc made. After couple weeks practice won 1896 Olympic discus competition with toss of 95′7 ½″. Also won shot put with 36′9 ¾″. Placed 2nd in long jump with 19′8 3/16″. Was 3rd in high jump going 5′7 3/8″. In 1900 Paris Olympics competed in shot and standing triple jump. Was scheduled to defend discus championship but boycotted event when it was rescheduled on Sunday. Finished 3rd in shot with put of 40′, improvement over 1896 gold medal performance. Bronze medal winner in standing triple jump with 31′2″.

GERMAR, MANFRED B. 3/10/35, Köln, Germany. Member 1956, 60

German Olympic teams. Co-held world 200-m record. Ran 20.6 on Oct. 1, 1958, at Wuppestal. Considered to be one of greatest, if not greatest, sprinters in European track history. In 1957, 58 ran 100-m in 10.2 three times and set 200-m world record. Had finished 5th in 1956 Melbourne Olympic Games. Undefeated from 1956 to July, 1960, in 200-m. Won 1958 European Championship in 200-m with 21.0, but lost to countryman Armin Hary in 100-m. Member Germany's world record-tying 400-m relay team in 1958. German foursome ran 39.5 at Cologne on Aug. 29.

GILBERT, A.C. B. 2/15/84, Salem, Oreg. D. 1/24/61. Member 1908 Olympic team. Won gold medal in London Olympics in pole vault. Tied with E.T. Cooke, also of U.S., at 12′2 1/16″ for 1st place. Height set Olympic record despite absence of vaulting box. As Yale student tied for 1908 IC4A pole vault title at 11′. Worked way through college as magician. Inventor of erector set, headed company which manufactured American Flyer electric trains.

GILL, HARRY B. 1/9/76, Feserton, Ontario. D. 8/31/56, Orillia, Ontario. Outstanding coach of Illinois track teams 30 years. Took over as Illini coach in 1904. Won first of 11 Big Ten team titles three years later. Teams finished 2nd 7 times, 3rd 4 times, and 4th 4 times. Worst finishes were trio of 5th place finishes and a 6th. Had dual meet record of 117 wins, 27 losses, 2 ties. Teams won 1921, 27 NCAA team crowns. Coached 4 NCAA individual titlists. Founder and owner of Harry Gill and Co. Athletic Equipment. Company made, and still does, widely used track and field equipment. Member Citizens Savings (Helms) Hall of Fame.

GOLLIDAY, JIM B. 4/23/31, Sacramento, Calif. D. 4/10/71, Chicago, Ill. Tied world 100-yd record. Ran 9.3 on May 14, 1955, at Evanston, Ill., Big Ten championships to tie Mel Patton and Hec Hogan for world record. Watches caught him in 9.2, 9.2, 9.3, 9.3, 9.4 and wind was under limit. Won 1952 NCAA 100-m title for Northwestern. Ran 10.4 into stiff wind. Looked like cinch for 1952 Olympic team but had muscle trouble and did not make team. After tour in army, came back to Northwestern in 1955. That year won Drake Relays 100-yd and Big Ten 100-yd before NCAA. In NCAA won 100-yd in 9.6 and 200-yd in 21.1. Ran in 1956 but plagued by muscle trouble and was again missing from U.S. Olympic team. Insurance man in Chicago until untimely death at age 39.

GONDER, FERNAND B. 1886. Member 1906 French team in unoffical Athens Olympics. Won gold medal in pole vault with 11′6″ which tied

Olympic record. French champion in 1904 with jump of 12′1″, world record. Also won title in 1905. Retired until 1913 when came back to win French title. Took 1914 French crown. Had official best of 12′4″.

GORDIEN, FORTUNE B. 9/9/22, Spokane, Wash. Member 1948, 52, 56 Olympic teams. Held world discus mark 10 years. First set mark in 1949 with 185′2¾″. Broke mark again same year with 186′11″. Personal best and world mark 194′6″, Aug. 22, 1953, at Pasadena, Calif., stood 10 years. Best year 1953–8 throws over 185′. Won 3 straight NCAA disc crowns for Minnesota. Six AAU titles—1946–50, 53–54. AAU record 183′9½″ in 1953 lasted 6 years. Made Olympic team 3 times. Won silver, bronze, but no gold. Third in 1948 with 166′7″. Fourth at Helsinki in 1952 with 172′9¼″. As favorite in 1956 was second with 179′9½″. In 1960 at age 38 had 187′10″ throw. In 1971 U.S. Masters, won with 147′ at age 48. Now track coach at San Bernardino Junior College in Calif.

GORDON, EDWARD B. 7/1/08, Jackson, Miss. Member 1928, 32 Olympic teams. World class long jumper over 10 years. Made 1928 Olympic team but did not make finals. Went 24′1½″ in preliminary jump. Premier long jumper in U.S. from 1929–32. Won 3 NCAA championships while at Iowa. In 1929 went 24′8½″ for collegiate crown, 25′0″ in 1930 and 24′11⅜″ in 1931. Won 1929 AAU with 24′4¼″ and 1932 title with 25′3⅜″. In 1932 Los Angeles Olympics was not favorite as world record-holder Nambu of Japan was in field. But Gordon won gold medal with leap of 25′¾″. Stayed in competition many years. Won AAU indoor twice. Went 23′4″ in 1938 and 23′10⅛″ in 1939 for last big titles. Member Citizens Savings (Helms) Hall of Fame.

GREENE, CHARLIE B. 3/21/45, Pine Bluff, Ark. Member 1968 Olympic team. Co-holds world 100-m, 100-yd records. Ran 9.1 100-yd at Houston on June 15, 1967, to tie record held by Bob Hayes, Harry Jerome and Jim Hines. John Carlos tied record in 1969. In 1968 on June 20 at Sacramento, Calif., in greatest 100-m day ever, ran 10.0 to tie record in AAU prelims. In semis ran 9.9 as did Hines and Ronnie Roy Smith. In finals ran 10.0 to take 1968 AAU championship. Made 1968 Olympic team in 100-m. In Mexico City ran 10.0 to win his semi heat. In finals was 3rd behind Lennox Miller of Jamaica and gold medal winner Hines. Hines ran 9.9 to tie world mark, Greene was timed in 10.0. Greene led off U.S. 400-m relay team that ran world record 38.2. While at Nebraska won 3 NCAA 100-yd titles. Ran 9.4 in 1965, 9.3 in 1966 and 9.2 in 1967. Won 1966 AAU in 9.4. Made comeback attempt for 1972 Munich Olympics but did not make team.

GRELLE, JIM B. 9/30/36, Portland, Oreg. Member 1960 Olympic team. One of top milers in 1960s who brought U.S. back into prominence in that event. One of stable of top milers at Oregon under Coach Bill Bowerman. Was NCAA All-American 1957–59. Won NCAA mile in 1959 with 4:03.9. Had best of 4:01.7 in college. In 1960 was AAU champ in 1500-m with 3:42.7. Took silver medal in 1959 Pan-Am games with 3:49.9 in 1500-m. In 1960 Olympics made finals of 1500-m, but was 8th with 3:45.0. Was 1963 Pan-Am 1500-m gold medal winner with record 3:43.5. Failed to make Olympic team in 1964 when finished 4th in final trials. Continued to compete and had great success. Was 1965, 66 AAU indoor mile champion. In 1965 ran 3:55.4 mile at Vancouver and 3:39.0 in 1500-m at Cologne. Veteran of international competition, was 1st in U.S.-USSR duals in '58, '64, '65. Ran 3:39.2 in 1965 dual. Was 2nd in 1959, 61.

GUILLEMOT, JOSEPH B. October, 1899, Dorat, Vienna. Member 1920, 24 French Olympic teams. Won gold medal in 5000-m in 1920 Antwerp Olympics. Ran 14:55.6 to defeat Paavo Nurmi. Was 2nd to Nurmi in 10,000-m few days later. French 5000-m champ in 1919, 21–25 and cross country champ in '20, '22, '26. Won English cross country title 1920–22. Residing in Paris where is enthusiastic sports fan.

GUMMEL, MARGITTA B. 6/29/41, Magdeburg, E. Germany. Member 1964, 68, 72 E. German Olympic teams. Held world womens shot put record. First broke mark with put of 61′11″ on Sept. 22, 1968, at Frankfurt. Improved record twice more at Mexico City Olympics to 64′4″ for gold medal before losing it. After losing record for almost year, had put of 65′11½″ at Berlin on Sept. 11, 1969. Mark lasted only 5 days. In 1972 Olympics won silver medal with toss of 66′3½″. Was 2nd in 1966, 69 European Championships, 3rd in 1971. Won GDR titles in '66, '68, '69, '71, '72. Has competed for 17 years. Member phys. ed. staff of German College of Physical Culture, member County Parliament of Leipzig.

GUTOWSKI, ROBERT B. 4/25/35, San Pedro, Calif. D. 1960. Member 1956 Olympic team. Held world record in pole vault with 15′8¼″ in 1957. Jumped 15′9¾″ same year, but disallowed as world mark on technicalities. Was allowed as American record. Failed to make 1956 U.S. Olympic team in tryouts. Added when Jim Graham was injured. Placed second in Melbourne to Bob Richards with 14′10½″. In addition to being one of history's fine aluminum vaulters, was long jumper with 24′9″ best and sub 10.0 sprinter. Won 1957 NCAA with American record 15′9¾″ and tied for first in 1956 for Occidental. Tied for 1958 indoor at 15′3″. Died in car accident in 1960.

GUTTERSON, ALBERT B. 1887, Vermont. D. 4/7/65. Member 1912 Olympic team. Scored surprising upset in 1912 Stockholm Olympics. Jumped over foot better than previous best to win gold medal with 24′11 ¼″. Jump beat Olympic mark by nearly 5″. Lasted as record until 1928. Jump came within ½″ of world record. Must have been once in lifetime performance. Never won a national title.

HAGG, GUNDER B. 12/31/18, Sörbygden, Sweden. Set 15 world distance marks from mile to 3-mile during 1940s. In 1938 placed 2nd in steeplechase in Swedish championships to attract attention. Was in service and ill, putting career in temporary retirement until 1940. Improved to world record 1500-m of 3:47.6 at Swedish championships Aug. 10, 1941. Suspended from Swedish amateur ranks for 10 months. Came back July 1, 1942, and set world mile mark of 4:06.2 at Goteborg. Started record-breaking 82 days in which set 9 world records in distances ranging from mile to 3-mile. Made successful tour of U.S. in 1943 and captured AAU 5000-m title. Ran 4:05.3 mile for American record. In 1944 broke 1500-m world record, defeating arch-rival Arne Andersson with 3:43.0. Set mile record with 4:01.4, again beating Andersson in 1945. Also set 2-mile record twice in 1944. Bannished from amateur track in 1946 for financial irregularities. May have broken 4-minute mile with another year of competition.

HAHN, ARCHIE B. 1880, Milwaukee, Wis. D. 1/21/55, Charlottesville, Va. Member 1904, 06 Olympic teams. Co-held world 100-yd record with 9.8 in 1901. Broke world 200-m (straightaway) record in 1904 with 21.6. Won 3 AAU championships: 220-yd and 100-yd in 1903 and 220-yd in 1905. In 1904 St. Louis Olympics took gold medal in 60-m, 100-m and 200-m. Time of 21.6 in 200-m good for Olympic record which was not bettered until 1932. Added 4th gold medal to collection in 1906 in 100-m. Author of *How to Sprint*, considered by many a classic of track literature. Member Citizens Savings (Helms) Hall of Fame. Victim of heart ailment.

HALBERG, MURRAY B. 7/7/33, Eketahuna, New Zealand. Member 1960, 64 New Zealand Olympic teams. Held world 2-mile, 3-mile records. Ran 8:30.0 at Jyvoskyla, Finland, on 7/7/61, for 2-mile record. Eighteen days later broke 3-mile record with 13:10.0 at Stockholm. Overcame severe physical injuries suffered while playing rugby to become great distance runner. Only lasting effect of injury was withered arm. Won first major title in 1958 with 3-mile victory in 13:15.0 at Cardiff British Empire Games. Greatest victory came in 1960 Rome Olympics. Won gold medal in 10,000-m in 13:43.4. Made big move after 9 laps and opposition could not recover. Won 2nd British Empire Games. Very versatile runner. Had 800-m best of 1:51.7, 3:57.5 mile, 27:52.2 6-mile and 2:28:43.0 marathon. In 1964 Tokyo Olympics was 10,000-m favorite but was 7th in what has been called greatest 10,000-m of all time. Won many national titles in New Zealand and still holds national 5000-m record of 13:35.2 despite abundance of great Kiwi runners.

HALL, ALBERT B. 8/2/34, Manchester, N.Y. Member 1956, 60, 64, 68 Olympic teams. Member 1959, 63 Pan-Am Games teams. Along with Hal Connolly and Ed Burke, dominated U.S. hammer throw. Was AAU champion in 1962 with toss of 219′3″. Took 1963 AAU crown with 214′11″. Standout collegian at Cornell, made 1956 Olympic team and was 4th with toss of 203′3″. In 1959 was 2nd to Connolly by ½″ in Pan-Am Games with toss of 195′11″. Made 1960 Olympic team and was 14th at 196′¾″. Set record in 1963 Pan-Am Games with throw of 205′10″. In 1964 Olympic Games was 14th with toss of 209′4½. In 1968 wasn't given much of chance to make team. But in trials tossed 220′5″ on first throw for berth. First time since 1964 that he broke 200′. Did not make finals, despite throw of 215′6½″. In effort to make U.S. Olympic team for 5th time, competed in 1971, 72. In 1971 Pan-Am Games won gold medal with 216′. Finished 3rd in 1972 AAU with toss of 217′7″. In 1972 trials was 4th with best of 220′9″. Connolly, only other active 4-time Olympian, also failed to make team as he was 5th.

HAMILTON, BRUTUS B. 7/19/1900, Peculiar, Mo. D. 12/28/70, Berkeley, Calif. Member 1920, 24 Olympic teams. Coached 1952 Olympic team. U.S. won 13 gold medals under his guidance. Athletes set 2 world records, 7 Olympic marks and equalled two more. Head track coach at California 1932–1965. Cal teams took 2nd in 6 NCAA Championships, captured 14 NCAA individual crowns. Cal teams set several world records during Hamilton's career. Athletes included Harold Davis, Guinn Smith and Don Bowen. Coached U.S. international teams in 1965, including dual with Russia. Assistant Olympic coach in 1932, 36. Won silver medal in 1920 decathlon. In 1924 was 7th in pentathlon. Called one of the greatest track coaches by Ken Doherty, a former coach, in one of his books. Member Citizens Savings (Helms) Hall of Fame.

HAMM, EDWARD B. 4/13/06, Lonoke, Ark. Member 1928 Olympic team. Held world long jump record. Got off jump of 25′11″ at Cambridge, Mass., July 7, 1928, for world mark. Took 1928 AAU championship with 25′11″ world mark leap. Was 1927, 28 NCAA long jump champion while at Georgia Tech. Won 1928 championship with 25′0″ jump. In 1928 Amsterdam Olympics won gold medal with Olympic record 25′4¼″. Defeated Silvio Cator of Haiti, who became history's first 26′ jumper, for gold medal. Member Citizens Savings (Helms) Hall of Fame.

HAMMOND, KATHY B. 11/2/51, Sacramento, Calif. Member 1972 Olympic team. Holds U.S. 400-m record. Ran 52.1 at Warsaw on Aug. 29, 1969. In 1972 Olympic trials ran 51.8 to break her record. Bronze medalist in 1972 Munich Olympics. Ran 51.64 to break her record again and take 3rd. Won 1972 AAU in 52.3 and 1969 in 54.4. Was 2nd in 1967 AAU but won 220-yd and 440-yd. Was 4th in 1970. Won 1972 AAU indoor. Student at American River College in 1972.

HAMPSON, THOMAS B. 10/28/07, London, England. Member 1932 British Olympic team. Held world 800-m record. Ran 1:49.8 in 1932 Olympics at Los Angeles for gold medal on Aug. 2. Broke record by almost full second. British schoolteacher was actually timed in 1:49.7 but rounded off to 1:49.8 according to rules. Stayed back on first lap with time of 54.8. On final lap, gradually passed everyone and held off late challenge by Alex Wilson of Canada. Ran 54.9 on gun lap. First sub-1:50 800-m runner. Won British Empire Games in 1930 with 1:52.4 which was best time prior to 1932 Olympics. High point of career was 1932.

HANSEN, FRED B. 12/29/40, Cuero, Tex. Member 1964 Olympic team. Held world pole vault record. Vaulted 17′2″ at San Diego, Calif., on June 13, 1964. Improved mark to 17′4″ on July 25 of the same year at Los Angeles. First came into prominence in 1963 when tied for 1st in NCAA while representing Rice. Started off best year, 1964, by winning Texas Relays with jump of 15′6″. Then won Cal Relays with 16′4½″. After that, had 3 straight meets with vaults of 17′ or better. Won Texas Federation meet at 17′1″, San Diego Invitational at 17′2″ for world mark, and the AAU championships at 17′0″. Set record of 17′4″ in meet with USSR for career best. In 1964 Rome Olympics was only American left when bar was raised over 16′. Passed at 16′1″ and 16′3″. Cleared first try at 16′5″. Passed again at 16′6¾″, but Reinhardt of Germany attempted and made height. Bar then moved to 16′8¾″. If Hansen failed, Reinhardt would become first non-American to win gold medal. Hansen kicked bar off twice. On third try, with tremendous pressure on shoulders, cleared bar by 6″ to take gold medal. Ranked best vaulter in world by *Track & Field News* in 1964. Dentist in Houston.

HARBIG, RUDOLPH B. 11/8/13, Dresden, Germany. D. 3/5/44. Held world 400-m, 800-m and 1000-m records. Set 400-m record of 46.0 at Frankfurt on Aug. 12, 1939. Got 800-m record with 1:46.6 at Milan on July 15, 1939. Won 1938 European Championships with 1:50.6 over rival Lanzi of Italy. Ran during war and set 1000-m record of 2:21.5 at Dresdsen on May 24, 1941. One of first to use interval training. Died in war on Eastern front.

HARDIN, GLENN B. 7/1/10, Derma, Miss. Member 1932, 36 Olympic teams. Held world 400-m hurdle record. Record 52.0 in 1932 Olympics, 51.8 in 1934 AAU and 50.6 in Stockholm in 1934. Finished 2nd in 1932 Olympics. Set world record as winner knocked down hurdle. Rule was that downed hurdle disqualified world mark. After practically laying out of hurdles a year, made 1936 Olympic team. Won gold medal in 1936 Olympics with 52.4 clocking. Won '33, '34, '36 AAU 440-yd hurdles. Depended much on great speed. At LSU won NCAA 440-yd dash in 1933,34. Best in dash was 46.5. Son Billy was world class 440-yd hurdler in 1960s. World mark 50.6 of 1934 stood 19 years.

HARRIS, ARCHIE B. 7/3/18, Urbanna, Va. D. 10/29/65. Held world discus record. Tossed disc 174′9″ at 1941 NCAA championships at Palo Alto, Calif., on June 20, competing for Indiana. Only black man to hold world record in discus. Recaptured world record for U.S. after being held by Andersson of Sweden and Schroder of Germany since 1934. Had great season with throws of 170′-plus consistently. Won 1941 AAU with 167′9½″. Was 1940 NCAA champion with 162′4½″. His 1941 NCAA toss lasted 12 years before being smashed by Sim Iness of Southern Cal, breaking world mark with 190′. Like many other athletes of 1940s, never had chance for Olympic honors because of WW II.

HART, EDDIE B. 4/24/48, Martinez, Calif. Member 1972 Olympic team. Was 1970 NCAA 100-yd champ for California with 9.4. In 1971 took 2nd in NCAA. Had best of 9.3 in 1971. In 1972 trained hard for Olympics. Won Kennedy Games 100-yd in 9.4 for only major win before Olympic trials. At trials ran 10.1 in 100-m first heat, 10.1 in quarterfinals and 9.9 in semis. Did not win any of three races. But in finals, won in 9.9 to tie world record. At Munich was denied chance to run in his second 100-m heat when was late due to communications breakdown. Made up for some grief by anchoring U.S. 400-m relay team to gold medal and world record-tying 38.19.

HARY, ARMIN B. 3/22/37, Quierschied, Germany. Member 1960 West German Olympic team. Held world 100-m record with 10.0 at Zurich, June 21, 1960. Surprised fellow German Germar and England's Radford in 1958 European Championships with 10.3 win to gain world attention. Defeated impressive field in 1960 Rome Olympics, including Jerome of Canada, who also had 10.0 to credit; Sime, Budd and Norton of U.S.; and Radford of England. Time of 10.2 set Olympic record. Did not run 200-m in Games. Had 20.9 best. Also ran on winning 400-m relay team. U.S. placed first but was disqualified. Great start in Games gave win by fraction over Sime. Quick start out of blocks called phenomenal. Retired from track after auto accident in 1960s.

HAYES, BOB B. 12/20/42, Jacksonville, Fla. Member 1964 Olympic team. Won gold medal in 1964 with 10.0 in 100-m for Olympic record, but not world record because of wind. Anchored 400-m relay team, making up 2-m deficit to win by 3-m over Poland in Olympic and world record 39.0. Co-holder world 100-yd mark with 9.1 in semi heat of 1963 National AAU in St. Louis. Also timed at 9.1 in finals but disallowed because of wind. In 1963 Florida Athletic Club Invitational tied world 220-yd mark with 20.6 despite 8 mph wind in face and misjudging finish. Once clocked at 26.9 mph during 100-yd dash. Called "World's Fastest Human." Football, track star at Florida A & M, now star pass receiver with Dallas Cowboys. Member Citizens Savings (Helms) Hall of Fame.

HAYES, JOHN B. 1889, New York, N.Y. D. 10/25/68. Member 1908 Olympic team. Won gold medal in 1908 London Olympic marathon in one of most famous incidents in Olympic history. With 6 miles to go, South African Charles Hefferon led with Dorando Pietri of Italy good deal behind. But Pietri made mad dash to catch and pass Hefferon. As Pietri entered stadium he began to waiver and took wrong turn, going right instead of left. Fell down and was helped to feet. Meanwhile, Hayes overtook Hefferon. Pietri was pointed in direction of finish line and crossed line .32 before Hayes. Pietri was disqualified for being helped after collapse, Hayes was given gold medal. Both Hayes and Pietri turned pro and ran exhibitions with Italian beating Hayes, a New York store clerk, regularly. Only second American to win gold medal in marathon.

HEIN, KARL B. 6/11/08, Hamburg, Germany. Member 1936 German Olympic team. Unknown prior to 1935. In 1936 won German championship in hammer throw and set German record of 178′1½″. In 1936 Berlin Olympics won with 185′4 3/16″ and set Olympic record. Was second gold medal winner in Germany's history. In 1938 won European Championships with career best of 192′10″.

HEIN, VILJO AKSELI B. 3/1/14, Lahita, Finland. Member 1948 Finnish Olympic team. Held several world distance records. Set 6-mile record of 28:38.6 at Helsinki on Aug. 25, 1944. Also set 10,000-m record of 29:35.0 in same race. Improved 6-mile record to 28:30.8 on Sept. 9, 1949, at Kouvola. Broke Paavo Nurmi's 10-mile record which stood for 17 years, running 49:41.6 on Sept. 30, 1945, at Turku. Improved mark to 49:22.2 on Sept. 14, 1946. Set 1-hr run mark on same day as first 10-mile mark with 12 miles, 29 yds. Set 20,000-m mark at Turku on Sept. 22, 1949, with 1:02:40.0. In 1948 London Olympics 10,000-m, was heavy favorite. Took lead at start and led until 10th lap when Zatopak caught him. Ran together 6 more laps before Zatopek opened up 30-yd lead. Hein, admitting defeat, left the track and did not finish.

HELD, FRANKLIN (Bud) B. 10/25/27, Los Angeles, Calif. Member 1952 Olympic team. Held world javelin record, 263′10″ in 1953 and then 268′2½″ in 1955. Developed new type javelin with better weight distribution and shorter, lighter point. First man over 260′ and 80-m on Aug. 8, 1953, at Pasadena, Calif., with 263′10″. In 1952 finished 9th in Olympics with bad shoulder. In 1956 was injured and couldn't make Olympic team. Had throw of 270′ after tryouts. Won 1955 Pan-Am gold medal. Won NCAA 1948–50 while at Stanford. Won 5 AAU crowns, record 260′3″ in 1953. Unlike most, made great improvement after college. One of small number of great American javelin specialists. Member Citizens Savings (Helms) Hall of Fame.

HEMERY, DAVID B. 7/18/44. Member 1968, 72 British Olympic teams. Won gold medal in 1968 Olympics in 400-m hurdles. Set world record of 48.1 in winning by wide margin. In 1972 was bronze medalist, seeing his world record fall to John Akii-Bua. Hemery was edged by Ralph Mann, 48.51 to 48.52 for silver medal. Lived in U.S. for over 10 years, attended Boston U. There won 1968 NCAA 400-m hurdles in 49.8. Was 1966 British Empire Games 110-m hurdle champion in 14.1. Has high hurdles best of 13.4, won 1966, 71 English championships in event.

HILL, ALBERT B. 3/24/88. Member 1920 British Olympic team. In 1920 Antwerp Olympics won both 800-m and 1500-m. Feat has been accomplished by only Peter Snell since. Won 800-m first. Defeated Earl Eby of U.S. by yard, timed in 1:53.4. Two days later won 1500-m in

4:01.8. Set British mile mark of 4:14.2 in 1933 AAA (British AAU) championships on July 2. Had long career and won 4 AAA crowns, despite interuption by WW I.

HILL, THOMAS B. 11/17/49, New Orleans, La. Member 1972 Olympic team. In 1970 matched world 120-yd hurdle record with 13.2 at Wichita, Kans, USTFF meet. Was AAU champ in 1970 in 13.3. Won 1970 NCAA indoor for Arkansas State with 6.9 in 60-yd hurdles. Injured knee in 1971 indoor season and underwent surgery, missing entire season. Came back strong in 1972. In 1972 NCAA ran 13.3 in semifinals. In finals came in 2nd at 13.5. In 1972 AAU was 3rd in 13.6. In Olympic trial finals, surprised Rod Milburn and Willie Davenport by winning in 13.5. At Munich Olympics was 3rd with 13.48. Second Lt. in U.S. Army at time of Olympics.

HILLMAN, HARRY B. 8/9/81. D. 8/9/45. Member 1904, 06, 08 Olympic teams. Triple gold medal winner in 1904 St. Louis Olympics. Won 400-m in 49.6, 400-m (low) hurdles in 53.0 and 200-m hurdles in 24.6. In unoffical Olympics at Athens in 1906 was ill and placed fifth in 400-m. Became ill on boat trip to Greece. In 1908 London Olympics was close second to Charley Bacon in 400-m hurdles, Bacon setting world mark of 55.0. Won 1903 AAU 440-yd with 52.0 clocking and won again in 1908. Outstanding coach at Dartmouth College. Elected to Citizens Savings (Helms) Hall of Fame as coach.

HINES, JIM B. 9/10/46, Dumas, Ark. Member 1968 Olympic team. Co-holds 100-m and 100-yd world records. Ran 9.1 to tie 100-yd mark May 13, 1967, at Houston. In 1968 Olympic 100-m finals equalled world mark with 9.9. First appeared in limelight with 2nd-place finish in 1965 AAU 220-yd. Took 2nd in 1966 AAU 100-yd and 220-yd. In 1967 won AAU 100-yd with 9.3, 2nd in 220-yd. Also took NAIA 100-yd crown for Texas Southern. In 1968 was 2nd in AAU 100-m, but won Los Angeles Olympic trials with 10.0. In Mexico City Olympic 100-m finals, got best start of career took lead at halfway point. Won gold medal with record 9.9. Anchored U.S. 400-m relay team to gold medal, world and Olympic records. Timed on one watch in 8.2 for 100-m anchor leg. U.S. team clocked in 38.2. Went to pro football shortly after Olympics but failed with 2 teams.

HÖCKERT, GUNNAR B. 1910. D. 1940. Member 1936 Finnish Olympic team. Held world 3000-m and 2-mile records. Ran 8:14.8 on Sept. 16, 1936, at Stockholm to break 3000-m record. Set 2-mile record on Sept. 24, 1936, at Stockholm with 8:57.4. At Berlin Olympics of 1936 won gold medal in 5000-m with Olympic record of 14:22.2. Won Finnish

5000-m title in 1936. Same year set national 3000-m, 2-mile, and 2000-m records. Economist at time of death.

HODGE, RUSS B. 9/12/34, Monticello, N.Y. Member 1964 Olympic team. Held world decathlon record. Set world mark at Los Angeles on July 23–24, 1966, with 8230 points. Got off to good start in 10-event test with 10.5 in 100-m. Long jumped over 24′ and put shot a tremendous 56′9″. High jumped 6′1″ and ran 48.9 in 400-m to end first day. Got off to slow start on second day with 15.0 in 110-m hurdles. But then threw discus 165′1″ to gain on record. Went 13′5″ in pole vault and tossed javelin 211′7″. Ran fine 4:40.4 in 1500-m to clinch record. Had long career but did not win AAU title, although always among top contenders. In 1964 Olympics did not exhibit speed and strength he later showed to break world mark. Finished 9th with 7325 points. Did not make 1968 Olympic team. Won 1971 USA-USSR World All-Star meet with 7698 points. On 1971 Pan Am team and won silver medal with 7445 points. Injured, as was during much of career, prior to 1972 Olympic trials. Scored 7025 points in 9 events, not competing in 1500-m.

HOFF, CHARLES B. 1902, Fredrikstad, Norway. Member 1924 Norwegian Olympic team. World record-holder in pole vault during 1920s. In 1922, second year of vaulting, set first record with 13′6½″ on Sept. 3 at Copenhagen. Europe's first 4-m (13′2¼″) vaulter. World mark progressed to 13′9¾″ in 1923, 13′10½″ and 13′11⅜″ in 1925. Did not compete in pole vault in 1924 Olympics. Injured ankle prior to Games. Did compete in 400-m and 800-m but failed to place. Broke American vault record at 1926 Drake Relays with 13′9¼″ during U.S. tour. Did not lose in tour of States. Declared pro and could not compete in 1928 Olympics. Vaulted 14′2″ as a pro. Versatile athlete; scored 6368 points in decathlon under present scoring system. Ran 10.8 in 100-m, 24′3¾″ in long jump, 49.2 in 400-m, and 47′2¼″ in triple jump. Said to be one of greatest athletes in European history.

HOLDORF, WILLI B. 2/17/40. Member 1964 German Olympic team. In his 21st decathlon, won gold medal at Tokyo Olympics in 1964. Started off with 10.7 in 100-m, 22′11½″ in long jump, 49′½″ in shot, 6′½″ in high jump and 48.2 in 400-m. His 889 points in 400-m was his best. Second day saw 15.0 in 110-m hurdles, 151′1″ in discus, 13′9½″ in pole vault, 188′2½″ in javelin and 4:34.3 in 1500-m. German champion in 1961, 63. Had best score of 8085 in 1963. Was junior decathlon coach. Now owner of sporting goods store.

HORINE, GEORGE B. 2/3/90, Escondido, Calif. Member 1912 Olympic team. Held world high jump record with 6′6⅛″ jump on March 29,

1912, then broke own record May 18, 1912, with 6′7″ leap. World's first 2-m (6′7″) high jumper. Developed "western roll" technique. New style led to greater heights in high jump. When at Stanford, abandoned style temporarily, but returned to it and set American collegiate mark of 6′4$\frac{3}{4}$″ and world marks in 1912. Competed in 1912 Stockholm Olympics. Won bronze medal with 6′2$\frac{1}{2}$″ jump behind Alma Richards of U.S. and Hans Liesche of Germany. Won 1915 AAU title with 6′$\frac{3}{4}$″ for only national title. Horine style of high jump proved invaluable contribution to track and field. Member Citizens Savings (Helms) Hall of Fame.

HOUSER, CLARENCE B. 9/25/01, Wennigin, Mo. Member 1924, 28 Olympic teams. Held world record in discus with 158′2″ at Palo Alto, Calif., April 3, 1926. One of select few to win Olympic gold medal in both shot and discus. In 1924 Paris Olympics captured shot with 49′2$\frac{2}{3}$″ and disc with Olympic record 151′5$\frac{1}{8}$″. In 1928 Olympics at Amsterdam, won second gold medal in discus. Advanced Olympic record to 155′3″. Won '25, '26, '28 AAU discus titles. Also won 1921, 25 AAU shot titles. Took 1925, 26 IC4A discus titles while at Southern Cal. Also won 1926 IC4A shot title. Won 1926 NCAA discus crown. Was dentist when won second Olympic gold medal. Practices dentistry in Palm Springs. Member Citizens Savings (Helms) Hall of Fame.

HUBBARD, WILLIAM DEHART B. 11/25/03, Cincinnati, Ohio. Member 1924, 28 Olympic teams. Held world long jump mark with 25′10$\frac{7}{8}$″ in 1925. Also co-held world 100-yd mark with 9.6 in 1926. King of long jump for 6 straight years. Won 1922–27 AAU titles, with 25′8$\frac{3}{4}$″ in 1927 best jump. Won 1923 NCAA long jump with 25′2″ for Michigan. In 1925 NCAA set world long jump mark of 25′10$\frac{7}{8}$″ and won 100-yd in 9.8. Won gold medal in 1924 Paris Olympics with 24′5$\frac{1}{8}$″. Also competed in triple jump but failed to reach finals. Made 1928 team in specialty, but did not make finals with poor 23′4″ jump. Six AAU long jump titles unequaled. Member Citizens Savings (Helms) Hall of Fame.

IBBOTSON, DEREK B. 6/17/32, Huddersfield, England. Member 1956 British Olympic team. Held world mile record. Ran 3:57.2 at London on July 17, 1957, for British, European and world best. Defeated Ron Delany, who had won gold medal at 1956 Olympics. Had lap times of 56.0, 60.4, 63.9, 56.9 in record run. In 1956 Melbourne Olympics entered 5000-m. Qualified for finals but was running against USSR great Vladimir Kuts. Won bronze medal behind Kuts and countryman Pirie, despite own best time of 13:54.4. Ran many races in 1957 and had excellent year. Bettered Roger Bannister's 3:58.8 British record. Amount of competition said to have burned out talent after 1957.

IHAROS, SANDOR B. 3/10/30, Budapest, Hungary. Member 1960 Hungarian Olympic team. Held several world distance marks. Set 3000-m record at Budapest with 7:55.6 on May 14, 1955. At London 16 days later, set 2-mile record of 8:33.4. Set 1500-m mark of 3:40.8 at Helsinki on July 28, 1955. In 1954 set European record of 3:42.2 but was 6th in European Championship. On Sept. 10, 1955, at Budapest, set 5000-m mark of 13:50.8. Advanced that record to 13:14.2 at same track on Oct. 23, 1955. Also broke 3-mile record with 13:14.2 in process. In 1956 set 10,000-m mark with 28:42.8 on July 15, lowering record 11.4 seconds. Missed 1956 Olympics due to injuries and Hungarian revolt. In 1960 Rome Olympics, entered 10,000-m and made finals. In finals finished 11th with 29:15.8, far below best time, but race considered one of best 10,000-m in history.

INESS, SIM B. 7/9/30, Keota, Okla. Member 1952 Olympic team. Held world discus record. Tossed disc 190′ ¾″ for world record on June

20, 1953, at NCAA championships. Also 1952 NCAA champion for Southern Cal with 173′2 3/8″. His 1953 throw was NCAA meet record until 1966 when Randy Matson of Texas A & M had throw of 197′0″. Made 1952 Olympic team and was not considered favorite as Fortune Gordien held world record with throw of 186′11″. But Iness broke Olympic record on each of his six final throws and took gold medal with best of 180′6 1/2″. Accomplishments at Helsinki Games, he says, are greatest thrills in career. Head football coach at Porterville College in California.

ISAKSSON, KJELL B. 2/28/48, Harosand, Sweden. Member 1968, 72 Swedish Olympic teams. Had thigh injury at time of 1972 Munich Olympics and did not make qualifying height. In 1968 was 10th at Mexico City Olympics with vault of 16′10 1/2″. Had good year in 1971 with vaults of 17′9 3/4″ and 17′9 1/2″. In great 1972 season, cleared 18′ five times. Jumps were 18′1″, 18′2″ (both good for world marks), 18′ 1/2″, 18′2 1/2″ and 18′4 1/4″. Latter was equaled by Bob Seagren at same U. of Texas–El Paso meet and set world record. Had vaults of over 17′ in 20 of 21 competitions. Was 2nd in 1969 and 1971 European Championships. Small (5′8 1/2″, 150 lbs), but strong. Gymnastics instructor.

ISO-HOLLO, VOLMARI B. 4/1/07, Tahti, Finland. Member 1932, 36 Finnish Olympic teams. Outstanding distance runner and steeplechase man in 1930s. In 1932 Olympics was entered in both 10,000-m and 3000-m steeplechase. In 10,000-m was one of favorites as Finns had won all previous gold medals. Led on last lap until backstretch. Janusz Kusociński of Poland took lead on straightaway and broke Olympic record with 30:11.4. Iso-Hollo was 2nd. In 3000-m steeplechase, things were different. Won handily in race that was one lap long because of officials' error. In 1936 Berlin Olympics, entered same events. In 10,000-m was 3rd behind two other Finns. In steeplechase set Olympic record of 9:03.8 in winning gold medal. Made him only man ever to win two gold medals in steeplechase.

JACKSON (MANNING), MADELINE B. 1/11/48, Columbus, Ohio. Member 1968, 72 Olympic teams. Holds American 800-m record. Ran 2:00 in Mexico City Olympics to win gold medal and set Olympic, American records. Was 1967 AAU champ in 2:03.6 and also 1969 AAU titlist in 2:11.1. Was 2nd in 1966, 68. Gold medalist in 1967 Pan-Am Games in 2:02.0. In 1969 was named "outstanding athlete" in U.S.-Europe meet. Ran 2:03.8 in U.S.-USSR meet to win. In 1972 Munich Olympics did not make 800-m finals. Ran 2nd leg for U.S. 1600-m relay team that won silver medal.

JACKSON, MARJORIE (Mrs. Peter Nelson) B. 9/13/31, Lithgow, Australia. Member 1952 Australian Olympic team. Won gold medals in 100-m and 200-m. Tied world and Olympic records in 100-m with 11.5 in both semis and finals. In 200-m heat ran 23.6 to set world mark, then lowered to 23.4 in semis. Won gold medal with 23.7 clocking. Improved 100-m mark to 11.4 on Oct. 4, 1952, at Gifu, Japan. Broke world 100-yd mark 3 times. A 10.4 clocking on March 1, 1958, at Sydney was best. Holds 3 Australian national titles in both 100-yd and 220-yd. Won titles in '50, '52, '54. Broke national 100-yd record 5 times, 10.5 in 1952 was best. Also set 100-m record (11.8 in 1950), 220-yd (24.7 in 1950) and 200-m (24.6 in 1950, 24.2 in 1954, 24.0 in 1954). Housewife.

JARVINEN, MATTI B. 2/18/09, Tampere, Finland. Member 1932, 36 Finnish Olympic teams. Held world javelin record. No other man has so dominated event. First set world record at Viipuri on Aug. 8,

1930, with throw of 234′9″. Improved record twice in same month to 235′10″. Increased record to 239′3″ on Sept. 14, 1930, also at Viipuri. Improved record six more times to final mark of 253′4″ set June 18, 1936, at Helsinki. Son of Finland's first gold medal winner Werner Jarvinen, who won Greek style discus in 1906. In 1932 Los Angeles Olympics, broke Games mark by over 20′ with throw of 238′6½″ for gold medal. In 1936 Olympics finished 5th, mainly because of back injury. European champion in 1934 at Turin with world record throw of 251′6″, and in 1938 at Paris with 252′2½″. Added much to technique of javelin with smoothness. Brother Akilles twice silver medalist in Olympic decathlon and other brother Kaarlo competed twice in Olympic shot put.

JAZY, MICHEL B. 6/3/36, Oignies, France. Member 1956, 60, 64 French Olympic teams. Held world records in mile, 2-mile, 3000-m. Still holds 2000-m record of 4:56.7 set in 1966 at St. Maur on Oct. 12. Set mile record of 3:53.6 at Rennes on June 9, 1965, breaking Peter Snell's record. Cracked 3000-m record with 7:49.2 on June 27, 1962, at St. Maur. Improved mark to 7:49.0 on June 23, 1965, at Melun. In same race set 2-mile record of 8:22.6. Competed in 1956 Melbourne Olympics and 1958 European Championships but did not place. In 1960 Rome Olympics took 1500-m silver medal behind Snell with 3:38.4. In 1962 European Championships won 1500-m with 3:40.9. In 1964 Tokyo Olympics competed in 5000-m and 1500-m. Led most of 5000-m but Bob Schul of U.S. caught him and won. Jazy was also passed by Norporth of Germany and Bill Dellinger of U.S. and lost medal. Lost in 1500-m prelims. Ranked No. 1 in 5000-m in 1965 by *Track & Field News.* Winner 1965 Citizens Savings (Helm) World Trophy Award, Europe.

JENKINS, CHARLIE B. 1/7/34, New York, N.Y. Member 1956 U.S. Olympic team. Won 400-m gold medal in Melbourne Olympic Games. Surprised world record-holder Lou Jones and others in 46.7. Ran third leg for U.S. 1600-m team that won gold medal. Ran blistering 45.5 to give anchorman Tom Courtney 10-yd lead. Ran for Villanova as collegian. Won 1955 IC4A 440-yd in 47.2. Won 1957 IC4A 440-yd in 47.4. Was 1955 AAU champion with 46.7 quarter. Indoors, won IC4A 600-yd 1955-57. Was AAU 600-yd king in 1957, 58. Ran 1:10.4 in 1957 for meet record. Ran first leg for U.S. national team that set world mile relay mark of 3:07.3 on Nov. 11, 1956, at Los Angeles. Working for U.S. State Department in Washington, D. C.

JEROME, HARRY B. 9/30/40, Prince Albert, Saskatchewan. Member 1960, 64 Canadian Olympic teams. Held six world sprint records. Tied world 100-yd mark with 9.3 at Corvallis, Oreg., May 5, 1961, while student at Oregon. Twice in 1962 in Canada tied lowered 9.2 standard. On July 15, 1966, timed at 9.1 at Edmonton, Alberta, to tie Bob Hayes' world mark. Time of 10.0 at Saskatoon July 15, 1960, tied Armin Hary's 100-m mark. Won 1962 NCAA 220-yd title in 20.8 and 1964 100-m in 10.1. Also anchored Oregon team that equaled world 440-yd relay record of 40.0 on course with two turns. In 1960 Olympics was injured in 100-m semi heat and failed to qualify for finals. In 1964 Olympics won bronze medal in 100-m behind Hayes of U.S. and Figuerola of Cuba, despite 10.2 time. Was 4th in 200-m. Holds Canadian records with 10.0 in 100-m, 20.4 in 200-m and anchored record 440-yd relay. Won gold medal in 1967 Pan-Am Games in Winnipeg with 10.2. Member Canada's Hall of Fame.

JIPCHO, BEN B. 3/1/43. Member 1972 Kenya Olympic team. Took silver medal in Munich Olympic steeplechase with time of 8:24.6 behind teammate Kip Keino. In 1973 he ripped the world steeple record twice. Ran 8:19.8 at Helsinki on June 18. Nine days later, at same spot, ran a fantastic 8:14.0. On July 3 at Stockholm, ran 2nd fastest mile in history with 3:52.0. Next day ran 8:18.2 steeplechase. Is farmer with other agriculture interests.

JOHNSON, CORNELIUS B. 8/21/13, Los Angeles, Calif. D. 2/15/40. Member 1932, 36 Olympic teams. Co-held world high jump record with Dave Albritton. Both cleared 6'9¾" in 1936 Olympic tryouts in New York, July 12, 1936. Also held world indoor best of 6'8 15/16" done in N.Y.'s Madison Square Garden on Feb. 22, 1936. In 1936 Olympic Games in Berlin, won gold medal as Hitler watched black American shatter his racial theories. Broke 12-year record with 6'7 15/16" jump. In 1932 Olympics, competed as high school student. Finished 4th, clearing 6'5⅝" as did winner, but had more misses. Won 1933, 35 AAU titles outright and tied for '32, '34, '36 crowns. In 1934 tied with Walter Marty at 6'8⅝" for meet record and AAU best. Member Citizens Savings (Helms) Hall of Fame.

JOHNSON, JAN B. 11/11/50, Hammond, Ind. Member 1972 Olympic team. One of few men to clear 18' in pole vault. Went 18'½" at final U.S. Olympic trials. In 1970 as sophomore at Kansas, went 17'7" at NCAA outdoor championships at Drake. Vault was held indoors because of rain. Won 1971 USTFF with 17'3¼" vault. Also USTFF champ in 1970. Took 1971 AAU championship with leap of 17'0". Was 1971 Pan-Am Games champion at 17'5¾". In 1972, after transferring to Alabama, was USTFF champion again. Was 2nd in NCAA at 17'0". In Olympic trials, along with Steve Smith of Long Beach State, tied for collegiate record with 18′ ½″. In Munich Olympics won bronze medal with jump of 17′8 ½″. Hobby, collecting butterflies.

JOHNSON, PATTY JEAN B. 4/15/50, San Diego, Calif. Member 1968, 72 Olympic teams. Holds American 100-m hurdle record. Ran 13.1 at Cali, Colombia on Aug. 4, 1971. At 1972 Olympic trials lowered mark to 13.0. At 1971 Pan-Am Games won gold medal. Was 4th in 1967 AAU, 3rd in 1968 AAU and 2nd in 1970. Made 1968 Olympic team and was 4th, despite tying Olympic record of 10.5. Won 1971 AAU in 13.5. In 1971 U.S.-USSR World All-Star Meet, won in 13.6. In 1972 Munich Olympics did not make finals.

JOHNSON, RAFER B. 8/18/35, Hillsboro, Tex. Member 1956, 60 Olympic teams. Won gold medal in 1960 decathlon and silver in 1956. Had size, speed and ability, near perfection in ten-event decathlon test. Great natural talent, set world mark of 7985 points on fourth try at decathlon in 1955. Finished second to Milt Campbell in 1956 Melbourne Olympics. Duels with Russian Kuznyetsov and Yang of Formosa captured interest of world. In 1958 Kuznyetsov and Johnson met in Moscow where Johnson regained world mark, defeating Russian 8302 to 7897. Russian recaptured world record in 1959 when Johnson was injured in car accident and unable to compete. In 1960 Johnson made complete comeback to defeat Yang in record 8683 performance in Eugene, Oreg. At Rome Olympics, UCLA teammates Johnson and Yang staged dramatic duel. Johnson held on to lead in final event to beat both Yang (by only 58 points) and Kuznyetsov with 8392 points to Yang's 8334 and Kuznyetsov's 7809. Johnson truly an all-round performer with 10.3 in 100-m, 13.8 hurdles, 25′5 ¾″ long jump, 243′10 ½″ javelin, 54′11 ½″ shot and 170′9 ½″ discus. One-man track team. Now director of Kennedy Foundation. Member Citizens Savings (Helms) Hall of Fame.

JONES, HAYES B. 8/4/38, Starkville, Miss. Member 1960, 64 Olympic teams. Set world indoor 60-yd high hurdle record in 1962 with 6.9. Did not hold any world outdoor records, but was very consistent. Won 110-m hurdles gold medal at 1964 Toyko Olympics with 13.6. Was 3rd at 1960 Rome Games behind teammates Lee Calhoun (gold) and Willie May (silver). Had to defeat world record-holder Martin Lauer of Germany for bronze medal. Won 1958 AAU indoor and outdoor high hurdles with meet record 7.1 indoors and fine 13.8 outdoors. Won 1958 NCAA for Eastern Michigan in 13.6. Was AAU indoor champion 1960–62. Time of 7.0 in 1961 set meet record. Took AAU outdoor crowns in 1960, 61 with record-tying 13.6 both years. Had great start and 9.4 speed. Member Citizens Savings (Helms) Hall of Fame.

JONES, JOHN PAUL B. 1881. D. 1/5/70. Member 1912 U.S. Olympic team. First American to hold world record in mile. Ran 4:14.4 on May 31, 1913, at Cambridge, Mass. In 1911 IC4A, cracked unofficial world mark with 4:15.4 at Cambridge, running for Cornell. Also won half in same meet. In 1912 took 880-yd with 1:53.8 and tied Norman Taber in mile. In 1913, coming off disappointing 4th in 1912 Olympic 1500-m, set mile record of 4:14.4 for 3rd IC4A mile crown. Ran 58.3 last lap, fantastic time of era. Was IC4A cross-country champ 1911, 12. Member Citizens Savings (Helms) Hall of Fame.

JONES, LOU B. 1/15/32, New Rochelle, N.Y. Member 1956 Olympic team. Held world 400-m record. Set first mark of 45.4 in 1955 Pan Am Games in Mexico City for gold medal. Silver medalist Jim Lea, also of U.S., bettered old standard with 45.6. Jones' mark chopped .4 off old record set by George Rhoden of Jamaica in 1950. Rival Lea had defeated Jones in 1954 AAU championships, 46.6 to 46.7. At 1956 Olympic trials in Los Angeles on June 30, Jones lowered his world record to 45.2. Silenced doubters of Mexico City time who claimed rarified air aided runners. Lea was again second in trials. At Melbourne Olympics, Jones qualified for 400-m finals and Lea did not. In finals Jones was fifth with disappointing 48.1, losing in last 100-m. Ran lead leg for winning 1600-m relay team for gold medal and salvaged some glory. Won 1954 IC4A, running for Manhattan College.

JONES, SAMUEL B. 1879. D. 4/13/54. Member 1904 U.S. Olympic team. Won gold medal in high jump with 5′11″ performance. Was 3-time AAU champion in specialty. Won '01, '03, '04. Went 6′2″ in 1901 for best performance. Was 1900, 01 IC4A champion from Penn.

JORDAN, PAYTON B. 3/19/17, Whittier, Calif. Head coach 1968 U.S. Olympic team. Attended Southern Cal as fine sprinter. Ran at USC final 2 years in college after posting 9.6 in 100-yd and 21.1 in 220-yd at Santa Monica Junior College. Captain of track team, played rugby and was starter on Trojan football team. Captain of 1939 track team and ran on world record 440-yd relay team that ran 40.5 at Fresno, Calif, on May 14, 1938. Mark stood 16 years. Southern Cal won both Pacific Coast Conference and NCAA championships in 1938, 39 with Jordan's help. Equaled conference 100-yd record of 9.7 in 1938. Competed in football and track in navy after college. Won AAU 100-m in 1941 with 10.3. Also member of winning 440-yd and 880-yd relay teams. Had career bests of 9.4, 20.5, 10.3, 20.4. During WW II was Service All-American football player in 1944. Track coach at Occidental starting in 1946, and won 2 NAIA championships. Voted to NAIA Hall of Fame in 1967. Moved to Stanford in 1957 and built program into one of nation's best. Provided 4

Olympians and several world class performers. Under his guidance 1968 U.S. Olympic team got record-breaking total of 24 medals, 12 of them gold. Also coached Yugoslavian national team for European Championships; U.S. team in Maccabeth Games, University World Games and U.S. Deaf Games team.

KANNENBERG, BERND B. 8/20/42, Königsberg, Germany. Member 1972 West German Olympic team. Won gold medal in 50,000-m walk at Munich Olympics. First man to win on home track in event. Broke Olympic record with 3:56:11.6. Competed in 20,000-m walk but did not finish. In 50,000-m set blazing pace to chant of home crowd cheering, "Kannenberg, Kannenberg." Sergeant in West German Army, set world 50,000-m mark in 1972 of 3:52.44. Time bettered old mark by over 6 minutes. Was once weight lifter. Started walking competition in 1969.

KAUFMANN, CARL B. 3/25/36, New York, N.Y. Member 1960 German Olympic team. Held world 400-m record. Ran 44.9 in 1960 Rome Olympic finals on Sept. 6. Got credit for share of world record but finished 2nd to Otis Davis of U.S. Trailed Davis at 330-yd mark but closed gap to inches at tape. Timed in 44.93 to Davis' 44.9. Both were first to go under 45.0 in 400-m. Race was so close neither runner knew who won gold medal. Judges had to study photos to determine winner. Ran anchor on German 1600-m relay team that also broke world record with 3:02.7, but had to settle for silver medal behind U.S. Davis anchored U.S. to world mark of 3:02.2. Had only been concentrating on 400-m since 1958. Did finish 4th in European Championships and later set European record of 45.8. In 1959 won German Championship in record 45.4. Was 3rd in 1962 European Championships.

KEINO, KIPCHOGE B. 1/17/40, Kapschemoiywo, Kenya. Member 1964, 68, 72 Kenyan Olympic teams. Won gold medal in steeplechase at

Munich Olympics of 1972. Set Olympic record of 8:23.6 and became only man to hold Olympic records at two distances. Set 1500-m record in winning gold medal at Mexico City Olympics in 1968. Ran 3:34.9 in thin air to defeat world record-holder Jim Ryun of U.S. Has pair of silver medals in collection. Was 2nd in 1972 Olympic 1500-m with 3:36.8. Took 2nd in 1968 in 5000-m with time of 14:05.2. Held world records in 3000-m and 5000-m. Ran 7:39.6 in 3000-m on Aug. 27, 1965, at Halsingborg, Sweden, for mark. At Auckland in same year ran 13:24.2 on Nov. 30 for 5000-m record. Winner 1965 Citizens Savings (Helms) World Trophy Award, Africa. Chief inspector in charge of physical education at Kiganjo Police Training School. Owns tea plantation and has interest in Nairobi sports store. Turned pro in 1973.

KELLEY, FREDRICK B. 9/12/91, Beaumont, Calif. Member 1912 Olympic team. Won gold medal in 110-m hurdles in Stockholm Olympics. Ran 15.1 to lead American 1–2–3 sweep. U.S. had 5 of 6 finalists. Competed for Southern Cal. Was 1913 AAU champion in 120-yd hurdles. Ran 16.4 to take title.

KELLEY, JIM B. 7/3/93, Calhoun County, Iowa. D. 7/11/72, Canoga Park, Calif. Head coach 1956 Olympic team. Coach at Minnesota 1937–63. His 1948 team won NCAA title with Fortune Gordien, 3-time NCAA champ in discus, leading way. Gordien, world record-holder, was Kelley's top product. Gopher team won 1949 Big Ten Championship. Coached 1956 Olympic team which won 15 gold medals. Ironically, was 1936 U.S. Olympic basketball team coach. Member Citizens Savings (Helms) Hall of Fame.

KELLEY, JOHN J. B. 12/24/30, Norwich, Conn. Member 1956, 60 Olympic teams. Top American marathon runner in 1950s and early 1960s. Former Boston U. runner, Kelley won his first AAU marathon in 1956 with record 2:24:52.3. Proceeded to win the next 7 AAU titles in row. Lowered record to 2:21:00.4 with 1958 win. In 1956 Olympics was 21st with time of 2:43:40.0. In 1960 Rome Olympics was 19th with 2:24:58.0. Member 1955, 59 U.S. Pan-Am teams. Won 1959 Pan-Am marathon in 2:27:54.2, breaking Pan-Am record. Long-time contender for Boston Marathon crown. Was 1957 Boston Marathon champ with time of 2:20:05.0. Connecticut school teacher. Member Citizens Savings (Helms) Hall of Fame.

KING, LEAMON B. 2/13/36, Tulare, Calif. Member 1956 Olympic team. Co-held world 100-m and 100-yd records. Ran 10.1 twice within 7 days (Oct. 20–27, 1956) to tie 100-m record. Defeated Morrow, Murchison in both races. Had previously run 9.3 on May 12, 1956, at

Fresno, Calif., to tie 100-yd record. In 1956 Olympic trials had finished 4th in 100-m and did not qualify for individual, but made 400-m relay. Ran his 10.1s about month before 1956 Games. Had to be content to watch 100-m finals, but ran 2nd leg on U.S. 400-m relay team which broke world and Olympic record with 39.5. After Olympics ran on world record U.S. 800-m and 880-yd relay team that ran 1:23.8 in Sydney, Australia, Dec. 1, 1956. Smooth-striding sprinter with great finish.

KING, ROBERT W. B. 6/20/06, Los Angeles, Calif. D. 1965. Member 1928 Olympic team. Won gold medal in Amsterdam Olympics in high jump with 6′4⅜″. Won 1928 NCAA high jump title for Stanford at 6′5⅝″. Took 1927 AAU title with jump of 6′2⅝″. Following year tied for AAU with Charles McGinnis at 6′5″. Was obstetrician.

KINSEY, DANIEL B. 1/22/02, St. Louis, Mo. Member 1924 Olympic team. Won gold medal in 110-m hurdles at Paris. Ran 15.0 to take gold medal by inches over Sam Atkinson of South Africa. Competed for Illinois as collegian.

KIVIAT, ABEL B. 6/23/92, New York, N.Y. Member 1912 Olympic team. Held world 1500-m record. Ran 3:55.8 at Cambridge, Mass., on June 8, 1912. Was AAU mile champion in 1911 in 4:19.6, 1912 in 4:18.6, and 1914 with 4:25.2 clocking. Also AAU cross country champion in 1913. In 1911, 13 won both AAU indoor 600-yd and 1000-yd titles. In 1914 won 1000-yd only. Ran for strong Irish-American Athletic Club teams of New York. Made 1912 Olympic team in 1500-m. In Stockholm Games finals, took lead at bell lap with fellow Americans Norman Taber and John Paul Jones following. But Anthony Jackson of Great Britain passed U.S. threesome to win gold medal. Kiviat took 2nd by inch. Member Citizens Savings (Helms) Hall of Fame.

KLEMMER, GROVER B. 3/16/21, San Francisco, Calif. Co-held world record in 440-yd and 400-m. Ran 46.0 for 400-m and 46.4 for 440-yd at Berkeley, Calif., AAU Championships in same race on June 29, 1941, to tie both records. Had tied 440-yd record with 46.4 earlier in May of 1941. Won 1940 AAU with 47.0. Tall (6′2″) Californian was graceful runner and ran 46.9 at age 19. Still in his early 20s, war kept him from attaining full athletic promise and Olympic glory.

KOLEHMAINEN, HANNES B. 12/9/89, Kuopio, Finland. Member 1912, 20 Finnish Olympic teams. Held several long distance world records. Set first world record in 1912 Stockholm Olympics. Ran 14:36.6 for gold medal on July 10, in 5000-m. Had won 10,000-m prior to world mark. In heat of 3000-m team race, set record of 8:36.8 on July 12, but

Finns did not qualify for finals. In one of history's greatest athletic feats, won cross country for 3rd gold medal. In 1920 Antwerp Olympics, won marathon with Olympic record 2:32:35.8. First of great Finns in long distances. Set 20,000-m record in Helsinki with 1:07:40.2 on May 18, 1913. Got 25,000-m mark at Tampere on Oct. 10, 1920, with 1:26:29.6. Bettered mark at same place on June 22, 1922, with 1:25:20.0. Won 1912–14 U.S. AAU 5-mile titles. Set meet record with 25:43.4 in 1912. Lit Olympic flame in 1952 Helsinki Olympics.

KOMAR, WLADYSLAW B. 4/11/40, Kownie, Poland. Member 1964, 68, 72 Polish Olympic teams. Won shot put gold medal in 1972 Munich Olympics. On first throw tossed yellow shot 69′6″ to win gold medal and set Olympic record in beating American George Woods by ½″. In 1968 Olympics was 6th with put of 63′3″. At Tokyo Olympics in 1964 was 9th with toss of 59′8 ½″. Once suspended "for life" by Polish Track & Field Federation, but reinstated and came back in 1970 to world class.

KONOPACKA, HELENA B. 1900, Rawa Mazowiecka, Poland. Member 1928 Polish Olympic team. Rates as greatest Polish woman track athlete with 24 national titles. Won titles in long jump, high jump, shot put, discus and pentathlon. Held numerous Polish records. Gold medalist in discus in 1926 world championships in Gothenburg. In 1928 Olympics won gold medal in discus with toss of 129′11 13/16″. First Polish athlete to win gold medal. Lived abroad during war; now lives in U.S.

KRAENZLEIN, ALVIN B. 12/12/76. D. 1/6/28. Member 1900 U.S. Olympic team. Held world records in 110-m, 120-yd, 200-m, 220-yd hurdles and long jump. Set 110-m hurdle record of 15.2 in 1898 AAU championship. Broke long jump record twice in 1899 with 24′3 ½″and then 24′7 ½″. Set 200-m and 220-yd hurdle records in New York on May 28, 1898. In 1900 Paris Olympics, won 4 gold medals in individual events. Only man to accomplish this. Easily took 110-m hurdles in record 15.4 for first gold. Next was gold medalist in long jump with record 23′6 7/8″. Rival Myer Prinstein of Syracuse did not compete in finals when finals shifted to Sunday. Next won 60-m, then 200-m hurdles. Won 6 AAU titles. Took long jump, 120-yd and 220-yd hurdles in 1898. Won 120-yd and 220-yd hurdles in 1899. Was 1897 220-yd hurdle champ. Was IC4A 120-yd and 220-yd hurdle champ for Princeton 1898–1900. Won long jump from Prinstein in 1899 with 24′4 ½″. Father of modern hurdle form, tucking one leg under. Went to Germany in 1913 to help with development of German Olympic team. Member Citizens Saving (Helms) Hall of Fame.

KRAUSE, CHRISTIANE B. 12/14/50, Berlin, West Germany. Member 1972 West German Olympic team. Member West German 400-m relay team that won gold medal in Munich Olympics and tied world and Olympic record with 42.81. Young college student, did not think she would make 1972 Olympics. Was training for '76 Games. But in 1972 West German Championships, was 2nd in 200-m in 23.61 and 3rd in 100-m in 11.45. In Olympics, along with gold medal in 400-m relay, was 9th in 200-m final in 23.17. Studying to become physical education teacher. Hobbies: skiing, quitar, dancing, reading.

KRIVONOSOV, MIKHAIL B. 5/1/29, Mogilyev, USSR. Member 1956 Russian Olympic team. Held world hammer throw record. First set mark with toss of 207′9″at Berne on Aug. 29, 1954. Lost record for time but got it back at Warsaw on Aug. 4, 1955, with toss of 211′. Added 8″to mark at Belgrade on Sept. 19, 1955. Advanced mark to 216′ on July 8, 1956, at Minsk. After upping record to 217′9″, became first man to throw 220′. Tossed hammer 220′10″on Oct. 22, 1956, at Tashkent for career best. In 1956 Melbourne Olympics, met American rival Hal Connolly. Connolly had beaten world marks only to have them surpassed by Krivonosov going into Games. Krivonosov lost gold medal to Connolly by less than foot. Krivonosov had a toss of 206′9½″ to Connolly's 207′3½″. The 1954 European Champion lost touch after 1956 Olympics.

KRZESINSKA, ELZBIETA (Gold Ela) B. 1934, Warsaw, Poland. Member 1952, 56, 60 Polish Olympic teams. Held women's world long jump record with 20′10″ on Aug. 20, 1956, at Budapest. At 1956 Melbourne Olympics tied her world mark and won gold medal. In 1952 at age 18, was 12th in Helsinki Olympics. In 1954 European Championships took 3rd. In 1956 married pole vaulter Andregej Krzesinska, who became her coach. Her record-tying jump brought Poland its first gold medal since the war. Student at medical school while training, forced to stop training because of anemia. After becoming mother, won silver medal in 1960 Rome Olympics with jump of 20′6¾″. Got moniker because of hair and many victories. Now doctor and coach of youth team in Warsaw.

KRZYSZKOWIAK, ZDZISLAW B. 8/3/29, Wielichowo, Poland. Member 1956, 60 Polish Olympic teams. Held world steeplechase record. Ran 8:31.4 at Tula, USSR on June 26, 1960. Lost record to Taran of USSR in 1961, but regained it later in year. Ran 8:30.4 on Aug. 10 at Walez to get name back in record books. Excellent distance man on flat along with steeplechase achievements. In 1958 European Championships, won both 5000-m and 10,000-m. In 1960 Rome Olympics, set Games record of 8:34.2 and captured gold medal. Won handily despite great heat and opposition. Long career began in 1949. Had great stamina, evidenced by

1958 European Championships double. Speed proven by 5:44.8 best in 1500-m.

KUCK, JOHN B. 4/27/05, Wilson, Kans. Member 1928 Olympic team. Won gold medal in shot put in Amsterdam Olympics. Threw 16-lb iron ball 52′0¾″for 1st place and Olympic, world records. Was 1927 AAU champion with toss of 48′5″. Same year won NCAA title as student at Emporia (Kans.) State. Had put of 46′7⅜″to take collegiate title. Competed for Los Angeles Athletic Club. Now an innkeeper.

KUSOCINSKI, JANUSZ B. 1907, Oltarzewo, Poland. D. 1940. Member 1932 Polish Olympic team. Held world 3000-m record. Ran 8:18.8 at Antwerp on June 19, 1932, to break Paavo Nurmi's mark. In 1932 Los Angeles Olympics, won gold medal in 10,000-m. Set Olympic record of 30:11.4 over favored runners from Finland. Had knee injury that hampered him years after gold medal. In 1939 regained old form, set Polish 5000-m record of 14:24.2 and looked like contender in 1940 Olympics. But World War II ended his competition. Volunteer to defend Warsaw and was seriously wounded. Recovered and joined Polish underground. In 1940 was arrested and executed. Each year since 1954, international meeting is held in his memory. A memorial 3000-m race is run in his honor.

KUTS, VLADIMIR B. 5/1/27, Alesksino, Ukraine. Member 1956 USSR Olympic team. Held world records in 3-mile, 5000-m and 10,000-m. Got first world record and major championship at 1954 European Championships at Berne. Ran 13:56.6 in 5000-m, defeating Zatopek and Chataway. Run also good for 3-mile record with 13:27.4. Lowered record in 3-mile to 13:27.0 at London on Oct. 13, 1954. Also lowered 5000-m to 13:51.2 on Oct. 23, 1954, at Prague. Took 3-mile record down to 13:26.4 in same race. In 1955 lost 5000-m record to England's Chataway for 8 days. Ran 13:46.2 on Sept. 18, 1955, at Budapest. In 1956 Olympics entered both 5000-m and 10,000-m. In 10,000-m took over early, ran 14:06.6 in first 5000-m and won by 45 yds in Olympic record 28:45.6. In 5000-m went against Gordon Pirie of Great Britain. As usual, set burning pace and won gold medal with 13:39.6, beating Pirie by 100 yds. Set 10,000-m record of 28:30.4 in 1956 at Moscow on Sept. 11. Set final world mark in 5000-m with 13:35.0 on Oct. 13, 1957, in Rome. Same year developed stomach problems, forcing him to cut training with record 5000-m his last major race. Officer in Russian navy.

KUZNYETSOV, VASILY B. 2/7/32, Kalikino, Russia. Member 1956, 60 Russian Olympic teams. Greatest Russian, European decathlon performer in track history. Set world record of 8014 points in 1958. First man to score 8000 points. Lost record to arch-rival Rafer Johnson same year. Took record back with 8357 points in Moscow in 1959. Had 8350 performance in Philadelphia same year. Had many duels with Johnson. Johnson regained record in 1960 with 8683. Won bronze medal in 1956 Olympics behind Americans Campbell and Johnson. Same in 1960 behind Johnson and Yang of Formosa. Strong in almost every event. Made comeback in 1962 by winning third European Championship by 4 points.

LAIRD, RON B. 4/31/38, Louisville, Ky. Member 1960, 64, 68 Olympic teams. At one time held 24 American walking records. Won over 30 AAU walking titles in 2-mile, 10,000-m, 7-mile, 20,000-m, 25,000-m, 30,000-m, 35,000-m, 40,000-m from 1959–71. Won 1967 Pan-Am Games 20,000-m title in 1:33:05.2. In 1960 Olympics in Rome, finished 19th in 50,000-m walk in 4:53:21.6. In 1964 Tokyo Olympics was disqualified. In 1968 Olympics at Mexico City, was given an outside chance, but was 25th in 1:44:38.0. In 1971 won AAU 1-hr (7 miles, 1510 yd), 10,000-m (47.10.0), 25,000-m (2:01:48.4) titles. Left job as draftsman for city of Pomona, Calif., to concentrate on 1972 Olympics. In trials did not finish in either 20,000-m or 50,000-m.

LANDON, RICHMOND B. 11/20/98, Salisbury, Conn. D. 6/13/71, New York, N.Y. Member 1920 Olympic team. Won gold medal in high jump at Antwerp Olympics. Jumped 6′4 ¼″ to set Olympic record. At Yale won 2 IC4A high jump titles and tied for an other. Won 1919 IC4A at 6′2″and 1920 at 6′4″. In 1921 tied with H.P. Muller of Cal at 6′3 ½″. A 1921 Yale graduate, also competed for New York Athletic Club. Was sales executive in display advertising business.

LANDY, JOHN B. 4/12/30, Melbourne, Australia. Member 1956 Australian Olympic team. Held world mile, 1500-m records. On June 14, 1954, broke Roger Bannister's mile mark with 3:58, history's second four-minute mile. Time for 1500-m was 3:41.8. Met Bannister in Fifth British Empire Games on Aug. 7, 1954. In "Mile of Century," Bannister followed Landy, then overtook Aussie in stretch. Bannister timed in 3:58.8, Landy 3:59.6. Landy cut foot eve of race. Went into temporary retirement but came back in 1956. Ran 3:58.7 in losing to fellow Aussie Jim Bailey. Made 1956 Olympic team but finished 3rd behind Ron Delany, who set Olympic record 3:41.2, and Klaus Richtzenhain who ran 3:42.0. Landy also timed in 3:42.0 which bettered Olympic record. Retired shortly after Olympics. Set own pace as did most great Aussie milers. Did not rely on kick; ran at steady pace. Ran six 4-minute miles.

LARABEE, MIKE B. 3/12/33, Los Angeles, Calif. Member 1964 Olympic team. Held 400-m world record. Ran 44.9 at L.A. on Sept. 12, 1964. Was 1964 AAU champion in 400-m with 46.0. Also winner in U.S.-USSR dual meet. In final Olympic trials, ran for his world record and made Olympic team. Did not make 1956 team when at Southern Cal, and injured Achilles tendon in 1960 and missed team. In 1964 Tokyo Olympics, won his prelim heat in 46.8 and second round in 46.5. In semifinals lowered time to 46.0 and was again 1st. In final was slow in first 200-m but on final turn started to move. With final burst took lead 10-m from the tape and won gold medal. In 1600-m relay ran sizzling 44.8 leg to help U.S. to gold medal, world and Olympic records. Now regional distributor for Coors Brewing Co. in Santa Maria, Calif.

LARNEY, MARJORIE B. 1/4/37, Brooklyn, N.Y. Member 1952 Olympic team. Standout javelin thrower. Dominant woman in event during late 1950s. First came to national attention in 1952 when won AAU with toss of 126′3 ⅞″. Made Olympic team and was 13th with toss of 133′1 ¾″. Did not do well next 4 years far as titles, but improved tremendously from 1952 distances. Set AAU and national record in 1957 championships with toss of 187′8″ that stood until 1967. Won AAU titles 1958–60 with best of 153′7 ½″ in 1959. Won silver medal in 1959 Pan-Am Games with toss of 143′2 ½″. Member Citizens Savings (Helms) Hall of Fame.

LASH, DONALD B. 8/15/13, Bluffton, Ind. Member 1936 Olympic team. Held world 2-mile record. Broke Paavo Nurmi's record of 8:59.6 with 8:58.4 on June 13, 1936, at Princeton, N.J. One of favorites in 1936 Berlin Olympics but failed in both 5000-m and 10,000-m. Was 14th in 5000-m and 8th in 10,000-m. With 10,000-m time of 31:39.4, was left in dust by leaders. At Indiana won 1936 NCAA 5000-m in 14:58.5. Set American 2-mile record at 1936 Drake Relays with 9:10.6. Won AAU 6-mile in 1936, 40. Also won 3-mile in 1936. Was AAU cross-country champion 8 years, 7 of them in a row (1934–40). Won AAU indoor 3-mile in 1938, 39. Received AAU's James Sullivan award in 1938. Regional director of Fellowship of Christian Athletes and member of board of trustees of Indiana U. Member Citizens Savings (Helms) Hall of Fame.

LEA, JAMES B. 11/7/32, Little Rock, Ark. Member 1956 Olympic team. Held world 440-yd record. First man below 46.0. Ran 45.8 on May 26, 1956, at Modesto, Calif. World class quarter man for several years. Won 1953 NCAA for Southern Cal with 47.0. Won both NCAA and AAU in 1954. Ran 46.7 in NCAA and 46.6 in AAU. In Pan-Am Games ran 45.6 in 400-m but was 2nd to Lou Jones, also of U.S. Finished 2nd to Jones again in 1956 Olympic trials. In 1956 Melbourne Olympics lost out in quarterfinals and did not fulfill Olympic promise.

LEE, HUBERT H. B. 10/23/59, Erie, Pa. D. 3/1/33. First American to run 10 "flat" in 100-yd dash. Ran 10.0 on May 5, 1877, at Philadelphia. Tied world mark, although no official world records were kept then, of J. P. Tennent of Great Britain. Ran 23.5 in 220-yd dash in 1877 IC4A championships for Penn that was considered world best. Won 1877, 78 IC4A 100-yd and 220-yd dash titles. Ran 10.2 in '77 100-yd; 10.25 in '78. Ran 23.5 in '77 220 yd dash; 23.6 in '78.

LEHTINEN, LAURI B. 8/10/08. Member 1932, 36 Finnish Olympic teams. Held world 5000-m, 3-mile records. Set both marks at Helsinki on June 6, 1932. Clocked at 13:50.6 in 3-mile and 14:17.0 in 5000-m. Both broke Paavo Nurmi's records. At Los Angeles Olympics in 1932, won gold medal in 5000-m with 14:30.0, Olympic record. In 1936 Berlin Olympics took silver medal in 5000-m with 14:25.8, besting his Olympic mark as did gold medal winner Gunnar Hockert. Won British AAA 3-mile title with 14:09.2 in 1933. Finnish 5000-m champ in 1931, 35; cross country champ in '33, '35, '37. Held Finnish records in 3000-m and 5000-m. Ran 8:19.05 in 1933 for 3000-m record and 14:17.0 for 5000-m record same year. Formerly police officer, now retired.

LEMMING, ERIK B. 1880, Sweden. Member 1906, 08, 12 Swedish Olympic teams. Held world javelin record. Throw of 204′5″on Sept. 29, 1912, at Stockholm first mark to be listed in IAAF record books. First man to throw spear 50-m (164′0½″) and 60-m (197′). In 1906 unofficial Olympics at Athens, won gold medal with toss of 175′6″. In 1908 Olympics won in both "modern" and "free style". Pacesetter in style and was often copied. In 1912 Stockholm Olympics, pleased home folks with his 3rd gold medal. On first throw of final round had throw of 198′3½″. Did lose combined (left and righthand throws) to Saarista of Finland. Only man to ever win 3 gold medals in javelin.

LINDGREN, GERRY B. 3/6/46, Spokane, Wash. Member 1964 Olympic team. Held world 6-mile record. Holds American, collegiate records in distance events. Ran 12:53.0 in 3-mile on May 14, 1966, at Seattle for American and collegiate bests. Tied for American 6-mile record with Billy Mills. Both ran 27:11.6 at San Diego, good for world record also, on June 27, 1965. Set collegiate 10,000-m mark while at Washington State with 28:40.2 in nonwinning performance at Dusseldorf, West Germany, on Aug. 17, 1967. Phenomenal distance runner in high school. Once held schoolboy 1-mile, 2-mile and 3-mile national records. Was *Track & Field News* high school runner of year in 1964. Won 10,000-m in 1964 U.S.-USSR dual meet. The 5′6″, 120-lb runner made 1964 U.S. Olympic team as high school senior in 10,000-m. In Tokyo 10,000-m finals ran with slight ankle sprain but was 9th in 29:20.6 in greatest 10,000-m race of all time. At Washington State was NCAA 3-and 6-mile champion 1966–68. In 1966 set NCAA meet record of 13:33.7 in 3-mile. Was 1967 AAU 3-mile champ in 13:10.6. Hampered by injuries, did not make 1968 Olympic team. Continued to compete with good success, pointing towards 1972 Olympics. In 1972 5000-m trials, made finals but ran last. In 10,000-m finals did not finish.

LIQUORI, MARTIN (Marty) B. 9/11/49, Montclair, N.J. Member 1968 Olympic team. One of top milers in track history with career best 3:54.6 in 1971 Martin Luther King Games. As 19-year-old Villanova freshman, qualified for U.S. Olympic team. Finished 2nd behind Jim Ryun and ahead of Tom Von Ruden and Dave Patrick. In Olympics won opening heat in 3:52.7. In semis was 4th in 3:52.1. In finals, suffering from fatigue fracture, came home last in 4:18.2. In 1969 was ranked best miler in world. Was 2nd in NCAA indoor mile behind Ryun, but won NCAA outdoor over Ryun, 3:57.7 to 3:59.3. Also AAU king with 3:59.5. In 1970 again won NCAA outdoor, defeated Kip Keino in Martin Luther King Games. In 1971 won NCAA in 3:57.6, meet record. Also won AAU. In Pan-Am Games won gold medal with 3:42.1. Ranked first by *Track & Field News* in mile—1500-m. Ran 3:36.0 1500-m in 1971. In 1971 cross-country season injured left heel. Worked out but had to give up training in spring and Olympic hopes.

LISMONT, KAREL B. 3/8/49. Member 1972 Belgian Olympic team. Won silver medal in Munich marathon. Ran 2:14:31.8 behind Frank Shorter's 2:12:19.8. Ran in Olympic 10,000-m but did not qualify. Race was only 4th marathon for Lismont. Was 1971 European marathon champion. Ran 2:13:09.0 for meet record. Finished 16th in 10,000-m with time of 28:31.2. Won his 3 marathons before finishing behind Shorter. Won two Belgian marathons before his European triumph. One of youngest competitors in Olympic marathon.

LITTLEFIELD, CLYDE B. 10/6/92, Eldred, Pa. Member 1952 Olympic coaching staff. Coach Texas U. track teams. Outstanding athlete at Texas 1912–16. Won 4 letters in football, basketball and track. All-Southwest Conference in all sports. Hurdle champion, losing only once in highs and lows. After successful stint as Texas high school football and track coach, was named Texas track coach in 1920. While Longhorn coach for 41 years, won 25 Southwest Conference titles, coached 12 NCAA individual champs and 3 Olympians. Athletes hold 9 Southwest Conference records. Texas relay teams under Littlefield were highly successful. Set world records in sprint relays, sprint medley and distance relays. Longhorn teams broke 440-yd relay mark 4 times. Last mark was 39.6 on May 31, 1958, Modesto, Calif. His 800-m-880-yd team of 1957 set world mark of 1:22.7 on May 4 at Austin, breaking mark set in 1956 by U.S. All-Star team. Retired in 1961. Still lives in Austin. Voted to Texas Sports Writers Hall of Fame and Texas Longhorn Hall of Honor. Member Citizens Savings (Helms) Hall of Fame.

LITUYER, YURIY B. 4/11/25, Irbit, Russia. Member 1952, 56 USSR Olympic teams. Held world 440-yd, 400-m hurdle world records. Set 400-m hurdle record in 1953 on Sept. 20 at Budapest with 50.4. Broke Glenn Hardin's 19-year-old record. In 1954 ran 51.3 at London on Oct. 13, for world record in 440-yd. In 1952 Helsinki Olympics took silver medal in 400-m hurdles with time of 51.3 behind Charles Moore of U.S. Ran 50.7 in 1953 USSR Championships. In 1954 European Championships, finished 2nd behind Anatoliy Yulin of USSR. Was also 2nd in 1950 European Championships. In 1956 Melbourne Olympics, was 4th behind U.S. sweep of medals. Good all-round athlete, although not fast on flat. Had score of 6880 in decathlon.

LOEVLAND, HELGE B. 5/11/90, Froland, Norway. Member 1920 Norwegian Olympic team. Without doubt, the great all-round Norwegian track man. Won gold medal in 1920 Olympic decathlon, defeating Brutus Hamilton of U.S. Scored 6804.35 points in gold medal effort. Held total of 14 Norwegian marks. Bests were 15.3 in 110-m hurdles, 197′ in javelin, 4193 points in pentathlon, 7786 points in decathlon, 135′ in discus and 332′ in javelin with combined right and lefthand throws. Won 5 national championships in 110-m hurdles, one in long jump, 2 in pentathlon and 2 in decathlon. In spite of discus and javelin records, won no championships in those events. Officer in Norwegian army, was Lt. Col. when retired. President of Norwegian national sports body until WW II. Still very lively and wrote chapter on his gold medal for 75th anniversary booklet of sports federation.

LONG, DALLAS B. 6/13/40, Pine Bluff, Ark. Member 1960, 64 Olympic teams. Held world record for shot put with 65′10½″ on May

18, 1962, at Los Angeles. Put 12-lb shot 69′3 ⅛″ as Phoenix, Ariz., prep. Switched to 16-lb following prep career and put 61′0 ½″ for 3rd on all-time list at that time. As Southern Cal frosh put 63′7″. In 1960 set world mark of 64′6 ½″ but lost it to 1960 gold medal winner Bill Neider with 65′7″. Finished 3rd in 1960 Rome Olympics with 62′4 ½″ behind Parry O'Brien (62′8 ½″) and Games record-setter Neider (64′6 ¾″). Won world mark back in 1962 with 65′10 ½″ put. Won 1964 gold medal with Olympic record 66′8 ½″. Won 3 NCAA titles for USC 1960–1962, best of 64′7″ in 1962. Won 1961 AAU, 2nd in 1962. Won 1962 U.S.-Russia meet with meet record 64′1″. Now dentist in California. Member Citizens Savings (Helms) Hall of Fame.

LOOMIS, FRANK B. 8/22/96, St. Paul, Minn. Member 1920 Olympic team. Won gold medal in 400-m hurdles in 1920 Antwerp Olympics. Ran 54.0 on Aug. 16 to win gold medal, set world record. Was 1920 AAU champion in 440-yd hurdles in 55.0. Was 1917, AAU 220-yd low hurdle champion. Ran 24.8 in '17 and 24.2 in '18. Journalist by trade. Worked for *Chicago American* until retirement.

LOUIS, SPYROS B. 1872, Amoroussi, Greece. D. 3/26/40. Member 1896 Greek Olympic team. Won gold medal in first modern Olympic marathon. Shepherd and postal messenger, Louis ran 2:58.50 to defeat nearest competitor by over 7 minutes. Margin still widest in Olympic marathon history. Crown Prince and his brother greeted him as hero at finish line. Prayed and fasted day before race. Honored at 1936 Berlin Olympics.

LOVELOCK, JACK B. 1/5/10, Timaru, New Zealand. Member 1932, 36 New Zealand Olympic teams. Held world mile, 1500-m records. Set mile record at Princeton, N.J., July 15, 1933, with 4:07.6, defeating U.S. runner Bill Bonthron. Student in England at Oxford and set British mile record of 4:12.0 in 1932. Rhodes Scholar. In 1936 Berlin Olympics, won gold medal in 1500-m with world, Olympic record 3:47.8. Ran 56.8 last lap to defeat Glenn Cunningham of U.S. Time lasted 6 years as world record and 16 years as Olympic record. First 4 runners broke previous record. Lost to Archie San Romani in last race of career, 4:09 to 4:10.1, in 1936 at Princeton, N.J.

LOWE, DOUGLAS B. 8/17/02, Manchester, England. Member 1924, 28 British Olympic teams. One of 3 men to win Olympic 800-m twice. In 1924 Paris Olympics was 6th at bell. Made bid at 200-m mark and won by fraction. Timed in 1:52.4, his best at that time. Finished 4th in 1500-m with time of 3:57.0 in same Olympics. In 1926 AAA, lost to Otto Pelzer who set 800-m world record of 1:51.6. In 1928 Olympics was ready for world record-holder Hahn of U.S. and Martin of France, previous record-holder. Lowe, who ran to win, not set records, followed Hahn almost all the way. Pulled in front on backstretch to win 2nd gold medal. Time of 1:51.8 set Olympic record. Defeated Martin and Hahn shortly after Olympics in career-best 1:51.2. Track writer of note, with many hints on training that showed attitudes toward athletics in his day.

LUNDQUIST, ERIC B. 6/29/08, Grangesberg, Sweden. Member 1928 Swedish Olympic team. Held world javelin record. Had a toss of 232′11″ at Stockholm on Aug. 15, 1928, for world mark. Throw was world's first over 70-m. In 1928 Amsterdam Olympics was not favorite. Eini Penttila, who held world mark before Lundquist, was favored. Penttila injured foot and was 6th. Lundquist won with 218′6″, below his world mark but good for Olympic record. Had improved 26′ in one year. Forced to retire because of mental problems. Made comeback in 1936 and had career-best 233′5½″ that year.

LUSIS, JANIS B. 5/19/39. Member 1964, 68, 72 USSR Olympic teams. Lost gold medal in javelin in 1972 Olympics by ½″ to Klaus Wolferman of West Germany. Wolferman's throw of 296′10″ put him in lead going into last throw. On last toss, Lusis tossed spear 296′9½″, fraction too short. Was 1968 Olympic champion, winning on last throw. Had throw of 295′7″ which set Olympic record. In 1964 Tokyo Olympics was bronze medalist with 264′4″. Won 4 European championships, last in 1971 with 297′6″. Titles in '62, '66, '69 made him only athlete to take four European crowns. Set world mark of 301′9″ in 1968 but lost it year later. In 1972 had toss of 307′9″ to regain mark. Dominated event for over 10 years. Is Soviet army officer.

McCULLOUCH, EARL B. 1/10/46, Clarksville, Tex. Member 1967 U.S. Pan-Am Games team. Co-holder world 110-m hurdle record. Ran 13.2 at Pan-Am trials in Minneapolis on July 17, 1967. At Pan-Am Games won 110-m hurdles in 13.4, Games record. Also led off gold medal U.S. 400-m relay team. At Southern Cal won 1967, 68 NCAA high hurdle titles. Ran 13.4 in 1967 at 120-yds and 13.4 in 1968 at 110-m. Was 1968 AAU 60-yd hurdles champ in 6.9. Passed up chance to participate in 1968 Olympics to play pro football. Drafted 2nd by Detroit Lions and was *Sporting News* Rookie of the Year, 1968. As wide receiver, caught 40 passes for 680 yds.

McDANIEL, MILDRED B. 11/4/33, Atlanta, Ga. Member 1956 Olympic team. Held American women's high jump record. Set U.S. and Olympic mark in winning gold medal in 1956 Games with leap of 5′9 ¼″. Was AAU outdoor high jump champion in 1955 with jump of 5′6 ½″ for meet record that stood for 8 years. Also won AAU outdoor in 1953, 56. Took AAU indoor titles in 1955, 56. Latter jump of 5′4″ was good for meet record. Member Citizens Savings (Helms) Hall of Fame.

McDONALD, PATRICK (Pat) B. 1878, County Clare, Ireland. Member 1912, 20 U.S. Olympic teams. Great all-round weight man with national titles in shot and 56-lb weight throw. Twice Olympic gold medal winner. In 1912, surprise winner over world record-holder Ralph Rose. McDonald defeated Rose by 3 3/5″ with toss of 50′4″. Silver medalist behind Rose in now defunct 2-hand (left, right) shot with 90′3 17/20″. In 1920 Antwerp Olympics, won gold medal in 56-lb weight throw (no longer Olympic event) with toss of 36′11 5/8″. Did not do well in shot, finished 4th with put of 46′2 1/3″. New York City policeman, won AAU shot title in '11, '12, '14, '19, '20, '22. Was AAU champion in 56-lb weight throw in 1911, 14, 19–21, 26–29. Took AAU indoor shot title in 1916, 17, 19–21. One of many great Irish-American weightmen. Member Citizens Savings (Helms) Hall of Fame.

McGRATH, MATT B. 1878, Nenagh, Tipperary, Ireland. Member 1908, 12, 20, 24 U.S. Olympic teams. Held world hammer throw record. Tossed 16-lb ball and chain 187′4″ on Oct. 29, 1911, at New York City. One of line of Irish-American hammer throwers. Had long career beginning in 1906, lasting nearly 25 yrs. Had unofficial toss of 190′10″ in 1913. In Olympic competition won gold medal and 2 silvers. In 1908 London Olympics finished 2nd to rival John Flanagan of U.S. Set Olympic record of 179′7 1/8″ in 1912 Stockholm Olympics for gold medal. Record stood until 1936 Berlin Games. At Paris Olympics in 1924 was 2nd to Fred Tootell with 166′9 5/8″. In 1920 competed in Olympics at Antwerp, but handicapped by bad knee and was 5th. During long career took AAU hammer throw competition in '08, '12, '18, '22, '25, '26. Was AAU champ in 56-lb weight throw in '13, '16, '18, 22–25. Stocky (5′11″, 248) Irishman was New York City policeman. Member Citizens Savings (Helms) Hall of Fame.

McGUIRE, EDITH B. 6/3/44, Atlanta, Ga. Member 1964 Olympic team. In 1964 Tokyo Olympics, predicted to be next Wilma Rudolph. In 100-m was 2nd with 11.6. Teammate Wyomia Tyus won. In 200-m, was different story. Did not have Tyus to compete with. In first round ran 23.4, then 23.3 in semis. In finals broke Wilma Rudolph's Olympic record with 23.0 for gold medal. Member 1963 Pan-Am Games team and won gold medal with record-tying 11.5 in 100-m. Was 1963 AAU 100-m champion with 11.0. Won 1964, 65 AAU 200-m with 23.6 both years. One of many great sprinters from Tennesse State. Member Citizens Savings (Helms) Hall of Fame. Now schoolteacher.

McKENLEY, HERBERT B. 7/10/22, Clarendon, Jamaica. Member 1948, 52 Jamaican Olympic teams. Held world 440-yd, 400-m dash records. Had 440 times of 46.3 in 1947 and 46.0 in 1948; 45.9 in 400-m in 1948. Competed in U.S. for Illinois. Ran in competition without break for rest. Competition, rather than training, was schedule. Did not win individual gold medal in Olympics. In 1948 London Olympics was 2nd in 400-m, 4th in 200-m. In 1952 was 2nd in both 400-m and 100-m. Did collect gold for running great 44.6 leg on 1600-m relay. At Illinois won 1947, 48 NCAA 220-yd with 20.7 in 1947. Won '45, '47, '48 AAU Championships. Fast for first half of 440 and 400. Said could have been even greater with slower first half and stronger finish. Too much, too soon, many experts said.

MAKI, TAISTO B. 2/12/10, Rekola, Finland. Held several world distance records. Lowered 2-mile record to 8:53.2 at Helsinki on July 7, 1939. Set 3-mile mark of 13:42.4 on June 16, 1939, at Helsinki. In same race set 5000-m mark of 14:08.8. On Sept. 17, 1939, set both 6-mile and 10,000-m records at Helsinki. Ran 28:55.6 for 6-mile record. In 10,000-m, improved mark of 30:02.0 he set on Sept. 29, 1938, at Tampere to 29:52.6. In 1939 totaled 5 world records, all set at Helsinki. Won 1938 European Championships in 5000-m with 14:26.8. Versatile distance runner, capable from 1500-m to 10,000-m. Not able to compete in Olympic competition because of WW II.

MANN, RALPH B. 8/16/49, Long Beach, Calif. Member 1972 Olympic team. Holds world 440-yd hurdle record. Ran record 48.8 in 1970 NCAA championships at Des Moines, Iowa, on June 20. Was 3-time NCAA champ while at Brigham Young. Ran 49.6 to take titles in 1969, 71. Won 1970 AAU title with 49.8. In 1971 repeated in 49.3. In 1971 was Pan-Am Games gold medalist in Games record of 49.1 for 400-m hurdles. In 1972 was on-and-off. Came back off several bad races to win 1972 Olympic trials in 48.4, American 400-m hurdle record. In 1972 Munich Olympics ran 48.51, but had to settle for silver medal as John Akii-Bua of Uganda ran 47.82, world record. Engineering major at Brigham Young.

MANOLUI, LIA B. 8/25/32. Member 1952, 56, 60, 64, 68, 72 Rumanian Olympic teams. Won gold medal in 1968 Mexico City Olympics in womens discus with Games record 191′2½″. Bettered record by almost 4′. In 1960 took bronze medal with toss of 171′9⅜″ at Rome Games. At Tokyo was again bronze medalist with toss of 186′11″. In 1972 Munich Olympics made finals, but was 9th despite toss of 193′7″. Member Sporting Club of Metaul in Bucharest, won many Rumanian and Balkan titles. Is engineer, architect.

MATHIAS, ROBERT BRUCE (Bob) B. 11/19/30, Tulare, Calif. Member 1948, 52 Olympic teams. Won gold medal in 1948 Olympic decathlon at age 17 despite little experience in four of ten decathlon events. Youngest trackman ever to make American Olympic team at that time. Scored 7139 points to win, only competitor to score over 7000. Won only one event, discus, and tied for first in high jump and pole vault, but scored well in all events. Came to 1952 Games 3″ taller (6′3″) and 15 lbs heavier (205). Became first man in history to win two gold medals in decathlon with world, Olympic record 7887-point performance. Had set previous record in trials, breaking another world mark set in 1950. Won national decathlon championship four times. Also played college football as fullback at Stanford, played in 1952 Rose Bowl. Now representing California as Republican congressman in 18th District. Member Citizens Savings (Helms) Hall of Fame.

MATSON, RANDEL (Randy) B. 3/5/45, Kilgore, Tex. Member 1964, 68 Olympic teams. Holds world record in shot put. Tossed iron ball 70′7 ¼″ on May 8, 1965, at College Station, Tex. to shatter listed world record by almost 3″. Improved mark to 71′5 ½″ on April 22, 1967, at College Station. Only man to throw over 70′ until Al Feuerbach and George Woods reached in 1972. While student at Texas A & M, won 2 NCAA shot and discus titles. Won 1966 shot and discus with meet records in each event. Put shot 67′ ½″, discus 197′0″ for records. In 1967 improved shot mark to 67′9 ½″. Threw 190′4″ for discus title. As A & M frosh won 1964 AAU shot title with toss of 64′11″, meet record. Won AAU 1966–68. Improved meet record to 67′5″ in 1968. In 1964 Olympic Games won silver medal behind Dallas Long. Took lead on first of final tosses with throw of 66′3″, breaking Olympic record. But Long threw 66′8 ¼″ on next try to win gold medal. Took gold medal in 1967 Pan-Am Games with put of 65′4 ¾″. Did not compete extensively after won gold medal in 1968 Mexico City Olympics with record 67′4 ¾″ on first throw. Did win USTFF shot titles 1969–71. Made bid for 1972 Olympic team but was fourth in final trials with throw of 67′5 ¾″ and did not make team. Led qualifying round with put of 69′ 0 ¼″. Had best in 1972 of 69′6 ½″. Versatile athlete at Texas A&M, drafted by Atlanta Falcons in NFL, Seattle in NBA and Dallas of ABA. Played basketball one year at A & M and was star. Now executive director of booster club at West Texas State. Member Citizens Savings (Helms) Hall of Fame. Winner 1967 Citizens (Helms) World Trophy Award, North America. Pro 1973.

MATTHEWS, VINCENT (Vince) B. 12/16/47, Queens, N.Y. Member 1968, 72 Olympic teams. In 1968 ran 440-yd in 44.4 to better world record. In 1967 took silver medal in Pan-Am Games 400-m in 45.1. Won 1967 NAIA 440-yd for Johnson C. Smith College. In 1968 won AAU in 45.0. In 1968 pre-U.S. Olympic trials meet at South Lake Tahoe, ran his 44.4, besting world record. But IAAF disallowed mark because of "brush" spiked shoes. In final Olympic trials was 4th in 44.8 and missed place in 400-m. Did run on U.S. 1600-m relay team which set world record at Mexico City Olympics. Ran 45.0 leadoff leg in 2:56.1 run. Competed briefly in 1969, retired in 1970, 71. In 1972, after forming Brooklyn Over the Hill Athletic Association, returned to competition. In 1972 AAU, finished 2nd in 45.1. Made Olympic team with 44.9 for 3rd place. At Munich Olympics surprised world and won gold medal in 44.66. On victory stand, did not stand at attention and had silver medal winner Wayne Collett stand on top step with him. For "protest", he and Collett were banned from further Olympic competition. Matthews denied any protest. Youth worker by vocation. Turned pro 1973.

MATZDORF, PAT B. 12/26/49, Sheboygan, Wis. World high jump record-holder. Jumped 7′6¼″ at Berkeley, Calif., in U.S.-USSR dual meet on July 3, 1971. Took gold medal in 1971 Pan-Am Games at Cali, Colombia, with 6′10″ leap. Went 7′4″ in U.S.-Africa dual. Ranked top high jumper in world in 1971. Won 1971 Big Ten outdoor, indoor championships for Wisconsin. Went 7′3″ for indoor conference record, 7′1″ for outdoor record. Won 1970, 71 NCAA indoor crowns. Was 1970 NCAA outdoor champ. In 1972 was plagued by injuries. Was 2nd in NCAA indoor on misses to Colgate's Chris Dunn. Both cleared 7′2 ¾″ for NCAA indoor mark. After knee problems lessened and back trouble cleared up, suffered spike wound and missed NCAA and AAU outdoors. In Olympic trials went 7′ ½″, but suffered because of lack of competition in spring and was 5th. Winner 1971 Citizens Savings (Helms) World Trophy Award, North America.

MEADOWS, EARLE B. 6/29/13, Corinth, Miss. Member 1936 Olympic team. Co-held world pole vault record. Scaled 14′11″ on May 29, 1937, at Los Angeles, as did Southern Cal teammate Bill Sefton, but was 2nd on misses. Meadows and Sefton known as "Heavenly Twins" for vaulting performances. Twins tied for 1935 AAU vaulting title with 13′10⅜″. Also were NCAA co-champs for USC in 1935 with 14′1⅛″, and 1936 with 14′1¾″. In 1937 Meadows was 3rd in NCAA with 14′4⅞″ and Sefton took crown with 14′8 ⅞″. In 1937 AAU, Sefton, Meadows, George Varoff and Cornelius Warmerdam tied for 1st with 14′7 ⅝″. On misses Meadows was 3rd, Sefton 1st, Warmerdam 2nd and Varoff 4th. In 1936 Berlin Olympics, Meadows barely cleared 14′3″ to take gold away from 3 others, including Sefton who was 4th. Winning vault, cleared on 2nd try, broke Olympic record. Stayed active after Olympics and won 1940, 41 AAU indoors. Could still clear 14′ at age 35 in 1948. Member Citizens Savings (Helms) Hall of Fame.

MEISSNER-STECHER, RENATE B. 5/12/50, Suptitz/Torgau, Germany. Member 1972 E. German Olympic team. Won sprint double at Munich Olympics. Took 100-m gold medal by good margin with

11.07. Equaled world record of 22.40 in 200-m for 2nd gold medal of Games. Ran anchor leg on E. German 400-m relay that was 2nd behind W. German world record-equaling team. In 1971 European Championships, won gold medals in 100-m and 200-m. Ran 11.4 for 100-m victory, 22.7 for 200-m win. Has equaled world 100-m record two times. Ran 11.0 at Berlin on Aug. 2, 1970, repeated feat at Berlin on July 31, 1971. Tied world 60-m record of 7.1 on Feb. 28, 1971. Previously tied world 50-m record of 6.0 twice in the same month she tied 60-m mark. In 1973, set pending world marks of 22.1 in 200-m and 10.8 in 100-m on July 21 and 20 respectively. Student.

MEREDITH, JAMES (Ted) B. 11/14/92, Chester Heights, Pa. D. 11/2/57. Member 1912, 20 Olympic teams. Held world 440-yd and 400-m, 800-m and 880-yd records. Ran 47.4 on May 27, 1916, at Cambridge, Mass., for records in 400-m and 440-yd. Won gold medal in 1912 Stockholm Olympic 800-m, setting Olympic, world record of 1:51.9. Time for 880-yd of 1:52.5 good for world mark. Improved 880-yd record to 1:52.2 in Philadelphia, May 13, 1916. Ran on 3 world record-setting relay teams. Was IC4A titlist for Penn in 400-m 1914–16 and 880-yd in 1914, 15. Latter 880-yd time of 1:53.0 stood as meet record 11 years. Made 1920 Olympic team but did not qualify for 400-m finals. Ran on U.S. 1600-m relay team which was disappointing 4th. Won 1914, 15 AAU 440 titles. Did 47.0 with wind in 1915 AAU. Member Citizens Savings (Helms) Hall of Fame.

METCALFE, RALPH B. 5/29/10, Atlanta, Ga. Member 1932, 36 Olympic teams. Tied world 100-m record of 10.3 three times, 200-m record of 20.6 once. In 1932 NCAA won 100-m and 200-m with 10.2 and 20.3. Marks never submitted for world records. Won NCAA 100-yd and 220-yd in 1933, 34 for Marquette. Won AAU 100-yd 1932–34, and 200-m 1932–36. In 1932 Olympic trials defeated rival Tolan in 100 and 200. In Los Angeles Olympics in 1932, Tolan barely won 100-m, and also won 200. In 1936 Olympics, Metcalfe finished second behind great Jesse Owens in 100-m. Did win gold medal running on world record 400-m relay. "World's Fastest Human" 1934–35. Fast finish, but less than sensational start. Now Chicago businessman and Democrat congressman. Member Citizens Savings (Helms) Hall of Fame.

MEYFARTH, ULRIKE B. 5/4/56, Frankfurt, Germany. Member 1972 W. German Olympic team. As high school student won gold medal in 1972 Munich Olympics. Won Olympic high jump crown with 6′2¾″, second best jump by woman in Olympic competition. Surprising Olympic triumph, of course, ranks as greatest thrill in young career. At age 12 entered training for high jump career. Started out doing scissors style, but changed to "flop" style after Dick Fosbury's Mexico City win. In 1969 had best of 5′2″. In 1970 was up to 5′6″. In 1971 W. German Championships, was 2nd with 5′11″. Also won German junior title that year. Competed in 1971 European Championships but did not place. In 1972 was 3rd in German Championships and defended junior title. In July, prior to Olympics, placed 1st in meet with Canada with 6′ jump. In August took 1st in Switzerland meet and Hanna-Braun Sportsfest at 6′1″. In Olympics defeated many older, more experienced competitors.

MICKLER-BECKER, INGRID B. 9/26/42, Gesekel/Westfalen, Germany. Member 1960, 68, 72 W. German Olympic teams. Won gold medal in 1968 Olympics in pentathlon with 5098 points. In 1972 Olympics ran on W. German 400-m relay team that won gold medal in 42.81 to equal world, Olympic records. Competed in 1960 Olympic high jump and was 9th. Competed in '62, '66, '69, '71 European Championships. Was 1971 European long jump champion. In 1970 European Cup finals, won 100-m with 11.3, was 2nd in 200-m at 23.3 and ran on winning W. German 400-m relay team. One of best German woman athletes ever.

MIKAELSSON, JOHN B. 6/12/13. Member 1948, 52 Swedish Olympic teams. At London Olympics in 1948, won gold medal in 10,000-m walk. Set Olympic mark of 45:13.2. In 1952 at Helsinki, won Olympic gold medal in 10,000-m walk again and improved record to 45:02.8. Won English AAA 7-mile walk titles in 1937, 38 with best of 50:19.2 in 1937. Won 1946 European Championship in 10,000-m walk with 46:05.2. Set world 20,000-m walk mark on July 12, 1942, at Vaxjo with 1:32:28.4. Now lives in Los Angeles.

MILBURN, ROD B. 5/18/50, Opelousas, La. Member 1972 Olympic team. Holds world 120-yd hurdle record. Ran 13.0 in 1971 AAU heat at Eugene, Oreg. on June 25. Tied 110-m hurdle record in 1972 Olympics with 13.2 to win gold medal. Named World Track Athlete of Year in 1971 by *Track & Field News*. As Southern U. freshman in 1970, won NAIA and was 4th in AAU. In 1971 won NAIA (wind-aided 13.0), NCAA College Division (13.5), NCAA University Division (13.6), and AAU (wind-aided 13.1). Gold medalist at 1971 Pan-Am Games in 13.4. Had fine 1972 indoor season with 7.0 win in 60-high hurdle in U.S.-USSR indoor meet. In 1972 won NAIA in 13.5, AAU in 13.4. In Olympic trials, suffered first loss in over 2 years. Barely made team, as was 3rd in 13.6. But in Olympics, found form again and won handily in world record-tying 13.2. In 1973, won NCAA but lost in AAU. Set pending world record in 110-m hurdles of 13.1, July 6, 1973, at Zurich. Plans to play football when track days are over.

MILLS, BILLY B. 6/30/38, Pine Ridge, S.Dak. Member 1964 Olympic team. Held world 6-mile run record. Ran 27:11.6 at San Diego, Calif., on June 27, 1965, in AAU championships. Won by 5/100ths of second over Gerry Lindgren in unusual photo finish. Had mediocre career at Kansas, but made 1964 Olympic team. In 10,000-m at Tokyo scored what is considered by many as greatest upset in track history. Not considered among favorites as 1960 Olympic champion Murray Halberg of New Zealand, world record-holder Ron Clarke of Australia and Mohamed Gamoudi of Tunisia were among contestants. Thirty-eight runners started but at 5000-m mark, five were ahead of rest. Mills ran 14:04.6 first half, :07 off his best. On last lap, Mills, 7/16 Sioux Indian, had lead in home stretch but lost it to Clarke and Gamoudi. Mills did not give up. Managed to catch them with great sprint, passed them with 50 yds to go. Tremendous sprint enabled him to defeat what has been called greatest 10,000-m field in Olympic record 28:24.4. Won 1965 AAU 6-mile, but injuries prevented him from trying for 1968 Olympic team. Voted to Kansas Hall of Fame; one of 1972 "America's 10 Outstanding Young Men." Now assistant to commissioner of Bureau of Indian Affairs. Member Citizens Savings (Helms) Hall of Fame.

MILLS, CURTIS B. 10/6/48, Crockett, Tex. Held world 440-yd record. Ran 44.7 as Texas A&M sophomore on June 21, 1969, at Knoxville, Tenn., to win NCAA title. At 1970 Drake Relays ran anchor leg of A&M 880-yd relay team that set world record 1:21.7. At A&M was Southwest Conference 440-yd champ 1969–71. Was SWC 220-yd champ in 1970 with 20.7. Aggies won SWC 440-yd relay in 1970, 71 with Mills running anchor. Name in A&M record book in 10 different events, including relays. After 1969 record, never found form. Made try for 1972 U.S. Olympic team but was 8th in trial finals at 45.4. Competes for Philadelphia Pioneer Club.

MIMOUN, ALAIN B. January, 1921, El Telagz, Algeria. Member 1948, 52, 56 French Olympic teams. Won gold medal in marathon in 1956 Melbourne Olympics. Ran 2:25:00.0 for gold medal after previously winning 3 silver medals. In 1948 London Games was 2nd in 10,000-m with time of 30:47.4. In 1952 Olympics at Helsinki, took silver in 5000-m (14:07.4) and 10,000-m (29:32.8). Won total of 32 French national titles from 1947–66. Still competes in sports despite age.

MOENS, ROGER B. 4/26/30, Erembodegem, Belgium. Member 1952, 56, 60 Belgian Olympic teams. Held world 800-m record. Ran 1:45.7 at Oslo for world mark on Aug. 3, 1955. Record stood over six years before Peter Snell broke it with 1:44.3. Ran events ranging from 400-m to mile.

Had best of 47.3 in 400-m and 3:58.9 in mile. Ran 400-m in 1952 Olympics, eliminated in prelims. In 1954 European Championships, was favorite in view of 1:47.5 at Belgian Championships. But finished 5th despite 1:47.8. Injured foot prior to 1956 Melbourne Olympics and missed out on competition. In 1960 Rome Olympics was in good shape. Ran 3:41.4 for 1500-m few months before. In prelims came out ahead of Peter Snell, 1:48.5 to 1:48.6. In semis Snell was 1st. In finals could not hold off Snell and had to settle for silver medal. Said to be at best in small race, where could concentrate on few runners rather than large field.

MOORE, CHARLES, JR. B. 8/12/29, Coatsville, Pa. Member 1952 Olympic team. Held world record in 440-yd hurdles. Ran 51.9 on Aug. 4, 1952, in London. Five days later ran 51.6, also at London. Excellent 440-yd dash man. Won NCAA 440 with 47.0 while at Cornell. Won 1950 IC4A meet with time of 47.3. Took 1st in AAU 440-yd hurdles 1949–52. Meet record 51.9 in 1949 stood until 1956. Had world best in 1949 with 51.9; in 1950 with 51.5; 1951 with 51.4 and 1952 with 50.7. At Helsinki broke Roy Cochran's Olympic record of 51.1 with 50.8 clocking for gold medal on slow track. Also ran leg on silver medal 1600-m team, 46.2 leg being his fastest 400-m. Father, Crip Moore, was reserve 110-m hurdler on 1924 Olympic team. Member Citizens Savings (Helms) Hall of Fame.

MORRIS, GLENN B. 6/18/12, Simla, Colo. Member 1936 Olympic team. Held world decathlon record. Late starter in decathlon, beginning in early part of 1936. Good 440-yd hurdler until turned attention to decathlon. Won 1936 AAU championship with 7880 points (7275 under present point scale) which bettered world mark, but never entered into books. In 1936 Berlin Olympics, got into world and Olympic books with 7900 points for gold medal. Record stood 14 years until Bob Mathias broke it. Ran 11.1 in 100-m, 49.4 in 400-m, 14.9 in 110-m hurdles and 4:33.2 in 1500-m. Latter still best of all world record performances in last of 10 events. Member Citizens Savings (Helms) Hall of Fame.

MORROW, BOBBY B. 10/15/35, Harlingen, Tex. Member 1956 Olympic team. Co-holder world 100-yd dash record with 9.3 in 1957. Won 1955 AAU in Boulder, Colo., with 9.5 for first big win. Biggest year 1956. Won AAU 100-m, NCAA 100 and 200-m and finals in Olympic tryouts in same events. Won 100 and 200-m in 1956 Olympics in Melbourne. Tied 100-m record of 10.3 in prelims and set 200-m record with 20.6. Got third gold medal with anchor leg on 400-m relay team that set world, Olympic record 39.5. Won sprint double in 1956, 57 NCAA for Abilene Christian College. Was 1955, 56, 58 short sprint (9.4 in 1958 100-yd dash) AAU champion. Also won 1958 AAU 220-yd crown.

Anchored crack Abilene Christian sprint relay teams that set world 440 and 880-yd marks in 1958 with Morrow anchoring. Duels with Duke's Dave Sime were sprint classics. Member Citizens Savings (Helms) Hall of Fame.

MORTENSEN, JESSE B. 4/16/07, Thatcher, Ariz. D. 2/19/62, Los Angeles, Calif. Track coach at Southern Cal 1951–61. In 11 years as USC coach, Trojans never lost dual meet in 79 competitions. Won NCAA team titles 1951–55, 58, 61. Southern Cal was on probation for violations in other sports in two of four years Trojans failed to win NCAA. Coached 20 NCAA individual champions, including Parry O'Brien, Dallas Long, Sim Inness, all Olympic gold medal winners; and Ernie Shelton. Known as one of top USC athletes himself. Won 1929 NCAA javelin with 203′7¾″ toss. Also AAU champ at 204′11¾″. Member Citizens Savings (Helms) Hall of Fame.

MURCHISON, IRA B. 2/6/33, Chicago, Ill. Member 1956 Olympic team. Co-held world 100-m record. First ran 10.2 at Compton, Calif., June 10, 1956. Ran 10.2, as did Bobby Morrow, at Los Angeles, June 29, 1956. In International Armed Services Meet in Berlin Aug. 4, 1956, ran 10.1 to tie day-old record of Willie Williams. In 1956 Olympics finished 4th behind Hogon of Australia, costing U.S. sweep. Did start U.S. 400-m relay which won gold medal and set world, Olympic record 39.5. Great start put U.S. on record pace. One of shortest great sprinters in history at 5′4″. Consistant high finisher in major meets for several years. Was 1957 AAU indoor 60-yd dash champ in 6.2. Was 1958 NCAA 100-yd champ for Western Michigan with 9.5. Known for tremendous starts.

MURRO, MARK B. 6/4/49, Newark, N.J. Member 1968 Olympic team. American javelin record-holder. Threw spear 300′0″ at Tempe, Ariz., on March 27, 1970, for American citizen, collegiate record. Ninth in Mexico City Olympics at 262′8¾″ in 1969. Won 1969 NCAA for Arizona State with toss of 265′9″. Won USTFF meet with 280′2″ in 1969, and AAU same year with 284′3″. In 1970 was defeated by Tennessee's Bill Skinner in NCAA and plagued by injury. Did not have great success in 1970, but was 5th in 1971 AAU with throw of 255′2″. In 1972 looked like greatness had returned. Had best throw of 273′8″ and was given good chance of making U.S. Olympic team. But in AAU was 9th at 248′11″. Did not make top 6 in Olympic trials.

MYERS, LAURENCE (Lon) B. 2/16/58, Richmond, Va. D. 1899. Held world records in 440-yd, 880-yd. World's first sub-50 quartermiler. Set world mark in 1879 with 49.2. Lowered record to 48.6 in 1881. Ran 1:56 half in 1881 to first break into record books. Lowered standard to

1:55.4 on July 7, 1884, at Birmingham, England. Ran same time twice in 1885 to tie own record. One of greatest athletes in his time. Versatile performer, at one time held all U.S. records from 50-yd to mile. Won AAU 220-yd, 440-yd, 880-yd titles in 1879. In 1880 won 4 AAU titles: 100-yd, 220-yd, 440-yd, 880-yd. In 1881 took 3 AAU crowns with 100-yd, 220-yd, 440-yd wins. Ran 49.4 quarter which was meet record 15 years. In 1884 won 220-yd, 440-yd, 880-yd titles. Took single titles in 1882, 83 in 440-yd. Had best of 10.0 in 100-yd, 22.6 in 220-yd, 48.6 in 440-yd, 1:55.4 in 880-yd, 4:27.6 in mile. Retired from track in 1885 and was in betting business. Succumbed to pneumonia. Member Citizens Savings (Helms) Hall of Fame.

MYYRA, JONNI B. 8/24/92, Savitaipole, Finland. Member 1912, 20, 24 Finnish Olympic teams. Held world javelin record. Broke Erik Lemming's record by 12′5″ with toss of 216′10″ at Stockholm on Aug. 28, 1919. Said to have broken record before, but only last mark accepted by IAAF. In 1912 Olympics was 7th, but took gold medal in 1920 with throw of 215′9½″. Took 2nd gold medal in 1924 with 206′6½″. After 1924 Paris Olympics, moved to U.S. and settled in California. Had throw of 224′11″ in unsanctioned meet there in 1925.

NAMBU, CHUHEI B. May, 1906, Sapporo, Japan. Member 1932 Japanese Olympic team. Held world long jump, triple jump records. Long jumped 26′2 ¼″ on Oct. 27, 1931, at Tokyo. Went 51′7″ on Aug. 4, 1932, at Los Angeles Olympics for triple jump mark, gold medal. In long jump went 24′5 ¼″ for bronze medal. A 10.5 100-m sprinter, was one of line of top-flight Japanese jumpers. Chief of sports department of Osaka newspaper. Now retired.

NEMETH, IMRE B. 9/23/17, Kosice, Czechoslovakia. Member 1948, 52, 56 Hungarian Olympic teams. Held world hammer throw record. Tied mark of 193′7″ of Edwin Blask at Tata, July 14, 1948. Improved mark to 195′5″ at Katowice, Poland, Sept. 4, 1949. Boosted record to 196′5″ on May 16, 1950, at Budapest. In 1948 Olympics missed Games record by foot with 183′11 ½″ throw for gold medal. Competed in 1952 Olympics, was third with throw of 189′5 ½″. Throw bettered previous Olympic record by almost 5′. Winner Csermak was protege of Nemeth. In 1956 finished 5th in Melbourne Olympics.

NIEDER, BILL B. 8/10/33, Hempstead, N.Y. Member 1956, 60 Olympic teams. In 1960 shattered world shot put record with 65′7″ put on April 2, in Austin, Tex. Won 1955 NCAA for Kansas with 57′3″ toss. Most of career was Parry O'Brien's shadow. In 1956 Melbourne Olympics took silver medal behind O'Brien. But in 1957 topped world list with 62′2″ put. Won AAU shot title in 1957 with toss of 61′6″. In 1960 Olympic trials finished 4th due to ailing knee. After tryouts broke own record with 65′10″. Injury to Dave Davis made room on team. At Rome Games trailed O'Brien and Dallas Long going into final round. On next-to-last throw, broke Olympic record with put of 64′6 ¾″ for gold medal. Tried hand at boxing after Olympics but was knocked out in first try. Has own company that surfaces artificial tracks. Member Citizens Savings (Helms) Hall of Fame.

NIKKANEN, YIJO B. 12/31/14, Kanneljarvi, Finland. Member 1936 Finnish Olympic team. Held world javelin record. Threw 255′5″ on Aug. 25, 1938, at Karhula. Improved mark to 258′2″ on Oct. 16, 1938, at Kotka. In 1936 Berlin Olympics, third year of throwing, took silver medal with 232′2″. Great rival of Matti Jarvinen. Won 2 of 4 major confrontations with Jarvinen. Lost European Championship, but in last meeting set world record that lasted 15 years.

NORDWIG, WOLFGANG. B. 8/28/43, Siegmar/Chemnitz, Germany. Member 1968 German, 1972 E. German Olympic teams. Won gold medal in pole vault at 1972 Munich Olympics with record 18′ ½″. Made record height on last attempt. Made 17′10 ½″ on first attempt to clinch gold medal. One of central figures in pole controversy of Games. Said to have protested use of new type pole used by defending Olympic champion Bob Seagren. Became first non-American to win gold. In 1968 Olympics was bronze medalist at 17′8 ½″, same as winner, but had more misses. Won 3 European Championships. In 1968 went 16′6 ¾″ to win; in 1969 took title with 17′4 ¾″ and in 1971 set meet record of 17′6 ¾″. Ranked as top vaulter in world by *Track & Field News* in 1969, 70. Automation engineer.

NORTON, RAY B. 9/22/37, Tulsa, Okla. Member 1960 Olympic team. Co-held 7 world sprint records. Ran 10.1 in 100-m at San Jose, Calif., on April 4, 1959, for first world mark. Had three 100-yd times of 9.3 to tie world record. Time of 20.6 twice tied 200-m mark in spring of 1960. Had 20.5 time July 2, 1960, at Palo Alto, Calif., to regain share of record after it had been lowered. Won 1959, 60 AAU 100-m and 200-m championships. Was 1959 NCAA 220-yd titlist while at San Jose State. Triple gold medal winner in 1959 Chicago Pan-Am Games. Winning times of 10.3 in 100-m and 20.6 in 200-m. Anchored winning 400-m relay team. One of favorites in 1960 Olympic sprints. Performance one of greatest sports disappointments. Finished last in both 100-m, 200-m. On receiving end of illegal baton pass that disqualified U.S. 400-m relay team which had finished 1st. Had set 200-m mark of 20.5 in prelims. Despite Olympic failure, still one of world's greatest sprinters.

NURMI, PAAVO B. 6/13/97, Turku, Finland. Member 1920, 24, 28 Finnish Olympic teams. Won 7 gold medals in Olympic competition, set 20 world records in career as distance runner. Won 1500-m, 10,000-m cross-country run in 1920 Games in Antwerp. In 1924 at Paris, won 10,000-m cross country, 1500-m, 5000-m and ran on 3000-m team for 4 gold medals. In 1928 won 10,000-m at Amsterdam. Held 1500, 2000, 3000, 5000, 10,000, 15,000 and 20,000-m world records. Also mile, 2, 3, 6 and 10-mile runs, along with 1-hr run. Set first record in 1921 with 30:40.2 in 10,000-m. In 1924 set 1500-m and 5000-m world records on same day with hour rest between. In 1931 set last of 20 world marks with 8:59.5 two-mile on July 24 at Helsinki. Wanted to end career with gold medal in 1932 Los Angeles Olympics, but was suspended from amateur ranks. Continued to compete in Finland. Won national 1500-m at age 36. In 1925 tour of U.S., won over 50 races and lost only 2. Set many American indoor, outdoor marks on tour.

O'BRIEN, PARRY B. 1/28/32, Santa Monica, Calif. Member 1952, 56, 60, 64 Olympic teams. First shot putter to break 60′ barrier with 60′5 $\frac{1}{4}$″ at Los Angeles in 1954. "O'Brien Style" revolutionized event. Facing back of circle, made 180-degree turn, using speed and strength to shift weight towards front of circle. Held world mark seven years. Advanced world standard from 59′2 $\frac{1}{4}$″ in 1953 to 63′2″ in 1956. Outstanding in high school with 57′9 $\frac{1}{2}$″ (12-lb) best. Won first of eight AAU titles in 1951, two years out of prep ranks, at 55′9 $\frac{1}{4}$″. Won nine straight indoor championships. Best indoors of 61′8″. At Southern Cal won two NCAA firsts (1952, 53), 1953 mark of 58′7 $\frac{1}{4}$″. Won gold medal at 1952 Helsinki Olympics with record 57′1 $\frac{1}{2}$″. In 1956 Melbourne Games also took gold with record 60′11″ on first throw. Finished second at Rome in 1960 behind rival Bill Nieder of USA with 62′8 $\frac{1}{2}$″. Made 1964 Olympic team but finished fourth. Big, fast, strong perfectionist of style. Consistant. Won 116 straight in 1950s. Also fine discus man. Held record for combined (right, left-handed) shot put: 61′0 $\frac{3}{4}$″ right, 45′9 $\frac{1}{3}$″ left, 106′10 $\frac{1}{2}$″ total. Topped World Year Lists five times. Set World Senior record in 1971 with 53′4″ shot, 164′9″ discus performances. Now banker in California.

O'CALLAGHAN, PATRICK B. 1905, Kanturk, County Cork, Ireland. Member 1928, 32 Irish Olympic teams. After trying several events, settled on hammer throw. Made top-20 list in world his first year. Went to 1928 Olympics at Amsterdam as relative unknown. Lagged behind leader until 5th throw, then got off throw of 168′7″ for gold medal. In

1932 Los Angeles Olympics, waited until last throw to win gold medal with 176′11″. Missed Berlin Olympics because athletic federation he belonged to wasn't recognized by IAAF. Got off throw of 198′8 3/8″ in 1937 Cork County championships, but not considered by IAAF for world record because meet not sanctioned. Throw made in small ring and measured from center at first. Hammer was also 6 oz overweight. Coached by 3-time gold medal winner John Flannagan. Veterinarian.

ODA, MIKIO B. 3/30/05, Hiroshima, Japan. Member 1924, 28, 32 Japanese Olympic teams. Held world triple jump record with 51′1 1/2″ at Tokyo on Oct. 27, 1931. In 1924 Paris Olympics, was 6th at age 19. In 1928 Amsterdam Olympics, took gold medal with distance of 49′10 3/4″. Had set Asian record of 50′6 3/4″ before coming to Games. Led way for other Japanese athletes as first Japanese citizen to win gold medal. Injured in 1932 and did not do well in Los Angeles Olympics. Good all-round performer with 6′3 1/2″ high jump, 12′5 3/4″ pole vault and 24′8″ long jump. First of three consecutive Japanese gold medalists in triple jump.

OERTER, ALFRED (Al) B. 8/19/36, Astoria, N.Y. Member 1956, 60, 64, 68 Olympic teams. Held world discus mark. First man to throw disc 200′ with 200′5″ on May 18, 1962, at Los Angeles. Lost mark temporarily. Regained it July 1, 1962, at Chicago with 204′10 1/2″ toss. Advanced mark to 205′5″ at Walnut, Calif., April 27, 1963. Walnut again scene of world record performance April 25, 1964, as standard upped to 206′6″. Fantastic record of 4 gold medals in 4 Olympic Games! Standing jumper Ray Ewry only other man to accomplish feat. In 1956 Melbourne Olympics, broke Olympic record with 184′10 1/2″, beating teammate Fortune Gordien, world record-holder. Beat Rink Babka of U.S., who also held world mark, for gold in 1960 Rome Olympics. Advanced Olympic record to 194′2″. Again in 1964 beat world record-holder, Ludvik Danek. Won gold medal with Olympic record 200′1 1/2″ despite injured ribs. Surprised track world with attempt at 4th gold medal. In Mexico City 1968 Olympics, won gold with Olympic and personal best of 212′6 1/2″. Jay Silvester, world record-holder of U.S., was in field to complete Oerter's remarkable repeat performances. Was AAU titlist in '57, '59, '60, '62, '64, '66. Won 1959 Pan-Am Games with 190′8 1/2″. Won 1957 and tied for 1958 NCAA crowns for Kansas. Member Citizens Savings (Helms) Hall of Fame. Winner 1964 Helms World Trophy Award, North America.

O'HARA, TOM B. 7/5/42, Chicago, Ill. Member 1964 Olympic team. One of world's top milers in mid-1960s. Slim Irishman set world-best indoors with 3:56.4 on Jan. 6, 1964, at Chicago. Was 1963 NCAA cross country champion for Loyola. Best year 1964, with exception of Olympics. Besides world indoor mark, also won 3 other indoor championships. Opened outdoor season with 4:01 mile at Drake Relays. Ran 2nd at the Compton Invitational with a 3:57.6 mile. In 1964 AAU championships at New Brunswick, ran American record 1500-m with 3:38.1 clocking. Took 2nd in final Olympic trials with 3:41.5. In 1964 Olympics, held high hopes. Heavy cold halted training after turning in great times in practice. In first round at Tokyo ran 3rd in heat with 3:46.7. In semis failed to qualify as was 7th in heat with 3:43.4. Voted into Drake Relays Hall of Fame in 1970. Now successful insurance salesman in Chicago.

OLDFIELD, BRIAN B. 6/1/45, Elgin, Ill. Member 1972 U.S. Olympic team. Won berth on U.S. Olympic team by edging the great Randy Matson in shot put: 68′½″ to Matson's 67′5¾″. Was 6th in Munich Olympics with 68′7¼″. Turned pro after Olympics and was top money winner on tour with $10,375. On May 25 had toss of 70′10½″ for best indoor toss pro or amateur. Was over 70′ on all six tosses. Was teacher at Illinois State Training School before he turned pro in 1973.

ORTON, GEORGE W. B. 1872, Ontario, Canada. D. 6/26/58. Member 1900 U.S. Olympic team. Olympic pioneer from Penn, entered 3 events in Paris Games. Won 2500-m steeplechase, 3rd in 400-m hurdles, 4th in 4000-m steeplechase. Won IC4A mile in 1895, 97. Member Citizens Savings (Helms) Hall of Fame.

OSBORN, HAROLD B. 4/13/99, Butler, Ill. Member 1924, 28 Olympic teams. Set world high jump record of 6′8¼″ in 1924. Also set world decathlon record of 7710.775 same year. Tied for 1922 AAU high jump title with 6′5½″ jump but lost on misses. Also tied for 1922 NCAA crown for Illinois with 6′2⅝″. Set American collegiate record of 6′6″ at 1922 Drake Relays. Won 1923 AAU decathlon with 7351.89 points on old point scale. Was AAU indoor high jump titlist. Greatest year 1924. Set 6′8¼″ mark on May 27 at Urbana, Ill. At 1924 Olympics won high jump at 6′6″, and set Olympic, world record in decathlon with 7710.775. Won 1925, 26 high jump, decathlon AAU titles. Won 1923–26 AAU indoor titles. Competed over 16 years. Now osteopath. Helped coach Illinois track team in 1940s. Member Citizens Savings (Helms) Hall of Fame.

OSTERMEYER, MICHELINE B. 12/23/22, Berck sur Mer, France. Member 1948 French Olympic team. Won gold medals in womens shot put and discus in London Olympics, 3rd in high jump. Won discus on last toss with 137′6½″. Took shot with toss of 45′1½″. Jumped 5′3⅜″

for bronze medal in high jump. French shot champion from 1945–48, 50. Won discus in 1950, along with 80-m hurdles. In 1947 was French high jump champion. Won Grand Prix du Conservatoire de Music in piano. Mother of 2, vice president International Organization of French Athletes.

OUAFI, EL B. 1886, Ouled-Djellal, Algeria. D. 1956. Member 1924, 28 French Olympic teams. Won gold medal in 1928 Amsterdam Olympics in marathon. Toured course in 2:32:57.0 for first major victory. Took lead with about mile to go, defeated nearest competitor by 25 seconds. In 1924 Olympics was 7th after being blocked out. Turned professional in 1928 after Olympics. Auto mechanic who had served in French Foreign Legion.

OWENS, J.C. (Jesse) B. 9/12/13, Danville, Ala. Member 1936 Olympic team. Won four gold medals. Emerged world class in 1933 Interscholastic Championships in Chicago, winning 100-yd in 9.4 to tie world mark and long jumping 24′9⅝″. Continued career at Ohio State after prep days at Cleveland East Technical. In 1935 competed at Drake Relays, selected Athlete of Half Century by Drake officials in 1959 for lone performance. Ran 9.5 to win 100-yd and set American record in long jump with 26′1¾″. Long jump record stood 30 years, 100 mark for 20. Later in 1935 at Big Ten Championships, tied world 100-yd mark, set world long jump standard at 26′8½″, set 220-yd low hurdle straight course mark with 22.6 and set world 220-yd straight course mark with 20.7. Set or equaled 4 world marks in 70 minutes. Next came Owens' year to make history. Started with 1936 NCAA win in 100-m of 10.2, 200-m of 21.3 and long jump of 25′10⅞″. Qualified for Olympics at Berlin where thrilled world with four gold medals. Ran 10.3 in 100-m on Aug. 3 to tie Games record, 26′5¼″ long jump (Aug. 4) set Games mark, and won 200-m (Aug. 5) with 20.7. Anchored U.S. 400-m relay (Aug. 9) to record 39.8. After Olympics, Owens' performances anticlimatic. Called perfect natural talent by experts. Probably best known trackman in history of sport. Member Citizens Savings (Helms) Hall of Fame.

PADDOCK, CHARLES B. 11/8/1900, Gainesville, Tex. D. WW II. Member 1920, 24, 28 Olympic teams. "World's Fastest Human" in 1920s. Held world 100-m, co-held 100-yd records. Also 200, 300-m, 300-yd. Broke 4 world marks and tied one in one day, April 23, 1921. Ran 10.4 in 100-m, 21.6 in 200-m, 33.8 in 300-m, 30.2 in 300-yd, 9.6 in 100-yd. Won 5 AAU titles: 2 in 100 (9.6 in 1921, 24), 3 in 220 (21.4 in 1920, 21; 20.8 in 1924). Won gold medal in 1920 Antwerp Olympics with 10.8 in 100-m, 2nd in 200. At Paris Games was 2nd in 200, 5th in 100. Also ran on winning 400-m relay. Was on 1928 team in 200-m but failed to qualify. Unique finish–would leap last yards to tape. Died in WW II as captain in Marines. Member Citizens Savings (Helms) Hall of Fame.

PAPANICOLAU, CHRIS B. 11/25/41. Member 1964, 68, 72 Greek Olympic teams. First man to pole vault 18′. Vaulted 18′ ¼″ at N. Faliron on Oct. 24, 1970, for world record. In 1963 set European record of 17′4 ¾″. In 1964 Olympics settled for 18th place with subpar vault of 15′1 ¼″. Second in 1966 European Championships. In 1968 Mexico City Olympics, vaulted 17′6 ¾″ for 4th. Took 4th in 1969 European Championships at 16′5″. Competed in U.S. as student at San Jose State. Has dominated pole vault in Greece for almost 10 years. In 1971 was Greek champion at 17′1″, but did not make opening height in European Championships. Prior to Munich Olympics had jump of 17′8 ½″. In Olympics made 16′5″, then passed to 17′ ¾″. Failed 3 times and placed 11th. Winner 1970 Citizens Savings (Helms) World Trophy Award, Europe.

PATTON, MELVIN B. 11/16/24, Los Angeles, Calif. Member 1948 Olympic team. Held world 100-yd, 220-yd, 200-m records. Had 9.4 in 1947, then 9.3 in 1948. Latter tied 10 times but lasted 13 years. Broke Jesse Owens' 200-m, 220-yd record with 20.2. Favored in London Olympic 100-m, but had bad start and finished 5th. Did win 200-m with 21.1. Also ran on gold medal 400-m relay team. Ran 9.1 in 100-yd with wind and also set his 220-yd, 200-m world record on May 7, 1949. Won sprint double in 1948, 49 NCAA championships and 100-yd in 1947. Ran on Southern Cal world record 880-yd relay team with 1:24 in 1949. Never competed in AAU championships. Member Citizens Savings (Helms) Hall of Fame.

PEACOCK, EULACE B. 8/27/14, Dothan, Ala. Co-held world 100-m record. Tied world mark with 10.3 at Oslo on Aug. 8, 1934. Excellent sprinter-long jumper with misfortune of competing at same time as Jesse Owens and Ralph Metcalfe. In 1934 had successful tour of Europe, losing only twice. In 1935 AAU, defeated Owens in 100-m with wind-aided 10.2. Defeated Owens 3 of 5 times in outdoor meetings in 1935. Also won 1935 AAU long jump title over Owens with 26′3″. Hindered by muscle trouble and failed to make 1936 Olympic team. Tried to make comeback in 1937 but again forced out because of injuries. Probably feared more by Owens than any other trackman. Member Citizens Savings (Helms) Hall of Fame.

PELTZER, OTTO B. 3/8/1900, Ellernbock, Holstein, Germany. Member 1928, 32 German Olympic teams. Held 800-m, 880-yd, 1000-m and 1500-m world records. Ran 1:51.6 at London AAA meet on July 3, 1926, for 800-m, 880-yd records. Set 1000-m record with 2:25.8 at Paris on Sept. 18, 1927. Broke Nurmi's 1500-m record with 3:51.0 on Sept. 10, 1926. In 1928 Amsterdam Olympics, was eliminated in 800-m semifinals. In 1932 Los Angeles Olympics, made finals but finished out of running for medals in 800-m. Noted for great kick in last lap. Doctor.

PENDER, MEL B. 10/31/37, Atlanta, Ga. Member 1964, 68 Olympic teams. Ran on U.S. 400-m relay team that set world record 38.2 at Mexico City Olympics on Oct. 20, 1968. In 1964 Tokyo 100-m final, ran 10.4 but was 6th. Got off to fast start, as usual, and was leading with 20-m to go. But rib injury caused him to slow up and finish out of medals. In 1968 at Mexico City, story was same—6th place. Time was excellent 10.1. Did get gold medal for world, Olympic record 400-m relay performance. Helped pick up ground lost by injured Charlie Greene. Only U.S. sprinter to compete in both 1964, 68 Olympics. Holds world age bests for 26-year-old in 100-yd (9.3), 27 in 100-yd (9.3), 30 in 100-yd

(9.5) and 100-m (10.0 twice), 31 in 100-m (10.1), 33 in 100-yd (9.3). Excellent indoor sprinter due to great start. Ran 6.8 in 70-yd for world record in 1965, matched time in 1971. Ran 5.9 to tie indoor record in 1972. At age 34, Pender, captain in U.S. Army and assistant track coach at West Point, tried for 3rd Olympic berth. Ran in AAU but had cramp and withdrew. Ran 10.3 in first heat at 1972 Olympic trials, was 3rd in heat. In semis ran 10.1, but was 7th and did not make finals. Pro 1973.

PENES, MIHAELA B. 7/22/47. Member 1964, 68 Rumanian Olympic teams. Won gold medal in 1964 Olympics womens javelin with toss of 198′7½″. Beat existing record by almost 16′. With gold medal became youngest Olympic champion at age 17. Mark was age best also. In 1968 won silver medal with toss of 196′7″. In 1966 took 2nd in European Championships. Won several Rumanian national titles, was Balkan champion 1964–69. Now teacher.

PENNEL, JOHN B. 7/25/40, Memphis, Tenn. Member 1964, 68 Olympic teams. Held world pole vault record. First captured record with jump of 16′10″ on Aug. 5, 1963, at Santa Barbara, Calif. World's first 17′ vaulter. Went 17′¾″ on Aug. 24, 1963, at Coral Gables, Fla. Improved world mark, which had lost to Fred Hansen and Bob Seagren, to 17′6¾″ on July 23, 1966, at Los Angeles. Raised mark again, after losing it, to 17′10¼″ on June 21, 1969, Sacramento. Mark still stands, although several vaults are pending. Still U.S. citizens best. Often injured, missed entire 1967 season with various ailments. In 1964 Olympics was bothered by slipped disc, finished 11th with vault of 15′5″. Granted hope for making 1968 Olympic team by medical petition. After petition was accepted, hit old form and vaulted 17′4″. In 1968 Games, cleared 17′6¾″ but was only fifth. Made exceptional progress on fiberglass pole. Was 15′4″ vaulter in 1962, but went 17′¾″ for world record next year. Finished 2nd to U.S. teammates in 1963, 69 U.S.-USSR dual meets. In 1969 won both U.S.-West Germany and U.S.-Great Britain duals. Was 1965 AAU champion at 17′ and NAIA champ in 1962 for Northeast La. State. Attempted comeback for 1972 Olympic team but again fell victim to injury.

PETTERSSON, STEN B. 9/11/02, Stockholm, Sweden. Member 1924 Swedish Olympic team. Held world records in 110-m and 400-m hurdles. Only man ever to hold both hurdles record. Ran 14.8 to tie 110-m record, held by Earl Thompson of Canada, at Stockholm, Sept. 18, 1927. Set 400-m at Paris, Oct. 4, 1925, with 53.8. Set European record of 52.4 in 1928. Had career best of 14.6, done in 1930. Had 25.2 in 200-m hurdles. Highly successful in international competition, although could only claim bronze medal in 1924 Olympic 110-m hurdles with 15.7. Great name in Swedish athletics, won 22 national titles 1923–33.

PILGRIM, PAUL B. 1883, New York, N.Y. D. 1/7/58. Member 1906, 08 Olympic teams. Not originally selected for 1906 Olympic team. Added when Olympic fund drive successful enough to add one man. Selected with some reservation. Victory in 400-m heat dissolved misgivings. In finals won by meter in 53.2 upset over Lt. Wyndam Halswelle of Britain. In 800-m final again met Halswelle and 1500-m gold medalist James Lightbody of U.S. Lightbody and Pilgrim left field at 700-m and Pilgrim won by slim margin for 2nd gold medal, timed in 2:01.5. Games of 1906 his last hurrah in competition. In 1908 London Olympics was loser in prelims of 400-m. From 1914–53 was manager, athletic director of New York Athletic Club. Sent many athletes to Olympic competition.

PIRIE, GORDON B. 2/10/31, Leeds, England. Member 1952, 56, 60 British Olympic teams. Held several world distance records. Set world 6-mile record in 1953 at London with 28:19.4 on July 10. Got 5000-m mark, June 19, 1956, with 13:36.8. Tied Sandor Iharos' 3000-m record of 7:55.6 at Trondheim, Norway, June 6, 1956. Broke mark with 7:52.8 on Sept. 4, 1956, at Malmo, Norway. In 1952 Helsinki Olympics was 4th in 5000-m. In 1956 Melbourne Olympics ran in both 5000-m and 10,000-m. In 10,000-m was in strategic duel with Vladimir Kuts of USSR. Kuts set unbelievable pace in first 5000-m, then, after couple tries, prodded Pirie into taking lead. Kuts nearly slowed to walk. After trailing Pirie for few laps, Kuts took off again with 5 laps to go and won by 45 yards. Pirie, tired by fast pace of first half, finished 8th. In 5000-m, Kuts again took early lead and won easily in Olympic record 13:39.6. First 5 men beat Olympic record. Pirie, making great effort, finished 2nd. Competed in 1960 Rome Olympics in 10,000-m. Had career best of 29:15.2 but was 10th in one of greatest races ever. Never won major race, but was thought of highly.

PORTER, BILL B. 3/24/26, Jackson, Mich. Member 1948 Olympic team. Held Olympic 110-m hurdle record. In 1948 Olympic trials, Porter, Craig Dixon and Clyde Scott made team and world record-holder Harrison Dillard failed. But trio carried U.S. colors well. Porter, rangy 6′3″, set Olympic record of 13.9 in winning gold medal. Scott took silver medal, Dixon bronze. Both were inches behind Porter. Was 1948 AAU champion with 14.1 time. At Northwestern won 1947, 48 Big Nine (now Big Ten) 120-yd high, 220-yd low hurdle titles. In 1947 equaled American 70-yd high record of 8.5. In 1948 ran 7.7 in 70-yd lows to tie another American record. Now executive in hospital supply business.

POTGIETER, GERHARDUS B. 4/16/37, Retersmaritzburg, South Africa. Member 1956 South African Olympic team. Held 440-yd hurdle record. First set mark with 50.7 on April, 20, 1957, at Queenstown. Lost record to Americans Josh Culbreath and Glenn Davis for about year. Then ran 49.3 at 1958 Commonwealth Games at Cardiff on July 22, for record. In 1960, on April 16, ran 49.3 in South African Championships at Bloemfontein. Mark was good until Raplh Mann of U.S. ran 48.8 in 1970. In 1956 Melbourne Olympics was one of favorites in finals. Ran 51.3 in semis. In finals was 3rd going into last hurdle. Hit hurdle, fell and finished last. Set for another duel with Davis in 1960 Olympics. Few weeks before Games, however, was in car accident and missed Games because of major injuries. Made comeback few years later and ran 52.1.

PREFONTAINE, STEVE B. 1/25/51, Coos Bay, Oreg. Member 1972 Olympic team. American record holder in 5,000-m. Ran 13:30.4 at U.S.-USSR World All-Star meet on July 3, 1971, at Berkeley, Calif., for record. One of long line of distance men at Oregon under Coach Bill Bowerman. High school star at Marshfield High in Coos Bay with 4:06 mile, 3:49.1 in 1500-m, 13:43.0 for 3-mile, 13:52.8 in 5000-m and 8:41.6 in 2-mile that broke prep record by almost 7 seconds. At Oregon won NCAA 3-mile and Pacific-8 3-mile, along with NCAA cross country in freshman year, 1970. In 1971 won Pacific-8 mile, 3-mile; NCAA cross country and 3-mile titles. In 1972 NCAA on home track at Eugene, Oreg., won 5000-m in meet record 13:31.4. In Olympic trials ran 13:22.8 for 1st place and American record. In Munich Olympic Games ran fine race, but unable to stay with kickers. Finished 4th in 13:28.4, barely edged for bronze medal. Student at Oregon in senior year. Became first runner ever to win event 4 times when won 1973 NCAA 3-mile.

PRESS, IRINA B. 3/10/39, Russia. Member 1960, 64, USSR Olympic teams. Held womens world records in 80-m hurdles and pentathlon. Set 80-m mark with 10.3 at Moscow on Oct. 24, 1965. Had tied mark of 10.4 month earlier. In 1964 tied 10.5 world mark twice. Set pentathlon record in 1959 at Krasnadar with 4880 points. Improved mark 5 times to best of 5246 at 1964 Tokyo Olympics. Won gold medal with performance. Put shot 56′3½″, ran 10.7 in 80-m hurdles, 24.7 in 200-m, 20′5¾″ in long jump, and high jumped 5′4¼″. Won gold medal in 80-m hurdles in 1960 Rome Games with 10.8. Sister of Tamara Press, Russian weight specialist with 3 gold medals.

PRESS, TAMARA B. 5/10/37, Russia. Member 1960, 64 USSR Olympic teams. Won gold medal in womens shot put in Rome Olympics with record 56′10″. Was 2nd in discus with toss of 172′6½″. In 1964 won gold medals in both shot and discus. Upped own shot record to 59′6¼″ and set Olympic record in discus with 187′10¾″. Broke world shot record 6 times, discus mark 5 times. First broke shot record on April 26, 1959, with toss of 56′7 ¼″. Improved mark 5 times to 61′0″ on Sept. 19, 1965. First woman to pass 60′ mark. Claimed world discus record on Sept. 12, 1960, at Rome with 187′6″. Set last discus mark with 194′6″ at Moscow on May 11, 1965. Sister Irina was 1960 Olympic titlist in 80-m hurdles and 1964 Olympic pentathlon champ. Tamara winner 1963 Citizens Savings (Helms) World Trophy Award, Europe.

PRINSTEIN, MYER B. 1888. D. 3/10/28. Member 1900, 04, 06 Olympic teams. Held world long jump record with 23′8 ⅞″ in 1898. In 1900 Penn Relays, jumped 24′7 ¼″ to regain world record lost to Newburn of Ireland, then to Kraenzlein of U.S. Won 1898, 1900 IC4A for Syracuse. Was '98, '02, '06 AAU long jump champion. Won gold medal in 1900 Paris Olympics with 47′4 ¼″ in triple jump, won silver with long jump of 23′6 ½″. In 1904 St. Louis Olympics, won gold in both long jump and triple jump, 24′1″ in long jump. In 1906 Games in Athens, won gold medal in long jump. Versatile performer, competed in 400-m, 60-m and 100-m along with long jump and triple jump in Olympic competition. Member Citizens Savings (Helms) Hall of Fame.

PUTTEMANS, EMILE B. 10/8/47. Member 1968, 72 Belgian Olympic teams. Won 1972 silver medal in 10,000-m. Ran 27:39.6 behind Lasse Viren's world mark of 27:34.8. In first heat ran 27:53.4 to beat Olympic record. Also ran 5000-m, was 5th in 13:30.8. In qualifying heat set Olympic record of 13.31.8, which was smashed in finals. Holds European 3000-m mark with 7:39.8 run on Oct. 12, 1966, at Brussels. Has world 2-mile record pending with 18:17.8 run at Edinburgh on Oct. 21, 1971. Was 6th in 1971 European Championship in 5000-m, 1971 Belgian 5000-m champion in 14:01.0. Was 7th in 1969 European Championships, 12th in 1968 Mexico City Olympics 5000-m.

RAY, JOIE B. 4/13/94. Member of 1920, 24, 28 U.S. Olympic teams. Top U.S. miler in 1920s. Won AAU mile titles 1915, 17–23. Best of 4:14.4 in 1919. Won 1919 AAU 880-yd in 1:56. In 1920 Antwerp Olympics ran courageous race with leg injury and finished 8th in 1500-m. In 1923 anchored Illinois Athletic Club 4-mile relay team to world record 17:21.4. In 1924 Olympics was on U.S. 3000-m team race team that was 3rd. Ray finished 18th overall. In 1925 Ray, taxi driver, tied Paavo Nurmi's world indoor mile record of 4:12.0. In 1928 Amsterdam Olympics was 14th in 10,000-m. In marathon ran 2:36.04 and came in 5th. Gained much notoriety in dance marathons. Ran mile on birthday even in late 70s. Member Citizens Savings (Helms) Hall of Fame.

REMIGINO, LINDY B. 6/3/31, Elmhurst, N.Y. Member 1952 Olympic team. Surprise gold medalist in 100-m with 10.4. Also ran on winning U.S. 400-m relay team that ran 40.1. Standout sprinter at Manhattan College. Won IC4A 200-m in 1952 and 100-yd, 220-yd in 1953. Won 1952 Melrose Games and Knights of Columbus 60-yd. Ran on Manhattan's great 440-yd and 880-yd relay teams that won Penn and Colosseum relay titles during career. Had best time in 100-m of 10.2 at Oslo, Norway, in 1952. Best 100-yd time 9.4 at Fairfield, Conn., in 1954. Now highly successful high school track, cross country coach in Hartford Conn. Teams have won 6 state titles outdoors, 7 indoors. Teams won 48 dual meets in row.

RHODEN, GEORGE B. 12/13/26, Kingston, Jamaica. Member 1952 Jamaican Olympic team. Held world 400-m record. Ran 45.8 in Eskilstuna, Sweden, Aug. 22, 1950, to break record of countryman Herb McKenley. Came into own when went to college in U.S. at Morgan State in 1949. Won 1949 AAU 400-m with 46.4 at Fresno, Calif. Also 1950, 51 AAU champ with 46.0 in 1951. At Morgan State was NCAA 440-yd champ in 1950, 51 and 400-m champ with 46.3 in 1952. In 1952 Helsinki Olympics, Rhoden and McKenley met in 400-m finals. Battled it out with Rhoden winning by meter. Won second gold medal by anchoring Jamaica 1600-m relay team to world, Olympic record 3:03.9. Good sprinter, holding Jamaican 100-m record of 10.3. Now podiatrist in San Francisco. Member Citizens Savings (Helms) Hall of Fame.

RICHARDS, ALMA B. 2/20/90, Parowan, Utah. D. 4/3/63. Member 1912 Olympic team. Was 1913 AAU high jump champion with leap of 6′1 3/8″. Won gold medal in 1912 Stockholm Olympics over world record-holder George Horine. Set Olympic record of 6′4″. Versatile athlete. Won 1918 AAU shot put title with toss of 42′3 3/4″. Member Citizens Savings (Helms) Hall of Fame.

RICHARDS, ROBERT (Bob) B. 2/20/26, Champaign, Ill. Member 1948, 52, 56 Olympic teams. Only 2-time Olympic gold medal winner in pole vault. Personal bests 15′5″ outdoors, 15′6″ indoors. Had 126 vaults over 15′. Won or tied for nine AAU titles outdoors: 1948–52, 54–57. (ties '48, '52). Broke Warmerdam's 1942 AAU mark of 15′2 1/2″ with 15′3 1/2″ in 1954. Won 8 indoor crowns: 1948, 50–52, 54–57 (ties '52, '56). AAU record 15′4″ in 1955. Took bronze medal in 1948 London Olympics with 13′9 1/4″ vault. Won first gold medal with 1952 Helsinki vault of 14′11 1/4″. First in 1956 Melbourne Games with 14′11 1/2″. Versatile athlete. Won 1954, 55 AAU decathlon championships, best of 7313 points. Ordained minister. Called "Vaulting Vicar." Worked in national physical fitness program. Member Citizens Savings (Helms) Hall of Fame.

RICHTER, ANNEGRET B. 10/13/50, Dortmund, Germany. Member 1972 W. German Olympic team. Member W. German 400-m relay team that won gold medal, equaling world, Olympic record of 42.81. Also competed in 100-m at Munich and was 5th, timed at 11.3. First competed in W. German Championships in 1970, was 5th in 100-m at 11.5. In 1971 was 5th in 11.4, 4th in 1972 in 11.45. Has had good success competing indoors. In 1970 W. German indoor meet won 50-m in 6.4. In 1971 won 50-m in 6.3. In 1972 won 60-m in 7.2. In 1971 European indoor took 3rd in 60-m in 6.3, second in 1972 50-m in 6.2. Member W. German 400-m relay team that won 1971 European Championship. Stenographer by trade.

RITOLA, VILLE B. 1/18/96, Peräseinäjoki, Finland. Member 1924, 28 Finnish Olympic teams. Held world 10,000-m record. Ran 30:35.4 at Helsinki on May 25, 1924, to enter record books. Improved mark to 30:23.2 on July 6, 1924, at Paris Olympics, winning gold medal. Although U.S. resident, chose to compete for Finland. Also 1924 gold medalist in 3000-m steeplechase. Ran 9:33.6 for world best, although official records not kept for steeplechase. Also took silver medals in 10,000-m cross country and 5000-m behind "Flying Finn" Paavo Nurmi. In 1928 Amsterdam Olympics, defeated Nurmi in 5000-m with time of 14:38.0 for gold medal. Defeated Nurmi with comparative ease. Finished 2nd in 10,000-m behind Nurmi. In 3000-m steeplechase was favored. Tired from battle of 10,000-m and dropped out.

ROBERTSON, LAWSON (Robbie) B. 9/24/83, Aberdeen, Scotland. D. 1/22/51. Member 1904, 06 (unofficial Games), 08 U.S. Olympic teams. Coach 1924, 28, 32, 36 Olympic teams. In 1904 Olympics was 3rd in standing high jump. In 1906 at Athens, was 2nd in standing high jump, 3rd in standing long jump. Was 5th in 100-m and pentathlon. In 1908 London Olympics failed to place in 100-m, 200-m and standing high jump. Was 1904 AAU 100-yd champ in 10.4. Coach, Irish-American A. C. 1908–14, then took over at Penn where had great record. Had over 20 IC4A individual champions. One of best students was Bill Carr, who won gold medal in 1932 Olympic 400-m with world record 46.2. Robbie named head coach of 1924 U.S. Olympic team, called "greatest" by Robertson, which came back with 13 gold medals. Also coach 1928 team that had 8 golds. Team of 1932 under Robbie's guidance took 11 golds. Team took 12 gold medals in 1936 with Robertson at helm at "Nazi Olympics". Member Citizens Savings (Helms) Hall of Fame.

ROBINSON, ARNIE B. 4/7/48, San Diego, Calif. Member 1972 Olympic team. Top-rated long jumper in world in 1971. Was 4th in 1971 NCAA for San Diego State with jump of 25′ ¼″. Won AAU title the next week with jump of 26′10¾″ with wind. In U.S.-USSR World All-Star meet, won with 25′10¾″. Pan-Am Games champion with leap of 26′3¾″. In 1972, while in Army, won AAU with jump of 26′5¾″. Won Olympic trials with 26′4¾″, edging Randy Williams and Preston Carrington. In Munich Games had leap of 26′4¼″, but had to settle for bronze medal.

ROBINSON, REYNAUD B. 4/1/52, Ft. Mead, Md. Member 1972 Olympic team. Injured in 1971 but came back to make Olympic team. Won Vons Classic 100-m in 10.3, Compton Invitational in 10.3. In 100-m Olympic trials was edged by Eddie Hart for 1st. Both tied world record of 9.9. Robinson set collegiate mark with time. Ran for Florida A&M

where also played football. In semi heat ran another 9.9. In Munich Olympics ran well in first heat. Unfortunately, due to communications breakdown, missed next race, along with Hart. Did not run on 400-m relay team as Larry Black was selected to run leadoff.

ROELANTS, GASTON B. 2/5/37, Opvelp, Belgium. Member 1960, 64, 68 Belgium Olympic teams. Held world 3000-m steeplechase record. Ran 8:29.6 at Leuven, Sept. 7, 1963, to break world record. Improved to 8:26.4 on Aug. 7, 1965, at Brussels. Was 4th in 1960 Rome Olympics. Improved and took 1962 European Championships with 8:32.6 at Belgrade. Came to 1964 Tokyo Olympics with cast on leg. But when time to run came, was ready. Won gold medal with Olympic record 8:30.8. Was in lead nearly whole race. Prior to 1968 Mexico City Olympics, was bothered by knee injury. In Mexico City finals, led with 2 laps to go but could not stay in contention. Finished 7th with 8:59.4 in high altitude. Aside from steeplechase honors, holds 1-hr run world record of 20,664-m and 20,000-m with 58:06.2, both in same race at Leuven on Oct. 28, 1966. Public relations, salesman for Belgian liquor firm. Winner 1964 Citizens Savings (Helms) World Trophy Award, Europe.

ROSE, RALPH B. 3/17/84, Healdsburg, Calif. Member 1904, 08, 12 Olympic teams. Held world shot put record. threw 51′0″ at San Francisco on Aug. 21, 1909. Record stood amazing 16 years plus. Was AAU shot champ 1907–10 with best of 50.26′ in '09. Was AAU discus champ in 1905, 09 with best of 131.8′ in '09. Also won AAU javelin in '09 with 141.7′. Collected six medals in Olympic competition. In 1904 St. Louis Olympics, took gold in shot put (48′7″-world best), silver in discus (128′7 5/16″), and bronze in hammer throw (150′ 3/8″). In 1908 took gold in shot with 46′7 1/2″. In 1912 Games was very active. Won 2-handed shot put (90′10 9/16″), took silver medal in shot (50′ 2/5″), was 9th in hammer throw (139′8 7/20″), and 11th in discus (130′). Member Citizens Savings (Helms) Hall of Fame.

ROSENDAHL, HEIDEMARIE B. 2/14/47. Member 1968 German, 1972 W. German Olympic teams. Won gold medal in womens long jump, silver in pentathlon in 1972 Munich Olympics. Set Olympic mark in long jump with 22′3″. Finished 2nd to world record effort of 4801 points by Mary Peters of Great Britain with 4791. Ran anchor leg of W. German 400-m relay team that won gold medal with 42.81. In 1968 Olympics, pulled muscle while warming up for pentathlon and did not compete. Holds world long jump record. Jumped 22′5 1/4″ at Turin on Aug. 3, 1970, to set record. Versatile performer, has run 11.4 in 100-m, 23.1 in 200-m and 13.1 in 100-m hurdles. Great favorite of home fans at Munich Games. Teacher. Voted 1972 West German woman athlete of the year by W. German sports writers.

ROZSAVOLGYI, ISTVAN B. 3/30/29, Budapest, Hungary. Member 1956, 60 Hungarian Olympic teams. Held world records in 1000-m, 1500-m, 2000-m. Set 1000-m record of 2:19.0 at Tata, Sept. 21, 1955. Ran 3:40.6, Sept 3, 1956 for 1500-m record, also at Tata. Broke Gaston Reif's 7-year record in 2000-m by 4.8 seconds with 5:02.2 at Budapest on Oct. 2, 1955. Mark stood 7 years. In 1956 Melbourne Olympics, did not make finals. Had been timed around 3:41.0 just before Games. Like other Hungarians, upset by political troubles in country and not at best. In 1960 Rome Olympics, won bronze medal behind Herb Elliot and Michel Jazy. Ran 3:39.2.

RUDENKOV, VASILY B. 5/3/31, Zhobin, USSR. Member 1960 Russian Olympic team. In 1960 Rome Olympics, American Hal Connolly was favored in hammer throw but Rudenkov scored big upset. Rudenkov threw 220′1⅝″ to shatter Olympic mark of 207′3½″ set by Connolly. Held Russian record with toss of 226′2½″. Twice victor in USSR-U.S. dual meets. Won in 1956 with throw of 219′ to defeat Connolly. In 1960 meet took 1st at 217′7¾″ with teammate Bakrinin 2nd.

RUDOLPH, WILMA B. 6/23/40, St. Bethlehem, Tenn. Member 1956, 60 Olympic teams. Held womens world records in 100-m, 200-m and anchored 2 world record 400-m relay team. Tied 100-m record in prelim heat of 1960 Rome Olympics with 11.3. In 1961 on July 21, in Stuttgart, ran 11.2 to lower mark. Blasted 200-m world mark by 0.3 with 22.9 at Corpus Christi July 9, in 1960 AAU. In 1960 Olympics became first American woman to win both sprint gold medals. In 100-m, after tying world mark, ran 11.0 with wind, nullifying it as record. In 200-m set Olympic record of 23.2 in prelims. Won gold medal with 24.0 against strong wind. Anchored U.S. 400-m relay team to world record of 44.5 for gold medal. Became only American woman to win 3 gold medals. Member U.S. 400-m relay team in 1956 that won bronze medal. Was AAU 100-yd champion 1959–62. Ran 10.8 in 1961, 62. Also won 1960 200-m in 22.9 for world record. Had double pneumonia and scarlet fever at an early age, did not walk without braces until age 11. As school girl in Clarksville, Tenn., became star basketball player and unbeaten sprinter. Went to Tenn State in hometown and became world best under coaching of Ed Temple, who also coached her in 1960 Olympics. Member Citizens Savings (Helms) Hall of Fame. Winner 1960 Helms World Trophy Award, N. America. Assistant director of athletics for Mayor Daley's Youth Foundation in Chicago.

RYAN, PATRICK (Pat) B. 1/4/87, Pallasgreen, County Limerick, Ireland. Member 1920 Olympic team. Held world hammer throw record with 189′6″ on Aug. 17, 1913, in New York. Beat record by 2′2½″.

Record stood 25 years. Dominated U.S. competition in hammer for nearly 10 years. Was AAU titlist 1913–17, 19–21. Meet record of 183′3¾″ in 1914 stood 36 years. Was AAU 56-lb weight throw champ in 1912, 17. Fellow Irish-American Matt McGrath was chief rival for many years. Ryan broke McGrath's world mark of 187′4″ with his record toss. Competed in 1920 Olympics in hammer and weight throw. Took gold medal in hammer with 173′5½″, silver medal in 56-lb weight throw. Performances in hammer throw said to have been years ahead of time. Was New York City policeman. Member Citizens Savings (Helms) Hall of Fame.

RYUN, JAMES (Jim) B. 4/29/47, Wichita, Kans. Member 1964, 68, 72 Olympic teams. Holds world 880-yd, mile and 1500-m records. Ran 1:44.9 at Terre Haute, Ind., June 10, 1966, to break 880-yd record. In 1966 ran 3:51.3 mile at Berkeley Calif., on July 17 to set mile record. On June 23, 1967, ran 3:51.1 at Bakersfield, Calif., to break own mile record. Same year ran 3:33.1 in 1500-m at Los Angeles on July 8, to break world mark. Won 1967 NCAA mile for Kansas in 4:03.5. Was AAU mile champion 1965–67. Set world mark in 1967. In 1964 Olympics, still high school student at Wichita East, made U.S. Olympic team. Advanced to semifinals of 1500-m but ran 3:55.0 and did not qualify. Ill at time of semis. In 1968, after missing most of season because of mononucleosis, made Olympic team in 1500-m. In high altitude of Mexico City, finished 2nd to Kipchoge Keino of Kenya, who set Olympic record of 3:34.9. Ryun's silver medal, although considered failure by many, was remarkable considering June illness. Retired in 1969 after disappointing season. Came back in 1972 and had both good and bad outings. Ran 3:52.8 mile for best, 4:19 for worst. In Olympic trials ran 3:41.5 to win 1500-m and place on U.S. team. Did not qualify in 800-m. In Munich Olympics, fell in qualifying heat and was out of Games. Appeals to have him reinstated were rejected. Winner 1966 Citizens Savings (Helms) World Trophy Award, N. America. Turned pro 1973.

SALING, GEORGE B. 7/24/09, Memphis, Mo. D. 4/15/33. Co-held world 110-m hurdles record. Ran 14.4 in semi heat of 1932 Los Angeles Olympics on Aug. 2. Time also good for Olympic record by .4 second. In finals ran winning 14.6, despite knocking down last hurdle. In 1932, running for Iowa, ran 14.2 in NCAA finals for collegiate title. No wind factor, but time never made world record books. Took AAU 220-yd low hurdles title with 23.6. Ran 14.4 in 1932 Drake Relays for American collegiate and American records. Corydon, Iowa, athlete's life ended tragically in a car accident near Troy, Mo., year after Olympic triumph. Fine all-round hurdler with 22.8 best in 220 lows, 52.1 in 400-m.

SALMINEN, ILMARI B. 9/21/02. Member 1936 Finnish Olympic team. Held world 6-mile, 10,000-m records. Ran 29:08.4 at Kouvala on July 18, 1932, for 6-mile mark. Set 10,000-m mark in same race with 30:05.06 to break Paavo Nurmi's record. In 1936 Berlin Olympics, won gold medal in 10,000-m. Ran 30:15.4 to lead a 1–2–3 sweep by Finns. Congratulated by Hitler following win. European 10,000-m champion 1934, 38. Ran 31:02.6 for 1934 crown, 30:52.4 in 1938. Formerly sergeant in military, now retired.

SANEYEV, VIKTOR B. 10/3/45. Member 1968, 72 USSR Olympic teams. Won gold medals in triple jump in 1968, 72. Set world record in 1968 Mexico City Olympics with hop-step-jump of 57′¾″. In 1972 Munich Olympics, went 56′11″ with wind for gold. Owns 8 of world's top 12 jumps. Set world mark first at 1968 Olympics with 56′6¼″, but lost it in same meet. Came back to break mark on last jump to win gold medal. Was 2nd in 1971 European Championships at 56′1¾″. On Oct. 17, 1972, regained world record had lost in 1971. Jumped 57′2¾″ at hometown of Sukhumi for world mark. Following 2nd gold medal, was awarded Order of Lenin, one of highest honors given to Russian citizens.

SANTEE, WES B. 3/25/32, Ashland, Kans. Member 1952 Olympic team. In 1950s was called America's greatest miler. Set 1500-m world record with 3:42.8 at Compton, Calif., June 4, 1954. Ran 4:00.6 mile in same race to lower American record. First set American record with 4:02.4 in 1952. Competed in 1952 Helsinki Olympic 5000-m but did not qualify for finals. Won 1953 NCAA mile for Kansas with record-shattering 4:03.7. Member 1955 Pan-Am Games team and won silver medal in 1500-m. Mile champion in 1953, 55 AAU. Took 1st in 1952 AAU 1500-m. Won 1955 AAU indoor with record 4:07.9. Ran 4:00.5 at Austin, Tex., April 2, 1955, for personal best. Had run 4:00.7 on June 11, 1954, at Los Angeles. Ran 1:47.8 in 800-m for personal best at that distance. Banned by AAU for expense money violations in 1955 at age 23. Considering age and performances, could have been greatest of all time with career of normal length.

SCHMIDT, BILL B. 12/29/47. Member 1972 U.S. Olympic team. Became first U.S. Olympian since 1952 to win medal in javelin. Came through with toss of 276′11½″ for bronze medal. Won medal on second throw. Tossed 275′11½″ on fifth throw. Made finals by finishing in top 12. Did not surpass qualifying distance of 262′5½″. Qualified tenth with 259′½″. As student at North Texas State, was 2nd in 1970 NCAA. Same year set Missouri Valley Conference record with toss of 265′6″. In 1971 won World Military Games (CISM) with toss of 270′ at Turku, Finland. Was 4th in 1972 AAU at 256′2″. Took 1st at U.S. Olympic trials with 270′6″. Career best 280′7″.

SCHMIDT, JOZEF B. 3/28/35, Miechowice, Poland. Member 1960, 64, 68 Polish Olympic teams. Held world triple jump record. Hopped, stepped and jumped 55′10½″ at Olsztyn on Aug. 5, 1960. Jump still good for Polish record. Won 1958 European Championships, defeating world record-holder Ryakhovskiy of Russia in first big win. Before 1960 Olympics made world record jump in Polish Championships. Had hop of 19′8¼″, step of 16′5¾″ and jump of 19′8½″. In 1960 Rome Games shattered Olympic record with 55′1¾″ for gold medal. Jump was his 3rd best ever. Won 1962 European Championships on last jump with 54′3½″. In 1964 Tokyo Olympics won 2nd gold medal with leap of 55′3½″ to break own Olympic record. Won World Games in 1968 prior to Olympics with 54′3½″. In Olympics jumped 55′5″ to again beat

Olympic mark. Despite jump, finished in 7th place. Viktor Saneyev of Russia won with world mark 57′0¾″. Won 1970 Polish Championships with 54′2¾″ on Aug. 9, at Warsaw.

SCHMIDT, KATHY B. 12/29/53, Long Beach, Calif. Member 1972 Olympic team. Won bronze medal in 1972 Munich Games. Threw javelin 196′8″ for medal. Was 1969 AAU champion with toss of 177′4″. Was 1968, 69 AAU champion. Member 1969 U.S. international team. Did not compete in 1971, but in 1972 came back. Threw 197′9″ in Olympic trials to win place on team. Had illegal throw of over 200′ prior to Olympics. Was 3rd in 1972 AAU. Set American womens record with 205′6″ on March 3, 1973. Set American record of 208′1″ at Kennedy Games at Berkeley, June 2, 1973. Was 3rd record of year.

SCHOLZ, JACKSON B. 3/15/97, Buchanan, Mich. Member 1920, 24, 28 Olympic teams. Co-held world 100-m record. Ran 10.2 on Sept. 6, 1920, at Stockholm. In 1920 Olympics ran 2nd leg on U.S. 400-m relay team that won gold medal. Charles Paddock, Scholz, Loren Murchison and Morris Kirksey ran 42.2, good for world, Olympic record. Was 4th in 100-m. In 1924 Paris Olympics won gold medal in 200-m over Paddock in 21.6, equaling Olympic record. Finished 2nd to Harold Abrahams of Britain in 100-m. In 1928 Amsterdam Olympics, was 4th in 200-m, being barely edged out by Helmut Koernig of Germany. Competed for New York Athletic Club. Freelance writer. Member Citizens Savings (Helms) Hall of Fame.

SCHUL, BOB B. 9/28/37, West Milton, Ohio. Member 1964 Olympic team. Held world 2-mile record. Ran 8:26.4 at Los Angeles on Aug. 29, 1964, to smash Michel Jazy's mark by 2.4. Big year was 1964. Besides world record, set American and American collegiate records in 3-mile and 5000-m. Set marks at Compton Invitational on June 5 with 13:15.6 for 3-mile, 13:38.0 in 5000-m. Competed for Miami of Ohio. Won bronze medal in 1963 Pan-Am Games 5000-m with 14:29.2. Was 1964, 65 AAU 5000-m, 3-mile champion. Ran 13:56.2 in 1964 and 13:10.4 in 1965. Took 1st in U.S.-USSR dual meet in 1964 L.A. with 14:12.4 in 5000-m. Was 2nd in 1965 U.S.-USSR dual at Kiev with 13:54.4 in 5000-m. In 1964 Tokyo Olympics, was contender in 5000-m. No American had ever won gold medal in that event, but Schul was confident. In finals held back until last lap. Caught Jazy of France on home stretch and won gold medal with 13:48.8.

SCHULE, FREDRICK B. 9/27/84, Preston, Iowa. Member 1904 Olympic team. Won gold medal in 110-m hurdles in St. Louis Olympics. Ran 16.0 for gold, one of 21 (out of possible 22) won by U.S. Was 1903 AAU champion with 16.6.

SEAGREN, BOB B. 10/17/46, Fullerton, Calif. Member 1968, 72 Olympic teams. Holds world pole vault record. Vaulted 18′4 ¼″ on May 23, 1972, at El Paso, Tex. First American to jump 18′. First captured world mark in 1966 with vault of 17′5 ½″ at Fresno, Calif., on May 14. Upped mark to 17′7″ at San Diego, Calif., June 10, 1967, after losing mark to John Pennel. Lost mark to Paul Wilson 13 days later by ¾″. In 1968 U.S. Olympic trials at South Lake Tahoe, Calif., on Sept 12, went 17′9″ for record. Lost record again for 3 years before El Paso vault. Was 1967 Pan-Am champion with 16′7″. In 1968 Olympics at Mexico City, didn't vault until bar was at 16′6 ¾″. Made that height, then passed at 16′8 ¾″ and 16′10 ¾″. Made 17′ ¾″ on second try. Passed at 17′6 ¾″ in big gamble. Made 17′8 ½″ on second try to win gold medal on fewest misses. Claus Schiprowski of West Germany was 2nd, Wolfgang Nordwig of East Germany 3rd. Won 1969 AAU with 17′7 ½″ and 1970 AAU at 17′2″. Was NCAA champion for Southern Cal in 1967 at 17′4″, in 1969 at 17′7″. Injured much of 1970, 71. Injured knee and was operated on in fall of 1971. Trained hard and finally regained world record in magnificent comeback. Made U.S. Olympic team in 1972 with world best of 18′5 ¾″. In controversial ruling, IAAF banned carbon pole used by Seagren for Olympic Games. Pole was ruled legal, then banned again over protests said to have come from Nordwig. Using unfamiliar pole went 17′8 ½″, but didn't clear 17′10 ½″ and had to settle for silver medal. Nordwig won competition at 18′ ½″. Seagren presented pole to IAAF following event. Now an actor. Turned pro 1973.

SEFTON, WILLIAM B. 1/21/15, Los Angeles, Calif. Member 1936 Olympic team. Co-held world pole vault record with college teammate Earle Meadows. "Heavenly Twins" from Southern Cal both vaulted 14′11″ at Pacific Coast Conference meet in L.A. on May 29, 1937. Sefton won meet gold medal on fewest misses. High-vaulting twosome tied for 1935 AAU with 13′10 ⅜″. Tied for 1935 NCAA at 14′1 ⅛″ and 1936 NCAA at 14′1 ¾″. In 1937 Sefton took NCAA honors with 14′8 ⅞″. Meadows was 3rd at 14′4 ⅞″. In 1937 AAU, won on fewer misses over Cornelius Warmerdam, Meadows and George Varoff at 14′7 ⅝″. Made 1936 Olympic team as did Meadows, but was 4th. Meadows took gold medal with Olympic record 14′3″. Retired from competition in 1937 with much potential left untapped.

SEXTON, LEO B. 8/27/09, Danvers, Mass. D. 9/6/68, Perry, Okla. Member 1932 Olympic team. Won gold medal in shot put in Los Angeles Olympics. Set Olympic record with toss of 52′6 $^{3}/_{16}$″. Set world record with put of 53′ ½″ at Freeport, N.Y., on Aug. 27, 1932. Won 1932 AAU with 52′8″, meet record. Honor student at Georgetown. Was 6′4″, 240-lbs in prime. Also competed for New York Athletic Club. Insurance executive at time of death.

SHAVLAKADZE, ROBERT B. 4/1/33, Tbilisi, USSR. Member 1960, 64 USSR Olympic teams. Came into own as world class high jumper at age 25 with 6′10¼″ in 1958. Ready for meeting with John Thomas in 1960 Rome Olympics. In Games Shavlakadze was first to clear 7′1″. Thomas failed 3 times. Teammate Valery Brumel made height on 2nd try. Shavlakadze won gold medal on fewest misses, Brumel 2nd and world record-holder Thomas 3rd. Win considered one of track's greatest upsets. In 1964 USSR Championships, defeated Brumel, who developed into world record-holder, with 7′1½″. In 1964 Tokyo Olympics failed at 7′1″ and had to settle for 5th place. Phys. ed. instructor, wrote thesis *Stability in Results in the High Jump*. Winner in 1959 USSR-U.S. meet with jump of 6′9″.

SHELTON, ERNIE B. 9/28/32, Chanute, Kans. Member 1955 Pan-Am team. Top high jumper in mid-1950s. Was 6′5⅛″ high jumper at Los Angeles' George Washington High School in 1951. Improved to 6′7⅛″ as freshman at L.A. Valley College. Transferred to Southern Cal for remainder of college career. As Trojan, made mark as high jumper. As soph jumped 6′10⅛″, vast improvement in two short years. In 1954 set collegiate record with leap of 6′11⅛″. Also won NCAA crown at 6′10¼″. In same year was AAU outdoor champ at 6′9¾″. In 1955 raised collegiate mark to 6′11¼″ and was NCAA champ with 6′11⅛″. Was AAU indoor co-champ with 6′8¾″ and outdoor co-champ with 6′10″ leap. In collegiate career became known as one of most consistent performers in track history. Won 60 straight meets. Took gold medal in 1955 Pan-Am Games with jump of 6′7⅛″. Thought to be man who would break 7′ barrier. But in 1956 was plagued by injury. Failed to make Olympic team and Charlie Dumas became first 7′ jumper. Shelton now says greatest thrill never really came; that he considers his athletic career a failure as it ended "on such a sour note." Looking back on his performances, track historians beg to differ. He does consider his travels as trackman his greatest thrill. Now sculptor and instructor at L.A. Valley College. Regarded by critics as one of leading young U.S. sculptors. One of his works is 7′ statue of Amelia Earhart, which stands on corner of Tujunga Ave. and Magnolia Blvd. in North Hollywood, Calif.

SHEPPARD, MELVIN B. 9/5/83, Almonesson Lake, N.J. Member 1908, 12 Olympic teams. Held world records in 800-m with 1:52.8 and 1500-m with 4:03.4, both set in 1908 London Olympics, where became first man to win gold medal in both events. Also ran on gold medal 1600-m relay team. Won AAU 800-m titles 1906–8, 11, 12. At Stockholm Olympics in 1912, was not as fortunate as in 1908. Did not place in 400-m, 6th in 1500-m and 2nd in 800-m. Time for 800-m was 1:52.0. Did get gold medal for leg on Olympic, world record-setting 1600-m relay team clocked in 3:16.6. Had run on world record U.S. national two-mile relay team in 1910, mile relay in 1911, and 1600-m relay team in 1911. Member Citizens Savings (Helms) Hall of Fame.

SHERIDAN, MARTIN B. 1871, County Mayo, Ireland. Member 1904, 06, 08 U.S. Olympic teams. Versatile weightman who won 5 Olympic gold medals. In 1904 Games at St. Louis, won discus with throw of 128′10″. Was 4th in shot with put of 42′. In 1906 unofficial Games at Athens, was busy performer. Won shot with put of 40′4 4/5″ and discus with toss of 137′. Won silver medals in 56-lb weight throw, standing long jump and high jumps. Also competed in Greco-Roman wrestling in 1906. In 1908 London Olympics, won both regular discus (134′2″) and "Greek Style" discus (124′8″). Won bronze medal in standing long jump. Held unofficial world record in discus for 10 years. Had mark of 120′7 3/4″ in 1901 which he improved to 141′4 3/8″ in 1911. Won AAU shot crown in 1904 with 40′9 1/2″, discus crown in '06, '07, '11 with best of 133′9 1/2″ in 1911. Member Citizens Savings (Helms) Hall of Fame.

SHILEY, JEAN B. 11/20/11, Harrisburg, Pa. Member 1928, 32 Olympic teams. Won gold medal in 1932 Olympics in womens high jump at 5′5″. Set world high jump record with leap. Babe Didrikson also jumped 5′5″, but Shiley won jump-off. In 1928 Olympics was 4th with jump of 4′11 1/2″. Was AAU high jump champion 4 times, 1929–32. Went 5′3 1/2″ for best in AAU competition. Now housewife in Los Angeles. Member Citizens Savings (Helms) Hall of Fame.

SHORTER, FRANK B. 10/31/47, Munich, Germany. Member 1972 U.S. Olympic team. In 1969 won first major championship, NCAA 6-mile, running for Yale, in 29:00.2. In 1970 tied with Florida Track Club teammate Jack Bacheler for 1st in AAU 6-mile in 27:24.0. Won 3-mile in AAU indoor with 13:10.6. Took AAU 6-mile outdoors in 1971 with 27:27.2 time. Named 1970 outdoor AAU Most Outstanding Performer. Named Most Outstanding in 1971 indoor meet. In 1971 Pan-Am Games won 10,000-m in Games record 28:50.8, marathon in 2:22.40. At 1972 Olympic trials won spot in 10,000-m with winning 28:35.6. Also took 1st in marathon, along with Ken Moore, in 2:15:57.8. In 1972 Munich Olympics, "warmed up" for marathon with 10,000-m. Was 5th with 27:51.4 in what has been called greatest 10,000-m. On last day of Olympics won marathon in his birthplace. Ran 2:12:19.8 for gold medal. Won 1972 Sullivan Award as AAU Athlete of Year. Named World Athlete of Year by *Track & Field News*. Also U.S. Athlete of Year.

SHRUBB, ALFRED B. 12/12/78, Slinfold, Sussex, England. Held several long distance records. One of first great distance men. First record came in 3-mile with 14:17.6 in London on May 21, 1903. Set 2-mile mark with 9:09.6 on June 11, 1904. On Nov. 5, 1904, had remarkable day. Set 6-mile, 10-mile, 1-hr marks. Ran 29:59.4, 50:40.6, and 11 miles, 1137 yards to better world records in 3 events, respectively. Won 10 British AAA titles in events ranging from mile to 10 miles from 1901–04. Suspended from amateur ranks in 1904. Ran as pro for years. Once ran against a relay team of men and horses over 10 miles and won.

SIDLO, JANUSZ B. 6/19/33, Szopienice, Poland. Member 1952, 56, 60, 64, 68 Polish Olympic teams. Held world javelin record. Tossed spear 274′5″ on June 30, 1956, at Milan. Twice European champion. Won in 1954 at Berne with throw of 250′6″ and in 1958 Stockholm with 263′0½″. In 1952 Olympics failed to qualify, but in 1956 was favored. Led at end of semifinal round with 262′4½″. In final, lost world record and gold medal to Egil Danielsen of Norway. Won silver medal with semi best. In 1960 Rome Olympics had throw of 279′4″ in qualifying, but in competition was 8th with 250′10″. Co-favorite in 1964 Tokyo Olympics. Led after first round with 263′. Then fouled 3 times, had 2 lesser throws and finished 4th. In 1968 Mexico City Olympics was 7th with best of 264′3½″. Ranked first 5 times in long career, although never won major title. Had career-best 280′6″ in 1956.

SILVESTER, JAY B. 8/27/37, Tremonton, Utah. Member 1964, 68, 72 Olympic teams. Holds world discus mark. Threw disc 224′5″, Sept. 18, 1965, at Reno, Nev., to improve his old mark by over 6′. His first world record was 198′8″ on Aug. 11, 1961, at Frankfurt, Germany. Improved mark to 199′2″ nine days later at Brussels. Lost mark to Al Oerter, but regained it after Ludvik Danek had taken Oerter's place as record-holder. Had toss of 218′4″ at Modesto, Calif., on May 25, 1968. In 1961 took AAU title with throw of 195′8″. Won 1963 AAU with 198′11½″. In 1968 won another AAU crown with throw of 203′9″. Won 1970 AAU title with meet record 205′4″. In 1964 Rome Olympics was 4th with throw of 195′10½″. In 1968 Mexico City Games was 5th with 198′3½″. In 1971 competed often and was defeated only once. Had throws of 230′11″ and 229′9½″ as pending world records. In 1972 won AAU with 213′ and Olympic trials with 211′2″. In 1972 Munich Olympics came in 2nd behind Danek with throw of 208′4″. Now phys. ed. instructor at Brigham Young.

SIME, DAVE B. 7/25/36, Paterson, N.J. Member 1960 Olympic team. Held world 100-yd dash, 220-yd and 200-m dash and low hurdle records. Set American indoor 100-yd record in 1956 with 9.5 time. In same year set world marks. Ran 9.3 twice, 9.4 six times in 100-yd; 20.2, 20.3 both twice in 220. World 100-yd mark of 9.3, 220-yd and 200-m of 20.0, and 220-yd and 200-m hurdles in 22.2, all set in 1956. Running for Duke. Defeated by great Bobby Morrow in NCAA 100-m in 1956 and pulled muscle in 200-m. Injury cost spot on Olympic team. Came back and made 1960 Olympic team. Took silver medal in 100-m despite great diving finish. Hary of Germany took gold with both Sime and Hary timed in 10.2. Never won major title, but had great times. In 1971 at Miami, Fla., ran 9.6 at age 36. Surgeon in Miami.

SMITH, JOHN WALTON B. 8/5/50, Los Angeles, Calif. Member 1972 Olympic team. Top 400-m, 440-yd man in 1971, but plagued by injury and illness in 1972. Won 1971 NCAA 440-yd while at UCLA with 45.3. Next week ran 44.5 to break world record in 440-yd for AAU title. In World Games ran 45.7 for 400-m title. Ran 45.7 in 400-m for 1st place in U.S.-Africa meet. Won gold medal in Pan-Am Games in 44.6. Had 400-m best of 44.2 in 1971. Won 1970 AAU title in 45.7. Suffered severe case of hepatitis and mononucleosis late 1971, but came back for 1972 outdoor season. Won 1972 NCAA 400-m in 44.5 for his best time. In Olympic trials ran 2nd to Wayne Collett, timed in 44.3. In Munich Olympics made finals, despite pulled muscle. In finals pulled up lame.

SMITH, OWEN GUINN B. 5/20/20, McKinney, Tex. Member 1948 Olympic team. Won gold medal in pole vault. Vaulted 14′1¼″ despite torn cartilage in knee. Was 28 at time of Olympic triumph. Was 18-month veteran of combat flying in Army Air Force. Was 1942 graduate of California. While at Cal, won 1941 NCAA title. Went 14′2″ to tie Hunt of Nebraska for title. Same year won Pacific Coast Conference, West Coast Relays and Big 10-PCC dual meet titles. In 1940 set Cal record of 14′4½″. Upped mark to 14′6⅜″, which stood 25 years. President of Boston Company of Pacific, investment firm in San Francisco.

SMITH, STEVE B. 11/24/51, Long Beach, Calif. Member 1972 U.S. Olympic team. Broke own world indoor pole vault record with jump of 18′¼″ at Milrose Games in New York's Madison Square Garden on Jan. 26, 1973. First to go 18′ indoors. Jumped 17′11″week before in Los Angeles to claim record. Won 1973 AAU indoor at 17′8″. Was 1972 indoor champ. In final U.S. Olympic trials in 1972, vaulted 18′½″to finish 2nd to Bob Seagren's 18′5¾″. Only his 2nd meet in 14 weeks due to groin injury. At Munich Olympics, in heat of pole controversy, went out at 16′5″ and did not qualify for starting height. Student, competes for Pacific Coast Club.

SMITH, TOMMIE B. 6/5/44, Clarksville, Tex. Member 1968 Olympic team. Holds world 200-m (straightaway), 200-m (turn) and both 220-yd world records. First put name into record book in 1965 with 20.0 in 200-m (straight) at San Jose, Calif., on March 13. Bettered with fantastic 19.5 at San Jose, July 15, 1966. Time was also good for 220-yd record. Set both 200-m and 220-yd (turn) records at Sacramento, Calif., on June 11, 1966, with 20.0. Was 1967, 68 AAU champion in 220-yd and 200-m, respectively. Won 1967 NCAA for San Jose State with meet record 20.2 in 220-yd. Top-ranked 200-m, 220-yd man in world in 1967, 68, according to *Track & Field News.* In 1968 Mexico City Olympics got world attention on and off track. Ran 20.2 in 200-m semis, but was suffering from leg cramps. In final was wrapped in tape from waist to edge of shorts. Was 2nd going into final straightaway. Turned on incomparable speed in stretch and took lead in final 60 meters. At finish, threw his arms up in elation. May have cost him time, but ran 19.8 for world, Olympic record. On award stand Smith and John Carlos, who was 3rd, lowered heads and raised black gloved fists during National Anthem. Both expelled from Games for controversial protest of U.S. racial discrimination. Protest approved by some, scorned by many.

SMITHSON, FORREST B. 1885. Member 1908 U.S. Olympic team. Won gold medal in London Olympics in 110-m hurdles, leading 1–2–3-U.S. sweep. Timed in 15.0, world and Olympic record for both 110-m and 120-yd. Was 1907 AAU 120-yd hurdle champ in 15.6. Won AAU again in 1909 with 15.1.

SNELL, PETER B. 12/17/38, Opunake, New Zealand. Member 1960, 64 New Zealand Olympic teams. Held world mile, 880-yd, 800-m records. Set 800-m and 880-yd marks on Feb. 3, 1962, at Christchurch, New Zealand: 1:44.3 in 800-m, 1:45.1 in 880-yd. Shattered records by well over second. Surprised track world at 1960 Rome Games by defeating world record-holder Moens of Belgium in 800-m. Time of 1:46.3 bettered Olympic mark and was 2 seconds faster than pre-Olympic best. Developed into world's best miler after 1960 Olympics. Ran world record mile at Wangonui, Jan. 27, 1962, with 3:54.4. At 1964 Tokyo Olympics, Snell became first man in 44 years to win 800-m and 1500-m in same Olympics. Won 800-m easily in 1:45.1, Olympic record. In 6th race in 8 days, won 1500-m in 3:38.1. Ran 52.9 final lap to win by 10 yards. Winner 1960 Citizens Savings (Helms) World Trophy Award, Australasia.

SNYDER, LARRY B. 8/9/96, Canton, Ohio. Head coach 1960 U.S. mens Olympic team. Won 8 gold medals under his guidance. Head track coach at Ohio State 1932–65. Three of greatest students were Jesse Owens, Mal Whitfield and Glenn Davis. Owens won 4 gold medals and set 4 Olympic records in 1936 Olympics. Also set 4 world records in career. Davis won three gold medals in two Olympics (1956, 60) and set 3 world records. Whitfield won 3 gold, 1 silver medal in Olympics of 1948, 52. Also set 880-yd world record twice. Snyder's athletes set 14 world records. Coached 52 All-Americans in long, successful career. Long association with track and field began in 1914 when convinced Canton High baseball team to switch to track. Won Ohio state high school high jump title in 1915. Entered Ohio State in 1917, but left to enter service in WW I. Was pilot instructor. Returned to OSU in 1923 after barnstorming and managing grocery store in California. Captained Buckeye track team in 1924, 25. Best day as competitor was at Penn Relays in 1925. Won triple jump, 120-yd hurdles, was 2nd in broad jump and 440-yd hurdles behind Lord Burghley, who set world mark two years later. Was 2nd in 1925 NCAA 120-yd hurdles. Retired in 1965 "after a wonderful life in a sport that I loved." Member Citizens Savings (Helms) Hall of Fame.

SOWELL, ARNOLD (Arnie) B. 4/6/35, Pittsburgh, Pa. Member 1956 Olympic team. Outstanding 880-yd runner. One of favorites in 1956 Olympic 800-m. Took 1955 AAU title with 1:47.6. In 1956 won NCAA 800-m for Pitt at 1:47.6. Then won AAU with 1:47.6. Had mastery over Tom Courtney until 1956 Olympic trials. Courtney won with blazing finish in time of 1:46.4. Sowell was second with 1:46.9. In Melbourne Olympic 800-m final, Sowell took lead at 150 meters. Sowell and Courtney were even going into stretch when Courtney took over. Courtney won with second stretch drive near finish. Sowell, who had tried to outrun field early, faded to 4th place. Great collegiate star at Pitt. Won NCAA 880 in 1954, 56. Was IC4A 880-yd champ 1954–56. Also IC4A indoor champ at 1000-yds. Member U.S. team that set world 2-mile relay record of 7:23.0 in Sydney, Australia, on Dec. 5, 1956. Member Citizens Savings (Helms) Hall of Fame.

STANFIELD, ANDREW (Andy) B. 12/29/27, Washington, D. C. Member 1952, 56 Olympic teams. Held world 200-m, 220-yd (both on turn) records. Timed in 20.6 at both distances on May 5, 1951, in Philadelphia. Ran 20.6 at 1952 Olympic trials at Los Angeles, June 28, 1952, to tie own mark. Had to pass up 100-m because of chronic leg injuries, and concentrate on 200-m. In Helsinki Olympic 200-m finals, took gold medal and equaled Jesse Owens' Olympic mark of 20.7. Also anchored U.S. 400-m relay team to gold medal by 4 yards. Made 1956 Olympic team in 200-m and finished yard behind gold medal winner Bobby Morrow. Morrow broke mark of Owens and Stanfield with 20.6. Had 4 AAU titles in career. Took 100-m and 200-m in 1949 with 10.3 and 20.4 (wind aided), respectively. Was 200-m champ in 1952, 53. At Seton Hall dominated eastern collegiate sprint scene. Won IC4A 100 and 220-yd titles in 1949, 51. Took 100-yd crown in 1950 with wind-aided 9.6. Was IC4A indoor champ at 60-yd 1949–51. Ran on U.S. 880-yd, 800-m relay team that set world records of 1:23.8 in 1956 at Sydney, Australia. Member Citizens Savings (Helms) Hall of Fame.

STEELE, WILLIE B. 7/14/23, Seeley, Calif. Member 1948 Olympic team. Probably top long jumper of 1940s. In 1942 jumped 25′7 ¼″before going in service during WW II. Following stint in Army, returned to athletics at San Diego State. In 1947 at NCAA championships, came close to Jesse Owens' record with winning 26′6″leap. Took AAU title same year, as had in 1946. Was NCAA titlist in 1948 also. Although hampered by injuries, took gold medal in 1948 Helsinki Olympic Games. Winning jump of 25′8 ¼″was 3rd-best in Olympic history behind great Owens and Germany's Luz Long, who finished 2nd to Owens in 1936 Games.

STEERS, LESTER (Les) B. 6/16/17, Eureka, Calif. Held world high jump record with 6′11″on June 17, 1941, at Los Angeles. Record stood 12 years. Had great 1941 season. Won NCAA title for Oregon with 6′10⅞″in 1941. Jumped 6′10¾″in Seattle meet and was over 6′10″in 6 meets for year. Lost 1941 AAU on misses. Won first national title in 1938 indoor championship when tied with 3 others at 6′6″. Took 1939 AAU with 6′8⅛″leap. Won again in 1940 with 6′8¾″. Had perfected straddle style to high degree. Could have been first 7′ jumper if competition not stopped by war. Made 7′ in practice once. Member Citizens Savings (Helms) Hall of Fame.

STEPHENS, HELEN B. 2/3/18, Fulton, Mo. Member 1936 Olympic team. Great sprinter in mid-1930s. Won AAU 100-m in 1935 in 11.6, in 1936 with 11.7. Won 1935 AAU 200-m at 24.6. In 1936 Berlin Olympics took 2 gold medals. Ran 11.5 in 100-m for 1st gold medal. Ran on winning U.S. 400-m relay team. Also competed in javelin and was 10th with toss of 112′7½″. Had been 1936 AAU javelin champion at 121′6½″. Member Citizens Savings (Helms) Hall of Fame. Now librarian.

STERNBERG, BRIAN B. 6/21/43, Seattle, Wash. Held world pole vault record. Broke mark of 16′2½″by Pentti Mikula of Finland with

16′5″vault at Philadelphia on April 27, 1963. Advanced official standard to 16′8″ on June 7, 1963, at Compton, Calif., Relays. Had vault of 16′7″at Modesto, Calif., May 25, 1963. Won 1963 NCAA for Washington with record 16′4¾″. Won 1963 AAU in St. Louis on June 21, 1963, his 20th birthday, with meet record 16′4″. On July 2, 1963, career came to tragic end. Also one of nation's best trampolinists, was injured while working out. Fell from 14 feet on back of head and neck; was paralyzed from neck down. Gymnastic letterman at Washington and had performed stunt, double somersault with twist, several times. Used tramp as training for pole vault. Did not feel fiberglass poles were true test of vaulting. Said several times Don Bragg, steel pole record-holder, was still man with record. With fiberglass pole went from 12′in 1960 to 14′3¾″in 1961 to world junior best of 15′8″. Winner 1963 Citizens Savings (Helms) World Trophy Award, N. America.

STOCK, GERHARD B. 7/28/10. Member 1936 German Olympic team. Won gold medal in 1936 Berlin Olympics in javelin. Had throw of 235′8 13/32″ to defeat world record-holder Matti Jarvinen. Won bronze medal in shot put with toss of 51′4½″. Despite gold medal in javelin, won only 1 German title in that event. In 1938, on his birthday, won title with throw of just over 228′. Silver medalist in shot in 1938 European Championships. Had best of 242′8″ in javelin, 54′1″ in shot and 153′5″ in discus. Excellent decathlete, nearly won 1935 German title. But did not make first height in pole vault and did not get any points in event. Has been executive director of athletic office of Hamburg 20 years.

STONES, DWIGHT B. 12/6/53, Los Angeles, Calif. Member 1972 Olympic team. Holds world high jump record for 18-year-old. Went 7′3″ at U.S. Olympic trials. Won place on team by winning trials. Was 3rd in 1972 NCAA with 7′2″ as UCLA freshman. Won Pacific-8 title in 1972. As high school senior went 7′1½″ for 2nd-best ever by prep. In Munich Olympics jumped 7′3″ to tie lifetime best and won bronze medal. Youngest member of U.S. Olympic track team. Set world record of 7′6⅝″ at Munich on July 11, 1973.

STRICKLAND, SHIRLEY (Mrs. Laurie de la Hunty) B. 7/18/25, Perth, Australia. Member 1948, 52, 56 Australian Olympic teams. Won total of 7 Olympic medals. In 1952 won gold medal in 80-m hurdles in 10.9, world, Olympic mark. In 1956 in home country, won Melbourne gold in 80-m hurdles and lowered Olympic record to 10.7. Also ran on Australian 400-m relay team that took 1st. In 1948, won pair of bronze medals. Was 3rd in 100-m in 12.2 and 3rd in 80-m hurdles in 11.4. Ran on Australian 400-m team that took silver medal. At Helsinki Olympics also took bronze in 100-m with 11.5. Won 3 national titles in hurdles. Set

Australian records of 10.7 in hurdles, 11.0 in 100-yd, 57.4 in 400-m, 440-yd. Now teacher, housewife.

SWARTZ (ROBINSON), ELIZABETH B. 8/23/11, Riverdale, Ill. Member 1928, 36 Olympic teams. Won gold medal in Amsterdam Olympics in 100-m with 12.2. Also ran on U.S. 400-m relay that won silver medal. In 1936 Berlin Olympics ran on 400-m relay team that won gold medal in 46.7. Was 1929 AAU champion in both 50-m and 100-m. Ran 100-m in 11.2 to break meet record. Now housewife. Member Citizens Savings (Helms) Hall of Fame.

SWENSEN, KEN B. 4/18/48, Clay Center, Kans. Member 1972 Olympic team. Held American 800-m record. Ran 1:44.8 at Stuttgart, W. Germany, on July 16, 1970. As senior at Kansas State, won 1970 NCAA 880-yd with 1:46.3 after hot season on relay circuit. Was AAU champ same year in 1:47.4. In summer of 1970 went on international tour where set American record and lost only one race. In 1971 AAU, while in Army, was 3rd. Won gold medal in 1971 Pan-Am Games with Games record 1:48.0. Due to Army commitment and injury, not at best in 1972. Did make U.S. Olympic team, edging Jim Ryun and running 1:45.1. In Munich Olympics dropped out in prelim heat due to injury.

SZEWINSKA, IRENA KIRSZENSTEIN B. 5/24/46, Leningrad, USSR. Member 1964, 68, 72 Polish Olympic teams. Co-held world 100-m record and held 200-m mark. Ran 11.1 in 100-m on Oct 14, 1968, Mexico City. Set 200-m record at Mexico City in 1968 with 22.5 on Oct. 18. In 1968 Mexico City Games, won gold medal in 200-m with world record. Was 3rd in 100-m in 11.1 behind world record of Wyomia Tyus. In 1964 at Tokyo Olympics was silver medal winner in 200-m in 23.1. Also won silver medal in long jump in Polish record of 21′ 7¾″. Ran on Polish 400-m relay team that won gold medal. In 1972 Munich Olympics won bronze medal in 200-m in 22.74. In 1966 European Championships won 200-m in 23.1, long jump in 21′6″, took 2nd in 100-m and ran on winning 400-m relay team.

TAJIMA, NAOTO B. 8/15/12, Twakuni, Japan. Member 1936 Japanese Olympic team. Held world triple jump record. Went 52′6″ in 1936 Berlin Olympics. Record lasted 14 years. First man to hop, step, and jump 16-m. Third Japanese gold medal winner in event. Won by over foot with Masao Harada of Japan 2nd. Better known as long jumper with best of 25′4¾″. That distance won bronze medal behind Jesse Owens and Luz Long in 1936 Olympics.

TARMAK, JURI B. 7/21/46. Member 1972 USSR Olympic team. Won gold medal in high jump at Munich Olympics. Using straddle style, jumped 7′3¾″ on second attempt to win competition. Missed only twice before missing all 3 attempts at 7′5″. Jumped 7′4⅝″ in 1972 for year's world best. Despite jump, not considered favorite in Olympics. Made best jump in qualifying for Soviet Championships, but in finals was 5th.

TARR, JERRY B. 8/27/39, Topeka, Kans. One of greatest all-round hurdlers in track history. Competed at Oregon, where also played football. Ran 13.9 in 120-yd high hurdles to take 1961 NCAA title. Greatest year 1962. Took NCAA 120-yd high hurdles title with 13.5, and 440-yd hurdles in 50.3. In 1962 AAU won 120-yd high hurdles in 13.4 and 220-yd low hurdles in 22.6. In 1962 U.S.-USSR dual meet, won 110-m hurdles in 13.7. Had best 120-yd high hurdles time of 13.3 done in 1962. Won 2 Pacific Coast Conference Northern Division titles in high, low, and intermediate hurdles. Named All-American in 1961, 62 by NCAA. Member Oregon 440-yd relay team that set world record of 40.0

on May 26, 1962, at Modestoa, Calif. After completing college eligibility, tried pro football with little success.

TAYLOR, F. MORGAN B. 4/17/03, Sioux City, Iowa. Member 1924, 28, 32 Olympic teams. Set world 400-m hurdle record with 52.0 in 1928 Olympic trials. Won gold medal in 1924 Olympics with 52.6 which broke world record. Time not accepted because knocked over hurdle. Won AAU titles 1924–26, 28. After setting world mark in 1928, was Olympic favorite. Upset by Lord Burghley of England and Frank Cuhel of U.S. Ran poor 53.8 for bronze medal. In 1932 Los Angeles Olympics, took bronze medal again. Time of 52.0 equaled best, but winner, Tisdall of Ireland, ran 51.8. Taylor also world class long jumper with best of 25′2″. Had 440-yd dash best of 48.2. Member Citizens Savings (Helms) Hall of Fame.

TAYLOR, ROBERT B. 9/14/48, Tyler, Tex. Member 1972 Olympic team. Not ranked among top U.S. sprinters in 1971, but came on to win place on Olympic team. Was 1970 NAIA 100-yd champ and took 2nd in 1972 NAIA for Texas Southern behind Jean-Louis Ravelomonatosa in 10.2. In 1972 AAU ran 10.2 and took title. In Olympic trials ran 10.0, but was 3rd behind Eddie Hart and Rey Robinson who ran 9.9. In Olympics, due to communications breakdown, just barely arrived in time for heat, but qualified. In finals, lone American took silver medal, timed in 10.33. Ran 2nd leg on U.S. 400-m relay team that won gold medal and tied world record with 38.19.

TEMPLETON, ROBERT (Dink) B. 1897, Helena, Mont. D. 8/7/62. Member 1920 Olympic team. Was 4th in Antwerp Olympics long jump with 22′9 3/5″. Football, track star at Stanford. Turned attention to coaching at alma mater in 1922 and went on to become one of all-time greats. Held post 19 years. While at Stanford started daily practices, unheard of at time. Methods of coaching paid off as Stanford won 77% of meets with Dink as coach. Teams won NCAA team titles in '25, '28, '34. Coached 19 individual NCAA champs. One of most famous coaches in sports history. Member Citizens Savings (Helms) Hall of Fame.

TER-OVANESYAN, IGOR B. 5/19/38, Kiev, Russia. Member 1956, 60, 64, 68, 72 USSR Olympic teams. Set world long jump record with 27′3 1/4″ at Yerevon on June 10, 1962. Lost record to Ralph Boston for over 5 years before regaining it with 27′4 3/4″ in 1967 at Mexico City. Mark still good for USSR national record. Great rival of Boston. Boston won regularly at first, but Ter-Ovanesyan beat Boston 3 times in 1963 U.S. indoor season. Took AAU indoor that year with 26′6 1/2″. Also took U.S. AAU indoor in 1965 with 26′2 1/4″. European champion several times. In 1960 Rome Games took bronze medal behind U.S. jumpers Boston and Roberson, despite 26′4½″. In 1964 Tokyo Games was behind Great Britain's Davis and Boston. Jumped 26′2½″ under adverse conditions for bronze medal. In 4th Olympics jumped 26′7¾″ but was out of medal running in 4th place. Jumped 25′6″ in 1972 Olympic prelims, did not qualify for finals. Europe's first 8-m (26′3″) jumper. Dominated event in Europe nearly 10 years. Father, Arom, once Russian record-holder in discus.

TEWKSBURY, JOHN B. W. B. 3/21/76, Tunkhannock, Pa. D. 8/23/67. Member 1900 Olympic team. One of greatest all-round trackmen in early track history. Well known as sprinter but won gold medal in 400-m hurdles in 1900 Olympics. Ran 57.6, upsetting Henri Tauzin of France, European record-holder. Also won 200-m dash title with 22.2. Showed versatility by entering total of 5 events. Finished 2nd in 60-m with 7.1, 3rd in 200-m hurdles and 2nd in 100-m with 10.8. As great Penn sprinter, won 100-m and 200-m in 1898, 99 IC4A meets.

THOMAS, JOHN B. 3/3/41, Boston, Mass. Member 1960, 64 Olympic teams. First came into prominence in 1958 at age 17 with 6′10¾″ jump in Japan. Less than year later cleared 7′ in indoor meet. Improved to 7′1¼″ that season, but caught foot in elevator shaft and missed most of outdoor season. In 1960 jumped 7′2½″ indoors and broke world record outdoors with 7′1½″ jump on April 30, in Philadelphia. Mark went up to 7′1¾″ on May 21, 7′2″ on June 24 and 7′3¾″ at Olympic trials at Palo Alto, Calif. Appeared to be sure thing at 1960 Rome Games, but two Russians made history with almost unbelievable upset. Thomas passed opening heights but made 7′¼″. Failed at 7′1″ while Russians Robert Shaviakadze (who won gold medal) and Valery Brumel (silver medalist who went on to set world mark of 7′5¾″ in 1963) made height. Thomas won disappointing bronze medal. Won AAU in 1960, 62 and NCAA for Boston U. in 1960, 61. Despite fall from position as world's best, continued as 7′ jumper after Olympic defeat. Made 1964 Olympic team and finished second to Brumel with jump of 7′1¾″. Member Citizens Savings (Helms) Hall of Fame.

THOMPSON, WILBUR (Moose) B. 4/6/21, Frankfort, S. Dak. Member 1948 Olympic team. Fine shot putter for Southern Cal, but not in limelight. In 1948 Olympic trials finished 2nd behind James Delaney and ahead of Jim Fuchs and injured Charles Fonville. Thompson, nicknamed Moose though only slightly over 6′, 195lbs, rose to occasion. Smashed Olympic record by more than 3′ in London Games and took gold medal. Winning toss of 56′2″ was career best. Delaney was 2nd with 54′8½″, Fuchs 3rd. Thompson won 1949 AAU indoor with throw of 54′10⅛″. Member Citizens Savings (Helms) Hall of Fame.

THOMSON, EARL B. 2/15/95, Prince Albert, Saskatchewan. D. 4/19/71, Annapolis, Md. Member 1920 Canadian Olympic team. Won gold medal in Antwerp Olympics 110-m hurdles with world record 14.8. Trained in U.S. at Dartmouth. Set world 120-yd hurdle mark of 14.4 in 1920 at Philadelphia on May 29. Was 1921 NCAA champ in 14.8. Won 3 AAU titles: 1918 in 15.2, '21 in 15.0, and '22 in 15.6. Took 2 IC4A titles while at Dartmouth. Set world record in 120-yd highs in winning 1920 title and won in 1921 with 14.8. Enrolled at Dartmouth in 1916, but left shortly for 2 years service in Royal Canadian Air Force in WW I. Came back and graduated in 1921. Coached track at W. Virginia and Yale before taking coaching post at U.S. Naval Academy. Coached Navy trackmen over 30 years before retiring. Great success despite being almost totally deaf. Member Citizens Savings (Helms) Hall of Fame.

THORPE, JIM B. 5/28/88, Prague, Okla. D. 2/28/53. Member 1912 Olympic team. Recognized as one of greatest athletes, if not greatest, of all time. Won gold medal in pentathlon and decathlon in 1912 Games in Sweden. Also competed in high jump, finishing fourth, and finished seventh in long jump. In pentathlon won long jump, discus, 200-m and 1500-m. Finished third in javelin, other event of now defunct pentathlon. Set short-lived world record in decathlon with 8412.96 points (point schedules have changed three times since then). Won high jump, hurdles, shot and 1500-m. Under present scoring system, Stockholm performance merits 6268 points. In 1913 was revealed Thorpe played pro baseball in 1909, and lost both gold medals, Olympic and world records. World record would have stood for 12 more years. Although reported lax in training methods, natural ability carried him to great performances. Besides track and baseball, Thorpe also played professional football. Died of cancer. Named Athlete of Half-Century, and Greatest Football Player of Half-Century by sports writers.

TINKER, GERALD B. 1/19/51, Miami. Fla. Member 1972 Olympic team. Did not run in 1971, but came through in fine shape in 1972 to make U.S. Olympic 400-m relay team. Was 9.3 sprinter and football player at Memphis State, but transferred to Kent State in 1971. Resumed sprinting competition in 1972. Was 2nd in Kennedy Games 100-yd, running 9.4. In AAU 100-m finished 4th in 10.3. Placed fourth in Olympic trials in 10.1. Won relay team spot with showing. In Munich Olympics ran 3rd leg for U.S. team that won gold medal, tied world record with 38.19. Played football at Kent State.

TISDALL, ROBERT B. 5/16/07, Nuwara Eliya, Ceylon. Member 1932 Irish Olympic team. Won athletic fame in one day. Came to 1932 Los

Angeles Olympics with only 3 competitions in 400-m hurdles. Had best of 54.2 on grass prior to Games. Expected to be also-ran behind Glenn Hardin of U.S. and Lord Burghley of Great Britain. Ran 52.8 in semis to raise few eyebrows. In finals beat field with world-best 51.7. Knocked hurdle down, which then disqualified world record. Hardin got silver medal and world record of 52.0. Tisdall got all-important gold medal. Also competed in decathlon in Los Angeles Olympics and finished 8th. Settled in South Africa and did not compete seriously.

TOLAN, EDDIE B. 9/29/08, Denver, Colo. D. 1/30/67. Member 1932 Olympic team. Held world 100-m and 100-yd records. Ran record 10.4 in 100-m twice in 1929. In 100-yd was first to run 9.5 in 1929 at Evanston, Ill. Won 1931 NCAA 220-yd in 21.5 while at Michigan. Won 1929, 30 AAU 100-yd championships. Also won AAU 220-yd in 1929, 31. Finished 2nd to rival Metcalfe in 1932 Olympic trials. But in 1932 Los Angeles Games, Tolan set Olympic record 10.4 in prelims. In finals edged Metcalfe by smallest of margins, both timed in 10.3. In 200-m Tolan won handily with Olympic record 21.2. Member Citizens Savings (Helms) Hall of Fame.

TOOMEY, MARY RAND B. 2/10/40. Member 1960, 64 British Olympic teams. Set world long jump record at Tokyo Olympics on Oct. 14, 1964. Went 22′2¼″ to win gold medal. Also won silver medal in pentathlon, bronze as member of British 400-m relay team. In 1960 Olympics led qualifiers with 20′9″, but finished 9th in finals. In 1958 Commonwealth Games took silver medal in long jump. In 1966 was gold medalist in Commonwealth Games at 20′10″. In 1962, following birth of child by earlier marriage, won bronze medal in European Championships. In 1968 married then Olympic decathlon champion Bill Toomey, also a world record-holder.

TOOMEY, WILLIAM (Bill) B. 1/10/39, Philadelphia, Pa. Member 1968 Olympic team. Holds world decathlon record with 8417 performance at Los Angeles, Dec. 11–12, 1969. As all decathlon performers, a great all-round athlete. Had 10.3 best in 100-m, 45.6 in 400-m and wind-aided 26′¼″ long jump. But worked hard to develop in field events. In first decathlon in 1959, scored 5349 points on old scoring tables. Went 8′4¾″ in pole vault. In 1969 world record went 14′¼″ in vault for personal best. Won 5 straight AAU championships from 1965–69. Was 1967 Pan-Am Games gold medal winner with 8044 points. Scored 8222 in 1968 Olympic trials and set sights on gold medal in Mexico City. In Mexico City Olympics, took lead with best first day ever of 4499 points. Had 10.4 in 100-m, 25′9¾″ in long jump, 45′ 1¼″ in shot, 6′4¾″ in high jump, and 45.6 in 400-m (decathlon record). On second day did 14.9 in 110-m hurdles and 143′5½″ in discus. In pole vault, disaster nearly took place. Missed twice at 11′9¾″. Made on 3rd attempt and went on to clear 13′9½″. In javelin lost ground to Bendlin and Walde of E. Germany. In heat of 1500-m took lead early and defeated German rivals for gold medal. Toomey set Olympic record with 8193 points. Walde close behind with 8111 for silver medal and Bendlin, 8064 for bronze. Had 12 performances of over 8000 points. Childhood hand injury handicapped field event progress, but through hard work and determination became world best. Married Mary Rand, English long jumper who won 1964 Olympic gold medal and set world long jump mark of 22′2¼″ at Tokyo Olympics. Was junior college English instructor. Member Citizens Savings (Helms) Hall of Fame. Winner 1969 Helms World Trophy Award, N. America.

TOOTELL, FRED B. 9/9/02, Lawrence, Mass. D. 9/29/64, Wakefield, R.I. Member 1924 Olympic team. Was 1923 NCAA hammer throw titlist for hometown Bowdoin College with toss of 175′1″. Same year set collegiate record of 181′6½″ in winning IC4A title. Was AAU champion in 1923 with 173′ 6⅝″ and in 1924 with 173′11½″. In 1924 was Olympic hammer throw champion. Tossed 174′10⅛″ to defeat nearest competitor by over 2′. Track coach at Rhode Island many years and had 17 unbeaten dual meet seasons. Cross country teams went unbeaten 18 times. Athletic director at Rhode Island 1953–62. Rhode Island tennis coach in 1964 when died. Member Citizens Savings (Helms) Hall of Fame.

TORRANCE, JACK B. 6/20/12, Weathersby, Miss. D. 11/10/70. Member 1936 Olympic team. Huge (6′2″, 280) LSU weightman set world record in shot put in 1934 at Norway with 57′1″. Record lasted 14 years. Broke world record 3 times that year, first at Drake Relays with 55′1½″ put. Later broke world and AAU marks at AAU meet in Milwaukee with toss of 55′5½″. Record lasted in AAU for 15 years. Won NCAA in 1933, 34, setting records both times. Latter record 54′6 9/16″. Won AAU 1933–35. Highlight of career was 1934. After leaving LSU in 1934, performances never approached records. Made 1936 Olympic team, but finished disappointing fifth with short toss of 50′5½″. Called "Baby Elephant" because of his size, also fondly referred to as "Baby Jack." Played for pro football's Chicago Bears. Member Citizens Savings (Helms) Football Hall of Fame.

TOWNS, FORREST B. 2/6/14, Fitzgerald, Ga. Member 1936 Olympic team. Held world 120-yd, 110-m hurdle records. Ran 14.1 in prelim heat of NCAA championships in 1936 while running for Georgia. In 1936

Olympics equaled record of 14.1 in prelims. Won gold medal with 14.2. In Oslo, Norway, on Aug. 27, 1936, became first man to break 14.0. His 13.7 was investigated two years before being accepted as world mark because time so unbelievable. Won 1936, 37 NCAA 120-yd hurdle championships with 14.3 each year. Won 1936 AAU championships with 14.2. Tall (6′2″) and fast (9.7) with near-perfect form. Member Citizens Savings (Helms) Hall of Fame.

TRUEX, MAX B. 11/4/35, Warsaw, Ind. Member 1956, 60 Olympic teams. First of great modern American distance runners. Top-flite collegiate distance runner for Southern Cal. Made 1956 Olympic team in 10,000-m at age of 20. Same year won AAU with 30:52.0. In Melbourne Olympics made 10,000-m finals, but did not finish. Also competed in 5000-m but did not qualify. Was 1959 AAU 10,000-m champion with 31:22.4. In 1960 made Olympic team in 10,000-m. At Rome qualified for finals. Finished 6th, first time American had ever placed in event. His 28:50.2 was one of 10 all-time bests in event. Broke his American record by:45. Mark stood until Billy Mills won gold medal in 1964 Olympics. Considers 1960 Games best performance, but making 1956 team or winning high school letter as freshman at Warsaw, Ind., as greatest thrill. Now civil trial lawyer for County of Los Angeles, Calif. Handles real estate, construction contract disputes and food damage suits.

TSIBULENKO, VIKTOR B. 7/13/30, Vyeprik, USSR. Member 1952, 56, 60 Russian Olympic teams. Was 4th in 1952 Olympic javelin competition at Helsinki. In 1956 Melbourne Games, bettered Olympic record with throw of 260′9½″. Bettered old mark by more than 18′ but was 20′4¾″ behind gold medal winner Danielson of Norway and 1′5″ behind Sidlo of Poland. In 1960 Rome Olympics in bad weather took gold medal. In lull during rainstorm, got off toss of 277′8″. Longest throw of career at most opportune time.

TSIKLITIRAS, CONSTANTIN B. 1888, Pylos, Greece. D. 1913. Member 1908, 12 Greek Olympic teams. Held world standing long jump record. Jumped 11′⅝″ in 1912 Olympic Games at Stockholm. In 1908 London Olympics took silver medal in standing long jump and high jump behind Ray Ewry of U.S. In 1912, with Ewry retired, won standing long jump with world record leap, defeating Platt and Ben Adams of U.S. Finished 3rd, behind Adams brothers, in standing high jump. Died following year at age 25.

TUULOS, VILHO B. 3/26/95, Tampere, Finland. Member 1920, 24, 28 Finnish Olympic teams. In 1920 Olympics won gold medal in triple jump. In poor conditions went 47′7″ for gold medal. In 1923 International Games in Goteborg, won both long jump and triple jump. Long jumped 23′11 ¾″, triple jumped 50′6″. Set European record with triple jump of 50′9 ½″ which lasted 16 years. Was only 1 ½″ short of Dan Ahearn's world mark. In 1924 Olympics was 3rd with jump of 50′5″, only 5 ¼″ short of gold medal effort. Was again 3rd in 1928 Amsterdam Olympics. Jumped 49′6 ⅞″ for bronze medal and was again close. Winner had only 3 15/16″ edge on Tuulos. Came in 4th in long jump. Had best of 51′1 ½″ in 1928, but was disallowed because of excessive wind.

TYUS, WYOMIA B. 8/29/45, Griffin, Ga. Member 1964, 68 Olympic teams. Holds world 100-m record, tied for 100-yd record. Ran 11.0 in 1968 Mexico City Olympics on Oct. 15 for 100-m record. Ran 100-yd in 10.3 on July 17, 1965, at Kingston, Jamaica, and June 8, 1968, at Dayton, Ohio, to tie record. In 1964 Olympics came through with best performance of life to date and won gold medal in 100-m. Ran 11.2 to tie world mark in prelims and 11.4 in finals. Won 1964 AAU 100-m in 11.5. Took 100-yd title in AAU championship in 1965, 66 with 10.5 times. Also won 220-yd in 1966 with 23.8. Was AAU indoor champ in 60-yd 1965–67. In 1968 Mexico City Olympics, set world record in becoming only woman to win 100-m twice. Was 6th in 200-m. Ran on gold medal winning 400-m U.S. team. Member Citizens Savings (Helms) Hall of Fame.

VANDERSTOCK, GEOFF B. 10/8/46, Chicago, Ill. Member 1968 Olympic team. Held world 400-m hurdle record. Ran 48.8 in final Olympic trials at South Lake Tahoe on Sept. 11, 1968. Almost unknown until world record run. Was 3rd in 1968 NCAA for Southern Cal in 50.7. In AAU finished 2nd in 49.6. In Mexico City was considered one of favorites. Was 2nd in first heat with 50.6 and 2nd in semi with 49.2. In finals saw his world record shattered and hopes for a medal gone. David Hemery of Great Britain won in 48.1, and John Sherwood edged Vanderstock for 3rd, both in 49.0. Ranked 3rd in world in 1968. Ran in 1969 while in Army and had best of 51.5 in 400-m and 50.7 in 440-yd. Had prep record of 35.7 in 330-yd intermediates. Had leg problems while at USC.

VASALA, PEKKA B. 4/17/48. Member 1968, 72 Finnish Olympic teams. Won gold medal in 1500-m at 1972 Munich Games. Defeated Kip Keino, defending champ, in home stretch and ran 3:36.3 in process. Was long shot with Keino and Jim Ryun favorites. Time was 3rd-best in Olympic history, 6th on all-time list. In 1971 was 9th in European Championships. Same year ran 3:36.8 in 1500-m and set European 800-m record with 1:44.5. In 1968 Mexico City Olympics, was 9th in first heat with time of 4:08.5 and did not advance. In 1969 won Finnish Championship in 1500-m. In 1970 took 800-m, 1500-m, and ran on 1500-m relay team. In 1971 won 800-m and 1500-m. Was 1972 champ in 800-m and ran on winning 800-m relay team. Holds Finnish 1500-m, 2000-m and mile records. Times of 3:36.3 in 1500-m and 3:57.2 in mile.

VIREN, LASSE B. 7/22/49. Member 1972 Finnish Olympic team. Won two gold medals in distances at Munich Games. Won 10,000-m in world record of 27:38.4, despite falling down and losing precious seconds. Race considered best 10,000-m of all time. In 5000-m duplicated 10,000-m finish. Set Olympic record of 13:26.4. Ran 55.8 on last lap to run off challengers and put Finland back as leader in distances. In 1971 European Championships was 7th in 5000-m with 13:38.6 and 17th in 10,000-m with 28:33.2. Set world 2-mile record of 8:14 in 1972. Viren's pair of gold medals and Vasala's gold were first since 1936 for Finland. Constable in Myrskla, was Finn 5000-m champion in 1969 and 1500-m champ in 1972. Set national records in 3000-m, 5000-m, 10,000-m, 2-mile, 3-mile and 6-mile in 1970. In 1971 bettered 3000-m, 5000-m and 3-mile. Winner 1972 Citizens Savings (Helms) World Trophy Award, Europe.

WALSH, STELLA B. 4/3/11, Wierzchownia, Poland. Member 1932, 36 Polish Olympic teams. Reared in U.S. but competed for native country. Held womans world records in 60-m, 100-m, 200-m and 220-yd dash. Ran 7.3 in 60-m at Lemberg, Sept. 24, 1933, for world mark. Set 100-m mark at Warsaw with 11.7 on Aug. 26, 1934, and improved to 11.6 at Berlin on Aug. 1, 1937. Broke 200-m record at Warsaw, Aug. 15, 1935, with 23.6 clocking. Set 220-yd mark at Cleveland, Sept. 6, 1935, with 24.3. Had career that spanned over 20 years. Won first U.S. AAU titles in 1930 with 100-m, 200-m and long jump wins. Had 11.2 in 100-m, 25.4 in 200-m, and 18′9⅜″ in long jump. Won 100-m again in '43, '44, '48; 200-m in '31, '39, '40, '42–48; and long jump 1939–46, 48, 51. Took indoor AAU 50-yd in 1934 and indoor 220-yd in '30, '31, '34, '35, '45, '46. At age 37 won 3 AAU championships; at 40 took AAU long jump. Career probably longest of any track and field athlete, male or female. In 1932 Los Angeles Olympics, Staniolawa Waladrewicz (full name in Polish) won 100-m gold medal in 11.9. In 1936 Berlin Olympics was 2nd to Helen Stephens of U.S. in 100-m. Member Citizens Savings (Helms) Hall of Fame.

WARMERDAM, CORNELIUS (Dutch) B. 6/22/15, Long Beach, Calif. Holder world pole vault record 1940–57. Best jump outdoors 15′7¾″ at Modesto, Calif., in 1942. Vaulted at Fresno State with best of 14′1⅞″. After collegiate competition was member of San Francisco Olympic Club. Won or tied for 7 AAU titles: 1937 (tie), 38, 40–44. World's first 15′ vaulter. Cleared 15′0″ at Berkeley, Calif., on April 13, 1940 to break barrier. Steadily progressed to best of 15′8½″ indoors in Chicago in 1943. Did well indoors, won 2 AAU indoor championships. In last competition won 1944 AAU at 15′0″. Had 43 vaults over 15′. Continually studied vaulting. Unlike most, improved after college. Good speed and build for vaulting. Had little competition during peak years. Probably greatest vaulter of all time considering type of pole used. Now track coach at Fresno State. Member Citizens Savings (Helms) Hall of Fame.

WEFERS, BERNARD B. 1873. D. 4/18/25. Co-held world record in 100-yd, set 220-yd dash record. Ran 9.8 in 1895–97 to tie world standard. Ran 21.2 in 1896 IC4A to break world 220-yd mark by .6. In 1895 as Georgetown freshman, took sprint double with 10.0 and 21.8, and emerged as great sprinter. Double AAU winner in sprints 1895–97. Ran 21.4 in 220-yd in 1897. Took IC4A 100-yd in 1896, 97 with world record tying 9.8 in 1896. Took 1896 IC4A 220-yd at New York on May 30, with aforementioned record 21.2. Also credited with 200-m record. Record was broken by Charlie Paddock 25 years later. Set 300-yd world mark with 30.6 in New York on Sept. 26, 1896. Mark stood 39 years. Said to be greatest sprinter in 19th century. Member Citizens Savings (Helms) Hall of Fame.

WHITE, WILLYE B. 1/1/39, Money, Miss. Member 1956, 60, 64, 68, 72 Olympic teams. Holds American citizens womens long jump record. Jumped 21′6″ at Los Angeles on July 26, 1960. As high school girl from Greenwood, Miss., won 1956 Olympic silver medal with leap of 19′11¾″. In 1960 Rome Olympics was 16th. In 1964 was 12th in long jump at 19′11″, but led off U.S. 400-m relay team that won silver medal. In 1968 was 11th with 19′11½″. At 1972 Olympics jumped 20′11½″ in qualifying, but in finals and was 11th with 20′7″. Won gold medal in 1963 Pan-Am Games with jump of 20′2″, Games record. Was 3rd in 1959, 67 Pan-Am Games. Won 11 AAU long jump championships (outdoors and indoors). Won outdoor 1960–62, 64–66, 68–70, and indoor in ’62, ’68. Member U.S. international teams 1958–72. Was 2nd in ’61, ’62, ’64, ’70 U.S.-USSR dual meets. Took 1st in 1971 U.S.-USSR World meet at 21′4″. Won 1969 U.S.-USSR-British Commonwealth meet with 20′4¼″. One of number of track greats from Tennessee State. Member Citizens Savings (Helms) Hall of Fame.

WHITFIELD, MALVIN B. 10/11/24, Bay City, Tex. Member 1948, 52 Olympic teams. Held world record in 880-yd with 1:49.2 in 1950 and 1:48.6 in 1953. Intelligent runner, ran to win, not for time. Best 800-m time 1:47.9. Had both speed (46.6 400-m in 1948 Olympics) and stamina. Won gold medal in 800-m in both 1948, 52 Olympics with identical 1:49.2. Was 3rd in 400-m and ran on first place 1600-m relay. In 1952 was 6th in 400-m and on second-place 1600-m relay. Won 1948, 49 NCAA for Ohio State. Finished college career at Los Angeles State in 1956. Won 1949–51, 53, 54 AAU 880-yd titles. Won 1000-yd in 1954 AAU indoor. Failed in bid for 1956 Olympic team with 1:49.3, just :00.1 off winning 1948, 52 times. Member Citizens Savings (Helms) Hall of Fame.

WILLIAMS, ARCHIE B. 5/1/36, Oakland, Calif. Member 1936 Olympic team. Held world 400-m record with 46.1 in 1936 NCAA prelim heat in Chicago on June 19, 1936. Won NCAA crown that year for Cal with 47.0. Prior to Olympic year was obscure runner with times around 49.0. In 1936 Olympics won semi heat. In final staved off rally from Lu Velle of U.S., Brown and Roberts of England to win by inches with 46.5. World record stood 3 years.

WILLIAMS, PERCY B. 5/19/08, Vancouver, British Columbia. Member 1928 Canadian Olympic team. Held world 100-m record. Ran 10.3 at Toronto, Aug. 8, 1930, to break Eddie Tolan's record. Worked way across Canada from home in Vancouver to Toronto Olympic trials on dining car, won trials at 10.6. In 1928 Amsterdam Olympics became only non-American to win both 100-m and 200-m gold medals. In 100-m Canadian schoolboy ran 10.8 for gold over Frank Wykoff of U.S., Jack London of Britain. In 200-m won in 21.8 after nearly losing in prelims. Defeated Walter Rangeley of Britain, defending Olympic champion Jackson Scholz of U.S. After Olympics won 100-yd title in first British Empire Games, held at Hamilton, Ontario. Ruled Canadian sprinting 1928–31. Lost form in 1932 and was not Olympian in Los Angeles Games. At age 15 was told to avoid strenuous exercise because of rheumatic fever. Weighed only 126 lbs when won medals.

WILLIAMS, RANDY B. 8/23/53, Fresno, Calif. Member 1972 U.S. Olympic team. At 1972 Olympics at Munich, won gold medal with jump of 27′½″. Led qualifiers with jump of 27′4″. Second youngest man on U.S. team. Freshman at Southern Cal, took NCAA title in 1972 with wind-aided 26′8¼″. Also ran leadoff on USC's winning 440-yd relay team. Won 1972 U.S. Jr. long jump title with 26′4″. Went 27′4½″ to win U.S.-USSR Jr. meet. In U.S. Olympic trials was 2nd with jump of 26′4″. In 1971 led U.S. high school performers in long jump with 25′4½″ and triple jump with 52′3½″. Won 1970 triple jump title with 50′11¾″.

WILLIAMS, WILLIE B. 8/12/31. Held world 100-m record. Ran 10.1 in international military meet Aug. 3, 1956, in Berlin. Ran 10.1 in heat as did Ira Murchison. On wet track in meet finals, won over Murchison by foot, again timed in 10.1. Ran 9.4 in 100-yd three times with wind before world record time. Won NCAA in 1953, 54 for Illinois. Ran 9.5 in 1954. Failed in 1956 Olympic trials when hampered by muscle pull. In 1957 ran 9.3 in 100-yd and 20.3 in 220-yd with wind.

WINT, ARTHUR B. 5/29/20, Manchester, Jamaica. Member 1948, 52 Jamaican Olympic teams. One of great Jamaican quartermilers. Also fine halfmiler. In 1938 made first noises as runner. Won 800-m at 4th Central American and Caribbean Games in Panama, clocked at 1:56.3. Was 3rd in 400-m. In 5th Central American and Caribbean Games, beat Herb McKenley, also of Jamaica, in 400-m with 48.0. Also won 800-m in 1:54.8. Had greatest hour in 1948 London Olympic Games. Underdog to world record-holder McKenley, won semifinals with 46.3. In finals took lead with 20 meters to go and defeated McKenley, 46.2 to 46.4. Won silver medal day before in 800-m. In 1952 Helsinki Olympics finished 5th in defense of 400-m title. Again 2nd to Mal Whitfield in 800-m. Led off Jamaican 1600-m relay team that set world, Olympic record and won gold medal, timed in 3:03.9. Had best time in 800-m of 1:49.3 in winning 1951 British AAA.

WINTER, JOHN A. B. 12/3/24, Perth, Australia. Member 1948 Australian Olympic team. Won gold medal in high jump at London Olympics. Jumped 6′6″ to win over 3 Americans. Pulled back muscle during competition when clearing 6′4 ¾″. Made 6′6″, then had to watch as other jumpers tried and missed at height. Australian champ in '47, '48, '50. Went 6′6 ⅞″ in 1948. Set national record 3 times, best 6′7 ¼″ in 1948. Bank clerk when won Olympic gold medal, now bank manager.

WOELLKE, HANS B. 2/18/11. D. WWII. Member 1936 German Olympic team. In 1936 Berlin Olympics broke Olympic shot put record with toss of 53′1 13/16″. Gold medal was first for Germany since start of modern Games. Great source of pride to Adolf Hitler. German champion 1934–38, 41–42. Had career best of 54′5 ½″ at Frankfort on Aug. 20, 1936, for European record.

WOHLHUTER, RICHARD (Rick) B. 12/23/48, Geneva, Ill. Member 1972 U.S. Olympic team. Came of age in 1972 and made U.S. Olympic team with a 1:45.0 clocking in 800-m trials. In Munich Olympics 800-m prelims, fell down and did not qualify. Continued to compete after his Munich tragedy. On May 12, ran a 9:44.8 anchor leg on U. of Chicago Track Club 2-mile relay team that set a world record of 7:10.4. On May 27, broke world 800-m record with 1:44.6 clocking at Los Angeles. Going into 1972, his best was 1:49. Was 1970 NCAA 600-yd champ for Notre Dame. Took 2nd in 1972 AAU and won 1973 AAU over Dave Wottle in 1:45.6. Was 1973 USTFF mile champ in 3:58.8.

WOLCOTT, FRED B. 11/18/17, Snyder, Tex. D. 1/26/72, Houston, Tex. Co-held world 120-yd, 110-m hurdle record with 13.7 in 1941 AAU meet at Philadelphia. Tied Forrest Towns' mark, stood 7 years. Broke Jesse Owens' 220-yd hurdle mark with 22.5 (200-m time 22.3) in 1940. First sub-14.0 time in 1938 Texas Relays. Ran 13.7 in 1940 college triangular while at Rice. Record not submitted for world mark. Had 8 sub-14.0 times in 4 years of top competition. Lost only twice in same period. Won 1938–40 NCAA 220-yd lows for Rice. Won NCAA 120-yd highs in 1938, 39. Won AAU lows 1938–41 and highs in '38, '40, '41. A 9.5 sprinter, ran on sprint teams at Rice. Member Citizens Savings (Helms) Hall of Fame.

WOLFERMAN, KLAUS B. 3/31/46, Altdorf/Nurnberg, Germany. Member 1968, 72 W. German Olympic teams. Scored upset of world record-holder Janis Lusis to win 1972 Olympic gold medal in javelin with Olympic record of 296′10″. Lusis was ½″ behind. Opened with toss of 284′4½″, good for 2nd. Had throw of 290′ on 4th effort, but was still over 3′ behind Lusis. Got gold medal on 5th throw. Lusis came up short on last throw of 296′9½″. Wolferman increased personal best by over 10′ with 296′7″ few weeks before Olympics. Was 1972 W. German champion at 280′6″. Was 6th in 1970 European Championships with 265′2″. Set pending world mark of 308′8″ at Leverkusen, W. Germany, May 5, 1973. In 1968 Olympics, entered with best of 296′7½″, but failed to make finals with throw of 248′7½″. Phys. ed. instructor. Named W. German Male Athlete of Year in 1972 by W. German sports writers.

WOODRING, ALLAN B. 2/15/98, Bethlehem, Pa. Member 1920 U.S. Olympic team. Won gold medal in 200-m at Antwerp Olympics. Did not qualify for team in trials, but was taken to Olympics anyway. On soggy track wearing new shoes, ran 22.0 to win. Competed for Syracuse, was 1921 IC4A champion in 220-yd. Ran 21.4, 3rd-best time in meet's history of 44 years. Was sporting goods salesman.

WOODRUFF, JOHN B. 7/5/15, Connellsville, Pa. Member 1936 Olympic team. Came to national attention in 1936 Olympic sectional trials by winning 800-m with 1:51.3. In 1936 AAU, as Pitt frosh, was 2nd to Charles Beetham. In 1936 final Olympic tryouts, blazed 1:49.9 in semi heat. Final heat Beetham fell with 300 meters to go and Woodruff won easily in 1:51. Entered 1936 Berlin Olympics as favorite, despite inexperience. Made finals without much trouble. In final was boxed in and nearly had to stop to get out of jam. When free, took off at mad pace to catch field. Caught field and took lead but lost it and became trapped again. Around last turn, again made big move and took lead. Defeated Mario Lanzi by 2 meters with 1:52.9 for zig-zag 800-m gold medal. Was

1937 AAU champion with 1:50.3. As college star at Pitt was unbeatable. Took 1937–39 IC4A titles in both 440-yd and 880-yd. NCAA champ in 880 in 1937–39. War cut career short. Ran anchor leg on world record 2-mile and 3200-m relay team for U.S. at London in 1936. Broke American 800-m record with 1:48.6 in 1940. Ran 1:47.8 on course 5 ft short of 800-m. World record was 1:48.4. Member Citizens Savings (Helms) Hall of Fame.

WOODS, GEORGE B. 2/11/43, Portageville, Md. Member 1968, 72 Olympic teams. Good college shot putter at Southern Illinois, came into own in 1968. Was 3rd in AAU at 64′2″ but won U.S. Olympic trials with put of 68′ ¼″. throw was his best by almost foot. In Mexico City Olympic Games took 2nd with toss of 66′ ½″. In semiretirement in 1969, 70. Injured in 1971, but made comeback in 1972. In 1972 USTFF Championships at Wichita, Kans., tossed shot 70′1 ¾″ to best Randy Matson with 3rd-best throw ever. Skipped AAU, but won final Olympic trials with 70′1 ¼″. In 1972 Munich Games had best toss of 69′5 ½″ and lost by ½″ to virtual unknown Wladyslaw Komar. Now admissions counslor at Southern Illinois at Edwardsville.

WOTTLE, DAVE B. 8/7/50, Canton, Ohio. Member 1972 Olympic team. Co-holder world 800-m record. Ran 1:44.3 at 1972 Olympic trials finals at Eugene, Oreg. on July 1. Was 1970 USTFF champion and was 2nd in NCAA mile same year. Missed 1971 outdoor and indoor seasons due to stress fractures in both legs. In 1972 came back and won USTFF indoor mile in 4:03.7. Won NCAA 880-yd, running for Bowling Green, in 1:51.8. Had equally fine outdoor season, with 1st in NCAA 1500-m in 3:39.7. In 1972 AAU won 800-m in 1:47.3. At Olympic trials attempted to make team in both 800-m and 1500-m. Ran 800-m in world record time, was 2nd behind Jim Ryun in 1500-m. Ran 3:42.3 in 1500-m. Prior to 1972 Munich Olympics, had knee problems. At Games ran easily in 800-m prelims. In finals poured on speed in final 100 meters and passed Russia's Yevgeniy Arzhanov for gold medal. Ran 1:45.9, wearing his ever-present golf cap. In 1500-m ran 4th in his semi heat in 3:41.6, did not qualify for finals.

WYKOFF, FRANK B. 10/29/09, Des Moines, Iowa. Member 1928, 32, 36 Olympic teams. Held world 100-yd record. Ran 9.4 on May 10, 1930, at Los Angeles to break record held by Eddie Tolan. As high school flash from California, made 1929 Olympic team in 100-m and 400-m relay. In 100-m was 4th, but won gold medal as member of U.S. 400-m team. After Olympics went to Southern Cal where won 1930, 31 NCAA 100-yd. Ran 9.4 for record in 1930 meet. Won 1931 AAU with 9.5 for meet record. In 1931 anchored USC 440-yd and 400-m relay teams to record 40.8. Qualified for 1932 Olympic team in 400-m relay. Anchored team to gold medal and world, Olympic record 40.0 at Los Angeles Games. In 1936 made comeback to gain Olympic berth in 100-m and 400-m relay. Again 4th in 100-m, but repeated as gold medalist on relay team. Anchored team of Jesse Owens, Ralph Metcalfe, Foy Draper to world, Olympic record 39.8 which stood 20 years. Member Citizens Savings (Helms) Hall of Fame.

YANG, CHUAN-KWANG (C.K.) B. 7/10/35, Taitung, Formosa. Member 1956, 60, 64 Nationalist China Olympic team. Held world decathlon record. Scored amazing 9121 points on 1950 point scale at Walnut, Calif., Aug. 8, 1963. Performance netted 8089 under new scoring table, which still ranks as No. 8 performance of all time. Went 15′10½″ in pole vault to clinch record. Also ran 14.0 in 110-m hurdles, 47.7 in 400-m and 10.7 in 100-m. Student at UCLA at time, still holds U.S. collegiate record. At UCLA was teammate of great Rafer Johnson. Finished 2nd to Johnson in 1958 AAU by 129 points. Took AAU crown in 1959 when Johnson was injured. In 1960 scored 8426 points at Eugene, Oreg., but Johnson took world record with 8683. In Rome Olympics followed Johnson closely. Defeated Johnson in 6 of 9 events going into 1500-m final. Johnson stayed close and Yang could only gain 9 points. Johnson won gold medal with Olympic record 8392. Yang took silver, also breaking record with 8334. Won 1962–64 AAU. In 1964 Olympics had slowed up considerably and finished 5th. Favored by many to win gold medal. Was 16′ vaulter, 14.0 hurdler, and 25′ plus long jumper in individual events in prime. Member Citizens Savings (Helms) Hall of Fame.

YOUNG, CY B. 7/23/28, Modesto, Calif. Member 1952, 56 Olympic teams. Won gold medal at 1952 Helsinki Olympics. Tossed javelin 242′¾″ to break Olympic record. In 1956 Olympics was out of running with throw of 225′2″. Graduate of UCLA in 1951, took 2nd in 1950 NCAA. A 6′5″, 220-pounder in his moment of glory now rancher in Modesto area.

YOUNG, GEORGE B. 7/24/37, Roswell, N. Mex. Member 1960, 64, 68, 72 Olympic teams. First runner to be member of 4 U.S. Olympic teams. In 1960 Rome Olympics ran 3000-m steeplechase and was eliminated in prelims when ran 8:50.8. In 1964 Olympics ran steeplechase and finished 6th in 8:38.2. In 1968 Mexico City Olympics won bronze medal in steeplechase in 8:51.8. Also ran 16th in marathon. In 1972 qualified for U.S. team in 5000-m in 13:29.4. In 1972 Munich Games ran 13:41.2 in prelims and did not qualify for finals. Won total of 12 AAU championships in indoor and outdoor meets. Won 3-mile, steeplechase titles. Competed on many U.S. international teams and won 1964 USSR meet. Schoolteacher in Arizona.

YOUNG, LARRY DEAN B. 2/10/43, Independence, Mo. Member 1968, 72 Olympic teams. Won bronze medals in both 1968, 72 Olympics in 50-km walk. In 1968 shocked track world when walked 4:31:55.4 for bronze. Time was best of all time for U.S. walker. In 1972 repeated feat with 4:00:46.0. Only man, other than George Bonhag (who won 1500-m walk in 1906), to win walk medal. Won AAU 50-km walk 1966–68, 71. Also won 20-km in 1972 AAU. Has won total of 15 national titles and American 30-mile record of 4:11:59.4 at Columbia, Mo., on April 17, 1971. Was 1967, 71 50-km gold medalist in Pan-Am Games. Navy veteran, had walking scholarship at Columbia (Mo.) College.

YRJÖLA, PAAVO B. 6/18/02. Member 1928 Finnish Olympic team. Held world decathlon record. First set mark in 1926 at Viipuri on July 17–18. Scored 7820.93 points on 1920 scale. Improved mark to 7995.19 on July 16–17 year later. Upped mark to 8053.29 on April 3–4, 1928, at Amsterdam Olympics. Mark, of course, good for gold medal, Olympic record. Large man, strong in weights. Had bests of over 48′ in shot, 180′ in javelin and 130′ in discus. Also had fine marks of 52.4 in 400-m and 4:41.1 in 1500-m in decathlon competition. Also high jumped 6′2″. Won Finnish decathlon title 5 times, 1925–29. Also won pentathlon title three times. Won high jump title. Now farmer in Manhala.

ZAHARIAS, MILDRED DIDRIKSON (Babe) B. 6/26/14, Beaumont, Tex. D. 9/27/56. Member 1932 Olympic team. Greatest female athlete of all time. Won first national honors at 1930 AAU meet in Dallas. Babe, so named because of ability to hit baseball like Ruth, won javelin and baseball throw, placed second in long jump with leap that bettered world mark. In 1931 AAU meet in Jersey City, won 80-m hurdles and long jump, set world record in baseball throw with toss most men would envy, 296′. Made 1932 Olympics and entered "only" three events. In meet before Games won shot, baseball throw, javelin, long jump and 80-m hurdles, tied for first in high jump. Set Olympic, world records in javelin (143′4″) and 80-m hurdles (11.7). Finished second in high jump after jump-off. Broke world, Olympic mark, but judges ruled style illegal and gave her second place. Later played professional womens basketball and baseball with House of David. In 1935 took up golf, went on to become one of all-time greats. Won three National Opens, four "World" championships. Voted Woman Athlete of Year five times by Associated Press. Named top woman athlete of first half of 20th century by AP. Made one of sports' greatest comebacks when won 1954 Women's National Open less than year after cancer operation. Authored *Championship Golf*, 1948. Victim of cancer. Member Citizens Savings (Helms) Hall of Fame.

ZATOPEK, EMIL B. 9/19/22, Koprivnice, Northern Moravia. Member 1948, 52 Czechoslovakian Olympic teams. Won 4 gold medals in Olympic distance competition. First gold in 1948 London 10,000-m in

29:59.6. In Helsinki Olympics in 1952, won 3 gold medals. Set Olympic records in 5000-m with 14:06.6 and 10,000-m with 29:17. Set world mark in marathon in 2:23:03.2. Won European championships in 5000-m and 10,000-m in 1950, and 10,000-m in 1954. Set 18 world records from 5000 to 30,000-m. On Sept. 15, 1951, set 1-hr (12 miles, 269 yd), 20,000-m (1:01:15.8) world records. On Sept. 29, 1951, set 10-mile (48:12.0); 20,000-m (59:51.6), and 1-hr (12 miles, 810 yd) world records. Had stamina, as evidenced in Olympic marathon win, and speed, especially in stretch. One of greatest to run on track.

ZEHRT, MONIKA B. 9/29/52, Riesa, E. Germany. Member 1972 E. German Olympic team. Co-holds world womens 400-m record. Ran 51.0 at Paris in June, 1972, to tie mark. Won gold medal at Munich Olympics in 400-m with Olympic record 51.08. Ran anchor leg on E. German 1600-m relay team that won gold medal, set world mark of 3:23.0. Was 1970 European junior champion in 400-m and ran on winning 1600-m relay team. Was 1970 E. German 400-m champ and won 400-m in European Cup. Also anchored winning 1600-m relay team. In 1971 was member E. Germany's European champion 1600-m relay team. Has competed 6 years. Student.